LETTERS OF NIKOLAI GOGOL

Nikolai Gogol

# LETTERS
## OF
# NIKOLAI GOGOL

Selected and edited
by Carl R. Proffer

Translated by
Carl R. Proffer
in collaboration with
Vera Krivoshein

Ann Arbor
The University of Michigan Press

# Preface

Gogol is one of literature's most curious and original figures. He is also one of the least understood. Apart from the dangers and difficulties of psychoanalyzing an artist who died more than a century ago, there are two particular reasons for this. First, Gogol was a practical joker as well as an eccentric, and it is often impossible to tell which is which. Gogol loved to put people on, to pull their leg—to exasperate a peddler by calmly insisting the cookies he was selling were actually pieces of soap, or to assure friends his stomach was in upside down. In reading through the numerous reminiscences about Gogol one must be careful to consider that most of them were written late in his life or after he died, that even during his lifetime he was the subject of many false rumors and apocrypha, and that strange incidents recounted as indications of his character may have simply been Gogol's diabolically serious and successful jokes. The second important reason why Gogol is often misunderstood is that he was made the rope in a tug-of-war between different political factions of the Russian intelligentsia. He was claimed both by Slavophils and by Westernizers; both groups used his works for their own propaganda purposes, stubbornly ignoring what he intended them to be or what they actually were. All of his works occasioned polemics characterized more by vituperation than by lucidity of thought; and when in 1847 Gogol published a book of essays entitled *Selected Passages from a Correspondence with Friends* the liberals and radicals accused him, quite unjustly, of being insincere and of betraying his earlier beliefs. And these charges were made so eloquently and vehemently that they have been passed down from one generation to another until the present day, when they can still be found in Soviet and American textbooks. Students learn

that Gogol was a traitor to liberalism and/or art, that his insistence that he had never basically changed his aspirations was a delusion, that he became a madman, that it is a waste of time to read anything he wrote during the last ten years of his life, and, above all, that nothing he said about his works should be believed because he was a notorious liar whose theory and practice of art had absolutely nothing in common.

Gogol's more than 1300 surviving letters contain over 600,000 words, and it is not surprising that few people have taken the trouble to read them. The letters do, indeed, reveal a strange and tortured man, but they also suggest that many critical clichés need reexamination. They show clearly how very much alike the Gogol of the 1820's and the Gogol of the 1840's were. This came as a surprise to me, and I think it will to students and teachers of Russian literature who will never have time to read the five volumes of Gogol's correspondence—as well as those interested in his work who do not read Russian. Gogol did, of course, mature and develop, but his whole life is cut from the same cloth. And his personality is as unique as his art.

This volume contains about a sixth of Gogol's epistolary prose. Deciding on the selections was a formidable task. It was essential to excerpt letters for Gogol is often prodigiously long-winded and repetitious (some letters run more than twenty printed pages), and much of what he says has no intrinsic interest. Selections in Russian sources, particularly Veresaev's *Gogol' v žizni*, were helpful guides in making my own choices. I tried to avoid long chronological gaps between letters and to keep the proportion of letters in any given period in approximately the same ratio to the total selection that one would find in the whole correspondence. There are examples of all of Gogol's different moods and different types of letters, with a fairly wide range of addressees from priests to Pushkin. The percentage of letters in which he discusses literary matters is higher here than in the total correspondence. There are examples of typically Gogolian humor, letters of advice (to his mother, sisters, friends, to newly weds, journal editors, poets, actors, censors, and Tsar), his impressions of the countries he traveled in, spiritual and literary confessions, apologies for insults, petitions for loans from friend and Tsar, descriptions of his illnesses, and home remedies for blindness. In the last analysis the letters are more significant as autobiography than as commentary on the literature of the time. The letters, together with the biographical introduction and the notes, should give the reader a picture of Gogol the man and artist. The Bibliography appended is the most comprehensive listing of works on Gogol in

common non-Slavic languages that exists; it can serve as a guide for study of Gogol, his works, and his relations to other European literatures.

Foremost among those who deserve recognition for help in preparing the manuscript is my patient and invaluable collaborator, Professor Vera Krivoshein of Reed College. The book would not exist if it were not for her. In the crucial middle step she compared my draft translation to the Russian text, filling in the lacunae, suggesting alternatives, and answering questions. Without this scrutiny there would be many more errors.

Indiana University

# Note on the Translation

The Russian text used is in Gogol's *Polnoe sobranie socinenij* (Moscow, 1937-52), Volumes X-XIV. Dates are given as they appear in this edition, some Old Style (Julian), some New Style. Occasionally, Gogol himself provided both dates, New Style first—separated from the Old Style by a slash. If it is not specified one can assume letters written in Russia are dated Old Style, those written abroad New Style.

The translation is intended to be accurate—by which I mean that *every* word is translated literally and that when Gogol uses the same word repeatedly there is a strenuous effort made to use the same English equivalent, even if it sounds unusual or awkward. (Sometimes it is impossible to realize the ideal; the words *sily, trudy,* and *delo* were particularly maddening in this respect.) When there are two different grammatical constructions in Russian there should be two in English—even if the English would be less labored if only one were used. When Gogol writes *gimn emu* it becomes an unfortunately homonymic "hymn to him"; the strange *nosovye nozdri* becomes an equally redundant "nose nostrils" (or "nasal nostrils"); and when in midsentence Gogol blunders in the tangle of his own grammar, the English does not correct him. When he uses a clumsy, roving sentence laden with relative clauses and participles the English is correspondingly long and (given the nature of literal translation from a concise language into a messy one) usually somewhat more ungainly. The reader should also bear in mind that Gogol uses many nouns, adjectives, and verbs in quite unusual combinations—his originality of word usage led some critics to claim he did not write in the Russian language. If at times the translation does not seem to be English, it is because it follows Gogol's Russian lead. I do not wish to blame Gogol for everything, for translators' errors of

Profanity is not present for the simple reason that the Soviet editors deleted all of it. These prim lacunae, as well as any other holes in the Russian text ( damaged autographs, friends' editing, etc.), are noted by four periods enclosed in brackets. From the context the reader will easily recognize which of these are profane hiatuses and be able to fill in any blank with an appropriate expletive.

# Contents

# Introduction: Gogol's Life

> My friend, well, what if we were to suppose that
> a sufferer were found who has been befallen by such a
> strange thing that everything he does and says is taken in a
> distorted sense, that almost to a man everyone has doubted
> him, and that a whole whirlwind of misunderstandings has
> started spinning before him.
>
> (Gogol to Pletnev, December 1-14, 1844)

Gogol was born on March 20, 1809. His parents had been married in
1805 when his mother was only fourteen, and he was the third child—
the first two were still-born. His father, Vasily Afanasevich Gogol-
Yanovsky,[1] the owner of between 130 and 200 serfs and a Ukrainian
estate of larger-than-average size,[2] was a risible sort given to entertaining friends with amusing anecdotes and writing his young wife
sentimental letters à la Karamzin.[3] He versified in Russian and
Ukrainian; he wrote, directed, and acted in comedies for the family
theater of a patronizing well-to-do relative. He died when Gogol was
only sixteen. Maria Ivanovna, Gogol's mother, was a kind but slightly
hysterical woman of little practicality or discernment. When her son
became a well-known writer she irritated him with unceasing praise
and her ascription to him of rubbishy works which appeared anonymously in various journals. Later, she composed many fanciful tales
about his life and went so far as to maintain that he had invented rail-
roads and the steamship.

Gogol's entrance into the gymnasium at Nezhin in 1821 followed
some three years of preparatory tutoring in Poltava. In the reminiscences of school chums Gogol appears as a sickly ectomorph who

promised little for the future. He was reasonably well liked, but he was a grubby little child whose sticky fingers repelled his classmates (his pockets were crammed with candies and gooey *galushki* which he munched dispassionately between and during classes). His laziness, audacious lies, refusal to wash, and general perversity alternately stupified and angered his superiors, but the punishment meted out was seldom harsh, though Gogol seems to have spent a good deal of time standing in the corner and was often shut up in his room without supper. On one occasion he was condemned to be thrashed, but the arrival of his executioners precipitated a startlingly realistic attack of make-believe madness; his wild eyes, spuming mouth, and horrific screams frightened the poor pedagogues, and he spent a few comfortable weeks luxuriating in the infirmary. Given this incident, it comes as no surprise that his favorite diversion at school was the theater; the Nezhin thespians performed Russian, French, and German plays, Gogol excelling in the comic roles—those of old women particularly. As he disliked virtually all games which required physical activity, the leisure hours of his uneventful adolescence were devoted to pleasant sedentary enterprises such as making copies of Pushkin's latest works (*The Gypsies*, the first chapters of *Eugene Onegin*) and embellishing the manuscripts with illustrations. N. P. Nikolsky, instructor of Russian literature in the gymnasium, declared Pushkin an empty but seditious libertine, but when on several occasions jokesters, Gogol included, handed in Pushkin's poems as if they were original compositions, the unsuspecting Nikolsky patiently rewrote and "corrected" them. In class the students were administered fatal doses of German Romanticism, Homer (read in Greek—which they did not understand), and eighteenth-century Russian relics such as Kheraskov and Sumarokov. Gogol contributed prose and verse to the school literary magazine which, in a fitting spirit of humility, was called *Parnassian Dung*. One poetic satire was entitled "Something about Nezhin, or, There's No Law Written for Fools." Indeed, Nezhin (from which Gogol graduated in 1828) was a good school only by the miserable standards of the time.[4] Gogol himself was not an outstanding pupil, and apparently he did not even consider going on to a university. He was the most poorly educated of all the great nineteenth-century Russian writers.

In December 1828 Gogol traveled from Vasilevka (the family estate) to St. Petersburg. His arrival created no stir whatever in the capital and, according to his childhood friend and traveling companion Danilevsky, was coupled with nothing more remarkable than that Gogol's nose got frostbitten, forcing him to spend several im-

patient days indoors. Confronted by the hostile climate, exorbitantly high prices, and surly inhabitants of Petersburg, the young provincial's enthusiasm soon turned as cold as his nose. Though for some time Gogol had been telling his mother and friends that he hoped to benefit his country in a post in the civil service, it appears that he already planned a literary career. Among the things he packed for Petersburg was *Hans Küchelgarten,* an ill-made verse idyll of about 1200 lines, which he published under a pseudonym and at his own expense in May 1829. When two reviewers tersely roasted the poem Gogol collected the unsold copies, burned them, and soon thereafter (July 24) decided to leave the country. He was to indulge in this kind of vicarious self-immolation with grim regularity later in life.

After a few weeks in Lübeck and Travemünde Gogol's loneliness, lack of funds, and resolve to try again induced his return to Petersburg. In the next year he failed to begin an acting career when, due to nervous self-consciousness, he bungled his audition, obtained a minor civil service post, had his first short story and a few fragments published in journals. Through the publications he met such established figures in the literary world as Vasily Zhukovsky and Peter Pletnev, who in early 1831 secured him a post as teacher in the Patriotic Institute (a school for girls) and as private tutor for a few gentry families. The appearance of two slim volumes of tales with Ukrainian settings—called *Evenings on a Farm near Dikanka* (1831-32)—was met warmly by the critics and the highest literary circles. Baron A. I. Delvig writes of the years 1831-32:

> At Pletnev's soirées I saw many literary people, including A. S. Pushkin and N. V. Gogol. Pushkin and Pletnev were very attentive to Gogol. This did not surprise me at all on Pletnev's part—in general he liked to patronize new talents—but on Pushkin's part it was totally incomprehensible to me. Pushkin always acted coldly and haughtily toward people whom he didn't know very well, who were not of the aristocratic circle, and toward talents who were little known.[5]

In mid-1832 Gogol returned to Vasilevka by way of Moscow where he met important members of the Russian literary and theatrical world, including Mikhail Pogodin, Mikhail Shchepkin, and Sergei Aksakov —all three destined to be among his regular correspondents. At the time, recalls Aksakov, Gogol's physical appearance was unflattering: the conceited Ukrainian was playing the Petersburg dandy; his smooth-shaven, nose-dominated face was perched on huge stiffly starched collars, a curly shock of hair was piled on top of his head, with the temple locks slicked down, and he sported a flashy vari-

colored vest with a shiny gold chain. But the trip was successful, the family reunion noisy and gay. Afterwards, accompanied by two servants and two sisters (bound for the Patriotic Institute) Gogol rolled back to Petersburg.

To his closest friends at this time (all Nezhin schoolmates such as Prokopovich, Danilevsky, Kukolnik, and Grebenka who were employed, or unemployed, in St. Petersburg) Gogol gave nicknames— Dumas, Hugo, and Balzac. For although the subject matter and style of *l'école frénétique* had some brief influence on Gogol he remained irreverent:

> Already at that time he didn't like French literature and didn't have much sympathy even for the [French] people themselves, because of "the fashion which they introduced in Europe," as he said, "of rapidly creating and immediately, childishly, destroying authorities." Incidentally, he read absolutely nothing from French *belles-lettres* and took up Molière only after a severe reproach from Pushkin for neglect of this writer. Also, he knew little of Shakespeare (Goethe and German literature in general barely existed for him), and of all the names of foreign poets and novelists one name—Walter Scott—was familiar to him otherwise than from guess and from rumors . . .

Perhaps Annenkov exaggerates a little, but one familiar with Russian literature of the early nineteenth century who remembers, say, the wide-ranging interests of Pushkin, cannot fail to be struck by how little Gogol says in any of his writings about non-Russian literatures and by the narrow limits of his culture and interests. The names of Shakespeare, Dante, Goethe, Schiller, and Molière do occur in his letters and essays, but almost always in the most general and vaguest terms—the kind of perfunctory praise expected for literary celebrities. Gogol was remarkably single-minded; he read and assimilated only what he needed for his own purposes, only what suited his own vision. In terms of Isaiah Berlin's hedgehog-fox dualism, Gogol would have to be classified as a superhedgehog.[6]

Reminiscences of the early and middle 1830's suggest that Gogol was a rather secretive person, disinclined to reveal himself to anyone; in the presence of strangers he was stubbornly clam-like, but with his Ukrainian friends he was usually relaxed, jovial, and ready to amuse the circle by employing his uncanny aptitude for ferreting out petty weaknesses and doing verbally annotated impersonations of people during their moments of vanity, inanity, affectation, and complacency. He also entertained the group with what might be called creative readings of newspaper advertisements— all with his own ridiculous or obscene animadversions—and by tell-

ing, with extreme solemnity, Rabelaisianly anus-oriented jokes. He enjoyed reading aloud (with his slight "o"-accenting Ukrainian intonation) from Derzhavin, Pushkin, and Yazykov. Virtually none of Gogol's contemporaries left memoirs without recalling his extraordinary talent as a reader, especially of his own works.

Gogol did not publish anything of import in 1833-34, but he continued to write. In early 1833 he repudiated the inconsequential stories of *Evenings,* saying he felt something great had to come. The following "Apostrophe to 1834" gives some insight into his mood and character as the year began:

> A great, solemn moment. Lord, how the waves of different emotions have mingled and crowded round it! No this is not a dream. It is that fateful and irresistible borderline between memory and hope . . . Already there is no memory, already it is flying away, already it is being overcome by hope. My past echoes at my heels; my still unpredictable future shines through the mist above me. I implore you, life of my soul, my genius. Oh, do not conceal yourself from me; be vigilant over me at this moment and do not leave me during the whole of this coming year which is beginning so enticingly for me. What will you be like, my future? Brilliant? Broad? Will you seethe with my great deeds, or . . . Oh, be brilliant! Be active and wholly devoted to my work and tranquility!
> Mysterious, inscrutable 1834! Where shall I mark you with my great works. Amid this huddle of houses cast one on the other, these thundering streets seething with merchantry, this hideous heap of fashions, parades, civil servants, wild northern lights, splendor, and base drabness? Or in my beautiful, ancient, longed-for Kiev, blest with orchards, rich in fruits, encircled by my lovely and wonderful southern sky, full of ravishing nights, where the hills are covered with shrubs, interspersed with seemingly harmonious ravines, and washed by my pure and my swift Dnieper? Will it be there? Oh! I do not know what to call you, my genius! You who flew past my ears with your harmonious songs even when I lay in my cradle, awakening in me inexplicable thoughts and fostering in me such infinite and entrancing dreams! Oh, look! I am on my knees, I am at your feet! Oh, do not part from me! Dwell on earth with me, if only for two hours each day, like my dear brother I shall achieve . . . I shall achieve! Life is seething within me. My works will be inspired. A divinity, inaccessible on earth, will hover over them! I shall achieve . . . Oh, kiss and bless me!

Gogol decided that the highroad to fame led through history, a subject he had been studying zealously but rather unsystematically

in connection with his teaching duties. With characteristic confidence and hyperbole he announced a grand plan to write a history of the Ukraine "in six small or four large volumes." Zhukovsky and Pletnev exercised their pull in high places, and in July 1834 our Ukrainian high-school graduate was appointed adjunct-professor of history at St. Petersburg University! Gogol's maiden lecture, an imaginative rhetorical achievement entitled "On the Middle Ages," was a success with the students, but in the performances which followed he revealed a lamentable lack of ability. When he did not cancel his class because of (he said) visits of relatives, or toothaches, or various other imaginary maladies, the lectures consisted of only thirty minutes of semiaudible mumbling supplemented by visual aids such as pictures of Palestine. The students (including young Ivan Turgenev) stayed away in droves, complaining it was obvious Gogol did not know much about history;[7] Gogol said the students were a sleepy lot of clods who could not recognize the truth when they saw it; and in January he was still maintaining that he was "writing a history of the middle ages which, I think, will consist of eight, if not nine, volumes."[8] He must have been busy, because at that very moment his *Mirgorod,* a collection of four more stories with Ukrainian settings, written between 1832 and 1834, was being published; it was followed later in 1835 by *Arabesques,* a collection of miscellaneous essays and stories about St. Petersburg. The short novel *Taras Bulba* was virtually the only concrete result of Gogol's studies in history.

When his undistinguished professorship was terminated in mid-1835, Gogol set out for the Caucasus, but lack of finances waylaid him in the Crimea. Between Kiev and Moscow on the return trip Gogol indulged in some play acting suggested by *The Inspector General,* the comedy on which he was then working. He sent his friend Pashchenko ahead to spread the story that a government inspector, traveling incognito, was following. The strategem was a complete success. At every post-station Gogol was met with great courtesy, and when he signed the register "adjunct-professor" the stationmasters were certain Gogol was the investigating official. Danilevsky wrote:

> Of course Gogol acted like a private person, but as if from simple curiosity he would ask, "Please, if possible, show me what kind of horses there are here; I would like to look at them."

Before there had always been long waits for horses at each station, but this time Gogol and Danilevsky rolled along with no arguments or delays.

Although anecdotes about travelers being mistaken for mas-
querading inspectors were not uncommon, and although *The Inspector General* bears some resemblance to Kotzebue's *Die deutschen
Kleinstädter* and Kvitko's *Arrival from the Capital,* it was Pushkin
who suggested the play's plot to Gogol. Count Sollogub, a minor
writer, said "Pushkin always called himself the god-father" of the
play, and Annenkov reports:

> It is well-known that Gogol took the idea for *The Inspector
> General* and *Dead Souls* from Pushkin, but it is less well-
> known that Pushkin did not relinquish his goods to him alto-
> gether willingly. In the circle of his friends he used to say,
> laughing, "You have to be careful with this Little Russian—he
> fleeces me so that I can't even holler."

Exactly how close Pushkin and Gogol were will probably always be
something of a mystery. Gogol's servant Yakim said Pushkin would
often visit Gogol and spend all night listening to his latest work or
reading Gogol his own poetry. If he didn't find Gogol home he would
rummage through his papers to see what was new. Gogol wrote several rhetorical tributes to Pushkin, but his letters on Pushkin's death
are curious schizophrenic combinations of effusive eulogy, cold
everyday news, and requests for money. The tone of the few surviving letters to Gogol from Pushkin suggests Gogol was not among his
intimates. The fox and the hedgehog do not live together.

Gogol read *The Inspector General* and "The Nose" at literary
soirées in early 1836. On April 9 Vyazemsky wrote:

> Zhukovsky's Saturdays are flourishing. . . . Only Gogol, whom
> Zhukovsky calls Gogolet, livens them up with his stories. Last
> Saturday he read us a story about a nose which all of a sudden
> disappeared from the face of some Collegiate Assessor. Kill-
> ingly funny!

*The Inspector General,* however, had snagged on the censorship, and
it was played only after Zhukovsky took Gogol's case to Nikolai I.
The tsar read the play and, uncharacteristically, authorized its publication; furthermore he attended the premier performance on April 19 with a number of his ministers and rocked with laughter. The
reports about this first performance are strangely contradictory.
Most of the witnesses say it was a great success, but the usually reliable Annenkov recalled that there was a good deal of silence, perplexity, and fear in the audience, that applause and laughter was
sporadic and strained, and even those who did laugh went away
grumbling, "It is impossible—slander and a farce." And after the
performance when Prokopovich presented Gogol with a freshly

printed copy of the play and said, "Admire your little son," Gogol
threw it to the floor, and leaning against a table said, "My God! Well,
if only one or two had cursed it. . . ." And soon after this he wrote:

> *The Inspector General* has been played, and my soul feels so
> disturbed, so strange. . . . I expected, I knew in advance how it
> would go, and nevertheless a sad, vexed, and painful feeling
> has enveloped me. My own creation seemed repugnant, bi-
> zarre, and as if it were not my own at all. . . .
>
> From the very beginning of the play's performance I sat in
> the theater bored. I didn't care about the rapture or the public
> or the way it received the play. Of all those who were in the
> theater, I feared only one judge, and this judge was I myself.
> Inside myself I heard rebukes and grumbling against my own
> play—which drowned out all the others. And in general the pub-
> lic was satisfied. Half of them even received the play with
> sympathy; the other half, as it usually happens, cussed it—for
> reasons, however, which do not relate to art. . . .

Gogol praises the actor who played the Mayor, but he says the main
role (Khlestakov) was completely lost; he curses Dobchinsky and
Bobchinsky, the caricaturistic costuming, and the actors' stubborn
refusal to heed any of his suggestions. "Again I repeat: melancholy,
melancholy! I don't know myself why melancholy possesses me,"
and concludes, "My play repels me. I would like to run away now,
God knows where."

Western Europe was the answer. On June 6 Vyazemsky bid
Gogol farewell and thus began a twelve-year period of European
wanderings filled with loneliness, illness, and the slow painful creation of *Dead Souls*—which he had already started to write. Between
1836 and 1848 Gogol visited Russia only twice—in the winters of 1839-
40 and 1841-42.

The summer of 1836 saw Gogol pass through Lübeck, Hamburg, Bremen, Düsseldorf, Aachen, down the Rhine to Mainz, to
Baden-Baden, then (August-October) to the main Swiss cities. Finally, in the first part of November, he went to live with Danilevsky
in Paris. There he moved in the society of the N. M. Smirnovs, A. I.
Turgenev, and Mickiewicz's Polish circle until spring, when he
moved to Italy, arriving in Rome on March 26. The Eternal City became Gogol's second home, and he was ecstatic about it. He spent
most of the next several years there, usually wandering about the
various German spas during the summer. Thus, we have the irony
of *Dead Souls* being written in Vevey, Paris, Rome, and Baden-
Baden. And so much did Gogol live within himself that one can find
hardly a trace of Western Europe in *Dead Souls*. Perhaps he could
have taught the impressionable Turgenev a lesson.

A. O. Smirnova relates an interesting incident from the summer of 1837. Gogol announced to her and the few Russians with whom he associated that he was writing something called "Dead Souls" and would read to them that evening. Gogol arrived with his notebook, but as he began chapter one a terrific storm broke loose with thunder and lightning and cascades of rain:

> Gogol looked through the windows and at first seemed disturbed, but then calmed down and continued reading. We were in rapture. . . . However, he didn't finish reading the second chapter and asked Karamzin to go with him to Graben where he lived. The rain began to die down and they set off. Later Karamzin told me that Gogol was afraid to go home alone, and to his question why answered that there were big dogs in Graben and that he was afraid of them and didn't have a stick. There were no dogs in Graben, and I suppose that the thunderstorm worked on his weak nerves—he suffered those nervous sufferings which are known only to nervous characters. The next day I asked him to read some more from *Dead Souls,* but he flatly refused and even asked me never to ask him for that again.[9]

In spite of such attacks of nerves, it would seem that the years 1837-38 in Rome were among the happiest of Gogol's life. I. F. Zolotarev, who shared Gogol's apartment, said he was generally jovial and talkative, enraptured over discovering the beauties of Rome and showing them off to others. But simultaneously there were signs of something else inside Gogol:

> In the first place, he was extremely religious; he went to churches often, and he liked to see manifestations of religiousness in other people. In the second place, a kind of stupor often possessed him: suddenly in the middle of an animated, gay conversation he would fall silent, and you couldn't get a word out of him. This happened to him without apparent cause.

Gogol also puzzled his acquaintances by the outlandish outfits he wore and by his stupendous appetite. He would go to a restaurant with Zolotarev and eat a complete dinner; but if a friend happened in as they were ready to leave, Gogol would order another complete dinner—stowing it God knows where in his skinny body. He displayed his own culinary prowess by preparing vast bowls of quivering macaroni and a goat's milk concoction which he dubbed "Gogol-mogol."

Among his acquaintances was Zinaida Volkonskaya, a Catholic convert, and her coterie of Polish friends and priests. Gogol learned to read Polish, discussed Mickiewicz's *Pan Tadeusz* and

Zygmunt Krasinski's *Undivine Comedy* and *Irydion,* and he made
the Poles (and some of his Russian friends) believe he was flirting
with Catholicism. Apparently, Gogol was just trying to please the
rich Princess Volkonskaya; nevertheless Gogol's considerable interest
in religious questions is fully attested by the memoirs of the period.

During the summer of 1838 Gogol traveled around Italy. According to N. V. Berg, Gogol gave this curious account of writing a
chapter of *Dead Souls:*

> Once in July I was traveling between the little towns of Gen-
> zano and Albano. Halfway between those towns on a little hill
> is a miserable inn with a billiard table in its main room—where
> the balls constantly clatter and there is chatter in various lan-
> guages. I stopped there too. I was writing the first volume of
> *Dead Souls* at the time and never parted from my manuscript.
> I don't know why, but precisely at the moment I entered the inn
> I felt like writing. I ordered a small table brought, sat down in
> a corner of the room, took out my paper-case, and in the noise
> made by the rolling balls, the indescribable noise, the rushing
> about of the waiters, the smoke, the suffocating atmosphere,
> I became completely lost in a marvelous dream and wrote a
> whole chapter without moving from my seat. I consider those
> lines some of the most inspired. I have seldom written with
> such animation.

Gogol's writing habits were indeed strange. On one occasion, in Russia, Aksakov and Zhukovsky entered Gogol's room (ordinarily kept
locked) unannounced and saw him standing at his writing desk:

> Before me stood Gogol in the following fantastic costume: in-
> stead of boots—long woolen Russian stockings reaching above
> his knees; instead of a frock-coat—a velvet spencer over his
> flannel vest; his neck was wrapped round with a large vari-
> colored scarf, and on his head was a crimson, velvet, gold-
> embroidered *kokoshnik* very much resembling the head-dress
> of Mordvinian women.

Gogol gazed unseeingly at the intruders for some time, quite unem-
barrassed by his weird costume. Others recalled that when Gogol
locked himself in his room to write they would often hear strange
voices coming from there—no doubt Gogol's conversations with
himself, his characters, and the mysterious gods of art.

In the spring of 1839 Pogodin and Shevyrev visited Gogol in
Rome. Pogodin noted it was amusing to travel with Gogol because of
another peculiarity—his extreme dislike of showing his passport or
revealing his name. He often gave fictitious names (like Gogel or
Gonel), and when required to produce his passport he would begin

swearing at the customs or police official in Russian—but in a sweet and apologetic intonation which, accompanied by appropriately humble gestures, often made the Italian relent and let him pass. If the official persisted, it often turned out Gogol had secreted his papers somewhere in his luggage:

> He would start to get mad, dig through his things without finding it anywhere, throw out everything that came to hand and, finally, finding it where one couldn't expect any documents to be, began to curse the passport itself—asking it why it got stuck in there—and to shout at the policeman: "There's the passport for you—eat it!"

The Russian visitors made it a happy spring, but the mood was broken by the slow death of a young man named Iosif Vielgorsky with whom Gogol had just recently become good friends. Before he died Vielgorsky presented Gogol with a Bible inscribed "To my friend Nikolai" which Gogol said was "doubly sacred" to him.

Gogol returned to Russia in September 1839 and remained there until June of the next year, living alternately with Pletnev, Zhukovsky, Pogodin, and the Aksakovs. Aksakov loaned him 2000 rubles in November, Zhukovsky 4000 in January; unfortunately for his friends Gogol's concepts of "loan" and "gift" had a disturbing tendency to overlap. Now he entertained by ritualistically preparing masses of macaroni and by reading the first six chapters of *Dead Souls*—both activities elicited cries of rapture. He was received as a conquering hero. Thus, the Pogodins and Aksakovs contained their exasperation when he fell asleep (or feigned sleep) at soirées arranged in his honor. Most of his eccentricities were politely ignored —as for example when, at dinner, he would methodically tear off pieces of bread, roll them into little balls, and coolly throw them at the ladies and gentlemen around the table (or put them in his glass as a sign he was displeased with the beverage). His main purpose in returning to Russia on this occasion was to take his two sisters from school in Petersburg and lodge them in some wealthy aristocratic lady's house in Moscow—a task which he did manage to arrange. Gogol was an accomplished freeloader. He celebrated his name day on May 9 at Pogodin's; among the distinguished guests was a young poet named Lermontov (he would be shot dead the next year) who read his narrative romantic poem *The Novice*.[10]

Gogol spent July and August in Vienna where a severe illness (or attack of nerves) put an end to a productive period and so terrified him that he made out a will. But in September he returned to Rome, saying as usual that the open road was salubrious for him, and continued the final work on *Dead Souls*, which Annenkov helped him

to copy in April-June 1841. Annenkov's memoirs give this picture of
Gogol at the time: The smooth-shaven face and foppishly combed
hair of Gogol's youth had been replaced by neat moustaches and light-
brown shoulder-length locks. He lived almost ascetically. He was un-
interested in politics. His reading consisted only of Dante, Pushkin,
and Gnedich's translation of the *Iliad*. He generally remained in a
good humor. (For example, he amused and annoyed his friends by
playing card games of his own invention, constantly changing the
rules during the course of play.) Sewing was a favorite pastime. He
was extremely fond of elaborate church services and religious pro-
cessions. Annenkov says the only really disturbing thing was Gogol's
sometimes morbid talk about death; for a while he even slept on a
divan just outside Annenkov's door (mussing his own bed to make
the maid think he slept there) because, Gogol said, he was afraid of
death. In spite of this he finished the first part of *Dead Souls* and in
October 1841 returned to St. Petersburg, remaining in Russia until
June 1842.

The difficulties he had getting *Dead Souls* passed by the beef-
witted censors are well documented by the letters which followed.
After the Moscow censors refused to pass it, Gogol sent the manuscript to Petersburg with Belinsky. This was done secretly, because
Gogol did not want to antagonize his Slavophil friends such as
Aksakov and Pogodin—people who considered Belinsky's Western-
izing politics anathema. Apart from the difficulties with the censorship, Gogol's second Russian sojourn was made unpleasant by quarrels with his friends, especially Pogodin. Besides loaning him money
Pogodin had lodged and fed Gogol, his sisters, and his mother on
various occasions (some of them lengthy), so it was reasonable for
him to expect repayment in the form of contributions to his journal,
*The Muscovite*. But except for the fragment *Rome* Gogol had nothing
to offer.

Though Gogol could be happy when *Dead Souls* was finally
published (1842), he considered the last two volumes much more
important, and he had been working on Part II for over a year
already. In these subsequent volumes Gogol intended to show the
good sides of Russian life, to introduce characters who should be
emulated, and in the end to show Chichikov's spiritual transfigura-
tion. Gogol maintained, and there is some reason to believe him, that
up to then his main characters were objectifications of his own personal vices and shortcomings. These he could create with genius.
But, he reasoned, he could not portray the good characters, the people who personify the moral excellence and potential strength of Russia, until he had something of their virtue in himself. So he had to make

himself better, to educate himself, to be reborn. And since, he believed, God gives the gift of artistic talent, religion had to play a fundamental role in the process of spiritual self-improvement. Although a bad soul could depict a dead soul, only a good soul could resurrect it. Before leaving for Rome Gogol astounded the Aksakovs by announcing he intended to make a pilgrimage to the Lord's Sepulchre, which he would describe for them, "but for that I have to purify myself and make myself worthy." It was to be six years before he made the pilgrimage.

Gogol then became a semimendicant troubador of unsung songs. The winter of 1843 saw him in Rome and Nice in the company of the painter Ivanov, the poet Yazykov, and his spiritual sister A. O. Smirnova—who provided an audience for his postprandial readings from Marcus Aurelius ("I swear to God," exclaimed Gogol, "all he lacks is being a Christian") and his beloved Gnedich translation of the *Iliad*. The postmarks of his letters provide the tortuous itinerary of the next years. Seeking a cure for his ailments he wandered despondently from spa to spa, from doctor to doctor. Biographers have always assumed that Gogol was a hopeless hypochondriac, with a penchant for making mountains out of hemorrhoids. This was the opinion of most of Gogol's friends and of his doctors. But Gogol's friends were not physicians—and neither were his doctors.[11] It is convenient to conclude that his pains were illusory, but I do not think we can exclude the possibility of some chronic organic illness, perhaps psychosomatic, which went undiagnosed and untreated. One suggested "cure" was bathing in the salt water at Ostend (fall 1844). There he took long lonely walks by the seashore; he was taciturn and avoided most of the other Russians, which made them regard him as a haughty crank.

He continued to work on *Dead Souls*. But in the summer of 1845 Gogol's anguished dissatisfaction with his manuscript culminated in another desperate act of literary pyromania—he gathered together and destroyed the drafts of Part II, the work of five arduous years:

> Volume II of *Dead Souls* was burned because it was necessary. "He will not come to life if he does not die," says the apostle. It is necessary to die in order to be resurrected. It was not easy to burn the work of five years—produced by such painful efforts where every line was achieved at the cost of violent agitation, where there was much that was my best thinking and interested my soul. But everything was burned, and at a moment when, seeing death before me, I wanted to leave at least something behind me which would be the best remembrance

of me. I thank God that he gave me the strength to do it. As soon as the flame had carried away the last pages of my book, its contents were suddenly resurrected in a radiant and purified form, like the phoenix from the fire. . . .[12]

In the meantime Gogol had conceived a new project. He would gather a number of the letters on religious, social, and moral topics he had written to various friends and publish them, along with several essays on aesthetic subjects (Russian poetry in particular), for the edification of Russia. He announced the project to Pletnev on July 30, 1846, saying the manuscript would soon be in the mail. This strange and original volume[13] entitled *Selected Passages from a Correspondence with Friends,* engendered controversy even fiercer than had *The Inspector General* or *Dead Souls.* Conservatives and radicals, Slavophils and Westernizers alike, were astounded and incensed by the book's pompous style, its sanctimonious tone, Gogol's patriarchal view of Russian society (he found justifications for tsardom, serfdom, and the censorship), and his insistence on the role of spiritual purpose in the highest and most Russian art. The stupid censors mangled the book, which did not help Gogol's cause; and about the only public defenders Gogol could find were the aging Vyazemsky and the astute but cloudy-styled Apollon Grigoriev. The usually mild-mannered Sergei Aksakov asked his friends not even to help Gogol publish the volume, grumbling that he should find some other executioner, and when it was published (1847) Gogol was the victim of a delayed-action bomb when in July the radical and consumptive Belinsky drafted an impassioned open letter (later sanctified by socialists) accusing Gogol of being insincere, renouncing art, being an apostle of ignorance and preacher of the knout—as well as a number of other equally misleading or totally false things.[14] Gogol confessed to the sins of pride and ignorance, but (and rightly so) lamented the fact that few people had read very carefully,[15] and consoled himself with the fact that the book had occasioned controversy and helped him learn something about Russia. In spite of the ferocious criticism Gogol did not recant; and though more cautious, even in the last years of his life he remained optimistic about continuing his career as teacher-artist and creating soul-transforming works which would justify his existence in the eyes of God and Russia. And from the memoirs of his contemporaries we know that in spite of some lugubrious letters written at the time he was under attack, Gogol was in good health and often in good spirits. In fact the humorless letters of his last ten years suggest a far more gloomy Gogol than do other sources, which frequently mention his cheerful disposition and talkativeness.

After a year and a half of ramblings around Germany and Italy Gogol at last realized his desired pilgrimage to the Holy Lands, leaving Naples on January 10, 1848. He was accompanied to Jerusalem by his Nezhin schoolmate Konstantin Bazili, then a high Russian diplomat on assignment in Syria. But the expedition was hot, uncomfortable, and spiritually unrecompensed. Gogol's letters reflect his disappointment and woe; he was disinclined even to set down his impressions. He returned to Russia for the last time. When he arrived at Vasilevka by way of Odessa, his sister Elizaveta wrote: How he has changed! He's become so serious; it seems that nothing cheers him up, and he's so cold and indifferent to us." He had reason to be: in addition to the frustrations of his last journey and the slow progress of *Dead Souls,* he had to endure the petting of emotionally solicitous relatives, hordes of visitors who drove by to gape at the famous writer, and a return to the scenes of carefree childhood with the realization that the best part of his life was irretrievably lost.

But he did cheer up, and in the fall of 1848 traveled to Moscow and Petersburg. Pletnev wrote:

> Judging by his appearance he is healthy, and even plumper than he has ever been. His exterior, elegant to the point of foppishness, does not suggest the author of *Correspondence.* He does not go into explanations of the state of his soul.

At a literary dinner four notable young writers—Goncharov, Nekrasov, Grigorovich, and Druzhinin—were introduced to him. Accounts of the occasion are somewhat contradictory. Panaev says things were at first strained, but went well when they started talking about literature—even though it was apparent Gogol had not read their works. Nekrasov says Gogol treated them as inferiors[16] and offended Goncharov by some comments about *A Common Story.*[17] If Gogol then knew nothing of contemporary literature he soon remedied his ignorance, for, in referring to the summer of 1849, L. I. Arnoldi reports:

> I had never seen Gogol with a single book except the works of the church fathers and an ancient botany, and therefore was extremely surprised when he started talking about Russian journals, about new Russian works, about Russian poets. He had read everything and kept up on everything. He spoke with great praise of the works of Turgenev, Grigorovich, Goncharov. "They are all signs favorable for the future," he said. "Our literature has made a sharp turn lately and has fallen onto the real road. Only our verse-makers are limping, and the times of Pushkin, Yazykov, and Baratynsky cannot return."

In one of his letters he praises Dostoevsky's *Poor Folk* (1846); however, judging by a remark made by Annenkov, Gogol was indifferent to his Siberian exile—or thought it was merciful. Gogol's old quarrels with Pogodin and Aksakov's indignation about *Selected Passages* were forgotten; again he lived with Pogodin in Moscow (1849-50), often visiting Kaluga, where A. O. Smirnova now lived, or Aksakov's charming estate, Abramtsevo, just to the north of Moscow, which meant he could often stop in Zagorsk to pray in the ancient churches of the hallowed Trinity Monastery. Aksakov said that in the winter of 1848-49 Gogol was stronger, healthier, and fatter than he had ever been before. And when Gogol read them the first chapters of Part II of *Dead Souls* Aksakov and most of his other friends felt assured there had been no diminution of Gogol's creative powers.

The story of Gogol during these last years is filled with the same antinomies that riddle his whole biography. He was truly a creature of incongruities.[18] He could ridicule man's passion for trivia—as with the lieutenant (in Chapter VII of *Dead Souls*) whose adoration of new boots continues long into the night, but his talent was often consumed by trivia—and, incidentally, it seems Gogol himself was a lover of boots, for in the battered case which during most of his life after 1836 contained his few modest possessions, he carried three or four fine pairs of boots, and in a few of his epistles we learn how fussy he was about choosing the leather and the bootmaker. Sometimes he dressed, or tried to dress, very foppishly; more often he looked slovenly. One day would see him wearing a peculiar combination of gaudy colors and starched white collars, the next he would be all in black with no linen showing. One day he would have his hair up in curlers, another he would appear at an important dinner uncombed and unshaven. He was alternately cheerless and cheerful. When he joked he always did so without smiling. He could be as humble as a monk or as vain as Satan. He prayed for salvation, but he spoke as if he were the savior. He gave thousands of rubles to needy students, but sponged off his friends for years. His sheer creative genius, the power to transmute the ridiculous into deathless poetry, is unparalleled in Russian literature, yet he was utterly ignorant of simple everyday facts known to every literate Russian. He could devote the morning to discourse on the works of the holy fathers and spend the afternoon telling dirty stories, childishly repeating some incontinent couplet he happened to remember from an unpublished Russian pornographer. Here is just one example of these two tendencies. Arnoldi says Gogol told him the following story in July of 1849:

"Do you know what happened to me the other day? It was late and I was walking along a remote back-street in a distant

part of town; religious singing was coming out of the lower floor of one dirty house. The windows were open, but shaded with light muslin shades such as windows in such houses are usually shaded with. I stopped, glanced in a window, and saw a terrible sight. Six or seven young women—whose shameful trade could immediately be recognized from the white powder and the rouge which covered their puffy worn-out faces—and one fat old woman of repulsive looks, were fervently praying to God before an icon set in the corner on a shaky little table. The small room, which by its décor recalled all rooms in such retreats, was brightly lit by several candles. A priest in vestments was conducting vespers; a deacon with his assistants was singing psalms. The profligates were bowing down fervently. I stood at the window for more than a quarter of an hour. . . . There was no one on the street, and I prayed with them, waiting for the end of vespers. It was terrible, very terrible," continued Gogol, "that room in disarray, with its own special appearance, its own special odor, those painted profligate dolls, the fat old woman, and right there in the same place— ikons, a priest, the Gospels, and religious singing. Isn't that all very terrible?"

But in 1850, according to Sollogub, Gogol told Countess Vielgorskaya this story:

"Several years ago," continued Gogol, and his face got all wrinkled from poorly disguised pleasure, "I had sat all evening with a friend. Since I was not entirely well that evening, my host undertook to accompany me home. We went along the street quietly chatting. In the east the dawn was already beginning to whiten—it was in the beginning of August. My friend suddenly stopped and started looking steadily at a rather large but plain and dirty house. Although he was a married man this place was familiar to him, because he muttered with surprise, "Why are those shutters closed, and why is it so dark? Wait for me, I want to find out." He clung to the window. Interested, I approached too. In a rather large room a priest was conducting a service in front of an altar-table, apparently praying for someone; a sexton was assisting him. Behind the priest stood a fat woman who glanced around threateningly from time to time; behind her, for the most part on their knees, were fifteen or twenty women with frizzled hair, with cheeks which glowed with an unnatural redness. Suddenly the gate was thrown open and a fat woman whose face very much resembled that of the first one appeared. 'Ah, Praskovia Stepanovna, how are you!' shouted my friend, 'What's going on at your place?' The fat lady said in a bass voice, 'Why my sister is planning to go to the Nizhny Novgorod fair with the girls, and she promised a service of prayers for good luck.'

"So there, Countess," added Gogol himself, "what is there to be said about rules and customs in our Russia?" Gogol's anecdote was met with a roar of laughter—and some embarrassment. The two versions of the story show how tears can be transformed into laughter.

In October 1850 Gogol went to Odessa, where he spent almost seven months during which he seemed to be in especially fine humor. He often read aloud passages from Zhukovsky's *Odyssey* or church writings and consented to read Molière's *School for Wives* for a local theater group planning to stage it. In Odessa as elsewhere he was treated as a precious vessel—to use Aksakov's phrase; all his hosts pampered and flattered him. A woman—her surname is unknown—who lived with the Repnins was his most fervent admirer; in fact the tone of her diary suggests she was in love with him, a fact of which he was apparently oblivious. Earlier that year he had proposed marriage to Iosif Vielgorsky's sister and was refused by the family.[19]

Gogol's last year, spent in Moscow, was as poor in external events as the rest of his life. He seems to have been in amiable spirits —he even attended a performance of *The Inspector General*, praised the actor who played Khlestakov, and later read part of the play for the actors. He was very articulate; numerous accounts of his manner in the last years mention his clarity and fluency in speaking always with well-chosen words. In the last months he continued working on and occasionally reading from *Dead Souls*. The story is told that often just after he had left Count A. P. Tolstoy's house for a walk, looking rather preoccupied, he would suddenly return to his room and add a few words to the manuscript. Up until two weeks before his death he was busy correcting proofs for the second edition of his *Collected Works*.

One of the greatest biographical mysteries in Russian literary history is what happened to Gogol in 1852 that made him act as he did and virtually commit suicide. As it is usually told, the first blow was the illness and death (January 26 O.S.) of Khomyakov's wife, a woman for whom Gogol felt special admiration and affection. It is reported that at one of the services for her Gogol said, "All is over for me," and commented on how terrifying a moment death is. However, he seems not to have been inordinately depressed during the following week; he wrote his mother of future plans for *Dead Souls* and continued correcting proofs until February 5. On that day he had a last disagreeable meeting with his strong-willed spiritual adviser, Father Matvey Konstantinovsky.[20] What happened is not known, but apparently it had a bad effect on Gogol. That day he complained to Shevyrev of pains in the stomach, saying they were a reaction to

some medicine he had been taking. During the next days he complained of pains in his stomach and intestines, saying his father had died at the same age of the same disease. There is a report by Gogol's servant that all during December and January Gogol had been "treating" himself by wrapping his body in a cold wet sheet. One wonders which of these various stories, if any, can be believed.

Then it was the beginning of Lent, and after a visit to church Gogol announced his intention of fasting. On the seventh he again went to church:

> However, even Communion did not calm him. That day he didn't want to eat anything, and later when he ate the Communion bread he called himself cursed, impatient, and a glutton . . .

After the sacrament Shevyrev begged him to eat, but Gogol assured him that he was eating quite enough. On the night of the ninth he sent for a priest, saying he was not satisfied with the communion he had in church and took the sacrament again at home. On Sunday the tenth he called in Count Tolstoy and, in what amounted to his last testament, gave him instructions on which of his manuscripts should be published, which entrusted to the metropolitan Filaret. On the eleventh and twelfth he was able to get up and attend vespers in Tolstoy's home, but he still ate virtually nothing. Pogodin leaves this account of what happened on the night of the eleventh:

> Tuesday night he prayed for a long time alone in his room. At 3 A.M. he called his servant boy and asked him whether the rooms on the other side of the house were warm. "Cool," he answered. "Give me a cloak; let's go, I have to arrange something there." And he went with a candle in his hands, making the sign of the cross in every room he passed through. Arriving he ordered the boy to open the flue as quietly as possible so as not to awaken anybody, and then asked for a portfolio that lay in a chest of drawers. When the portfolio was brought he took out a bundle of notebooks tied together with a lace, put them into the stove, and set fire to them with the candle in his hands. The boy, guessing what was happening, fell on his knees before him and said, "Master, what are you doing? Stop." "None of your business," he answered, "Pray." The boy began to sob and continued to plead with him. Meanwhile, the fire had gone out after only the corners of the notebooks had been charred. He noticed this, took out the bundle, untied the lace, placed the papers in so that they could start burning more easily, set fire to them again, then sat down on a chair in front of the fire, waiting for everything to be burned and reduced to ashes. Then he

crossed himself, returned to his former room, kissed the boy, lay down on a divan, and began to weep.

Gogol had destroyed Part II of *Dead Souls* (probably all eleven chapters); the manuscript represented twelve years of his life, twelve years of agonizing work. It is difficult even to conceive of the enormity of such an act of self-destruction. And Gogol immediately confused the issue by saying it was an accident:

> I wanted to burn a few things (I had long been preparing to do so), but I burned everything! How powerful the devil is—there is what he inspired me to do! I had clarified and stated much that is important there. It was the crown of my work; from it people could have understood what was unclear in my former works. . . .

If Gogol did burn *Dead Souls* accidentally it would make his death-wish more comprehensible, but it is hard to believe that Gogol, who was always extremely careful about keeping the manuscript safely locked or on his person, could have made such a disastrous error. And in any case it appears that he resolved to die several days before the destruction of *Dead Souls*.

Gogol died with his manuscript. When, near the end, Dr. Tarasenkov was brought in as a consultant, he was horrified by what he saw:

> A month had not passed since I had dinner with him; he had seemed to me a man of blooming health, brisk, fresh, strong—and now before me was a man who seemed to be wasted away to the extreme by consumption or brought to some extraordinary exhaustion by a prolonged process of wasting away. His whole body had grown extremely thin; his eyes had become dull and sunken, his face was drawn, his cheeks had become hollow, his voice had grown weak. . . .

Then during the last week Gogol resisted the clumsy efforts to treat him, crying out, "Leave me alone, don't torture me." The treatment he received from the council of five doctors was incredibly barbaric. Tarasenkov documented the last hours:

> I left so as not to be witness to the torturing of the sufferer. When I returned, three hours after my departure, at six o'clock in the evening, the bath had already been given; six large leeches hung on his nostrils; a lotion had been applied to his head. They say that when he was undressed and put in the bath he groaned intensely, cried out, said that they were doing it in vain; after they had put him in bed again—without any

underwear—he said, "Cover my shoulder, cover up my back!"
And when they put the leeches on he kept saying, "Take the
leeches off! Lift the leeches away!" (from his mouth) and attempted to grab them with his hand. They hung on there for a
long time after I got there—his hands were held by force so
that he didn't touch them. After seven o'clock Auver and Klimenkov arrived; they ordered the blood-letting continued a little
longer, to put mustard-plasters on his extremities, then a blis-
ter on the back of his neck, ice on his head, and internally a decoction of marshmallow root and laurel water. Their treatment of him was merciless; they handled him like a madman,
shouted at him as if he were a corpse. Klimenkov leaned
against him, poked at him, tumbled him over, poured some
kind of caustic spirits over his head, and when the patient
groaned from that the doctor asked, "What hurts, Nikolai
Vasilevich? Eh? Tell me!" But he groaned and didn't answer.

And he died at eight the following morning.

# Letters

*Marya Ivanovna Gogol. April 23, 1825. Nezhin.*

Don't worry, dearest mama! I have borne this blow with the firmness of a true Christian.

True, at first I was terribly stricken by this news; however, I didn't let anyone notice that I was saddened.[1] But when I was left alone, I gave myself up to all the power of mad desperation. I even wanted to make an attempt on my life. But God kept me from this—and toward evening I noticed in myself only a sadness, but no longer violent, which finally turned into a light, barely perceptible melancholy mixed with a feeling of reverence for the Most High.

I bless thee, holy faith! In thee only do I find a source of comfort and alleviation of my grief! So, dearest mama!—Now I am calm, although I cannot be happy having been deprived of the best father, the truest friend of all that is precious to my heart. But does nothing remain that would attach me to life? Don't I still have a sensitive, tender, good mother who can replace a father for me, a friend and all that is dearest and most precious?

Thus, I have you, and I still have not been abandoned by fate. Now you alone are the object of my attachment; you alone can relieve the sadness, quiet the grief. I am devoting my entire life to you. I am going to sweeten your every minute. I will do everything that a sensitive, thankful son can do. Oh, your grief troubles me more than anything else! Please, lessen it as much as possible, as I have lessened mine. Appeal, as I have appealed, to the Almighty. Why am I not with you now? You would be comforted. But in a month and a half it will be vacation, and I will be with you. Till then lessen your sadness, if only a little. Don't forget that connected to your well-being is the well-being of your son,

Who remains, with respect and tender love for you,
Nikolai Gogol-Yanovsky

P.S. Dearest mama, write to me. Are my sisters well: are my little sisters well; what are they doing now, what are they occupied with? Kiss them all for me; tell them that I will be home with them in a month and a half. Kiss grandmother, most respected Anna Matveevna for me; tell her that I owe her more than life. She comforts and returns my mother to me! And write me also, dearest mama: is Mashenka home or at boarding school? Oh, I would like very much to see her during vacation.

I am awaiting an answer with impatience. Please, write me quickly, as quickly as possible, at the next post. Every minute of delay will torment me.

Another P. S. If I don't trouble you with this and if you can, send me ten rubles for a book which I have to buy—its title is *A Course of Russian Literature*—because we study it here.[2] For my living expenses I need nothing.

## G. I. Vysotsky.[1] March 19, 1827. Nezhin.

. . . . We had a fine time during Shrovetide. We had a theater four days in a row; everyone played magnificently. All of the visitors who were here, people who have been around, said that they hadn't seen such a fine show at any provincial theater. The settings (four changes) were made masterfully, magnificently even. A fine landscape on the curtain completed the charm. The lighting of the hall was resplendent. The music also was outstanding; there were ten of our people, but they took the place of a large orchestra pleasantly; they were set up in the most advantageous place—a loud one. They performed four overtures of Rossini, two by Mozart, one by von Weber, one composed by Sevryugin,[2] and others. The plays presented by us were the following: *The Minor*, a work by Fonvizin, *The Unsuccessful Peacemaker*, a comedy by Ya. Knyazhnin, *Das Strandrecht* by Kotzebue, and in addition a French one by Florian,[3] and we still aren't surfeited—we are preparing several more plays for Easter. These activities have, however, amused me very much, and I have forgotten everything sad. But for how long? Lent has come, and with it deadly anguish.—There is absolutely no news; absolutely nothing curious has happened. . . .

—Baranov is on his own rightly acquired, ancestral estate; most cautiously, most cleverly, most interestingly he catches flies, puts them in a little jar, covers it with linen, seals it with his ancestral, hereditary coat of arms, and examines it in the light of the moon. . . .

## M. I. Gogol. March 24, 1827. Nezhin.

. . . . Spring is approaching. It is the gayest season when we can pass it gayly. This reminds me of the times of childhood, my burning passion for gardening. . . . It was papa's favorite exercise—my friend, benefactor, comforter. . . . I don't know what to call this

heavenly angel, this pure, elevated being who inspires me on my difficult path, enlivens me, gives me the gift of being able to feel my own self and often in moments of grief enters into me as a heavenly flame, brightening my clotted thoughts. At such a time I am joyful to be with him—I peer into him (that is, into myself) as into the heart of a friend. I am testing my strength for beginning an important, noble task: for the good of the fatherland, for the happiness of its citizens, for the good of the life of my fellow men; and, until now indecisive, not confident of myself (and rightly so), I am flaring up in a fire of proud awareness of myself and it is as if my soul sees this divine angel firmly, adamantly, continually pointing to the goal which is zealously being sought. Within a year I will enter the national civil service. . . .


## M. I. Gogol. April 6, 1827. Nezhin.

. . . . I refuse myself even the most urgent necessities in order to have even the slightest opportunity of keeping myself in a position such as I am in now—so that I have the opportunity of satisfying my thirst to see and feel The Beautiful. For this I collect my entire year's salary with the greatest of difficulty, putting aside a small part for the most essential expenditures. For Schiller, which I ordered from Limburg, I gave forty rubles—not at all insignificant money in relation to my means; but I have been rewarded and more, and now I spend several hours a day with the greatest of pleasure.[1] I don't forget the Russians either, and I only subscribe to the finest that is published. It goes without saying that I limit myself to some one item only; for six months at a time I do not acquire more than one book and this is extremely crushing for me. It is surprising how strong the attraction to the Beautiful can be. Sometimes I read an announcement of the publication of a work of the Beautiful—my heart beats strongly, and with a heavy sigh I drop the newspaper page of the announcement, recalling the impossibility of having it. Dreaming about getting it disturbs my sleep, and at such a time the receipt of money makes me more joyful than the most fervid greedy person. . . . I don't know what would happen to me if I still could not feel this joy—I would die of anguish and boredom. This sweetens my separation from you. You are silhouetted in my radiant dreams, and my soul embraces my entire life at once. You write that you didn't receive a letter from me in March; I think I wrote to you during the last days of March; perhaps you haven't received it yet. . . .

*Peter P. Kosyarovsky.[1] October 3, 1827. Nezhin.*

. . . . Perhaps about the time that I return home your regiment will set off God knows where and fate will drive me to Petersburg from where I will probably never be enticed to Little Russia. Yes, perhaps I will be able to live my whole life in Petersburg—at least I outlined just such a goal a long time ago already. Already in the most distant past, almost from the very years when I could understand nothing, I burned with an inextinguishable zeal to make my life necessary for the good of the nation, I seethed with desire to be of at least the smallest use. I was thrown into deep dejection by the uneasy thought that I might not be able to, that the road would be blocked in front of me, that I wouldn't be given the opportunity of being of the slightest use to the nation. Cold sweat broke out on my forehead at the thought that perhaps it would happen that I would perish in the dust not having marked out my name by one good and beautiful deed— to be in the world and not mark out one's existence was terrifying to me. In my mind I ran through all the classes, all the governmental jobs, and settled on one. On the department of justice.—I saw that here there would be more work than anywhere else, that only here could I be beneficent, only here could I be truly useful to humanity. Injustice, the greatest misfortune in the world, ripped my heart apart. I swore not to lose one minute of my brief life without doing good. For two years I constantly occupied myself with the study of the laws of other peoples—and, because they are basic to all others, the Natural laws; now I am studying those of my fatherland. Will my great plans be fulfilled? Or will Oblivion bury them in its dark cloud? During these years I hid these long-held thoughts within my- self. Distrustful of everyone, secretive, I entrusted my hidden de- signs to no one, I did not do anything which could reveal the depths of my soul. Indeed, whom would I trust and why would I express my- self; wouldn't my extravagance be laughed at, wouldn't I be con- sidered a zealous dreamer, an empty person? I didn't reveal my- self to anyone, not even to any of my comrades. . . .

*M. I. Gogol. March 1, 1828. Nezhin.*

. . . . I never said that I lost six years for nothing; I will say only that one must be amazed that in this stupid institution I could still learn so much. You expressed regret that you hadn't entrusted me to someone in the beginning, but do you know that thousands would have been needed for that. And what good would it have done? Here I

have seen those who were under special patronage; they just got better grades, but otherwise they were more stupid than others, because they studied absolutely nothing. I didn't upset you by informing you of this—knowing that you were not in a position to give me a better education and that one wouldn't as luckily get a state stipend at every institution. Apart from the unskillful science teachers, apart from the great negligence etc., languages are not taught here at all —those who arrive here with some knowledge of languages and leave having forgotten them serve as proof of this. If I know anything, it is entirely due to my own self alone. And therefore you shouldn't be surprised if I occasionally needed money for my study aids and materials, if I didn't achieve everything that I should have. I had no other guides besides myself alone, and can one perfect himself without the help of others? But I still have much time ahead; I have strength and diligence. My labors, although I have doubled them now, are not very difficult for me; on the contrary they serve me as nothing more than an amusement, and they will also serve as such during my state service, in hours free from other occupations.

As for thriftiness in my standard of living, be assured that I know how to make use of little. I have experienced more grief and need than you think. When I used to visit you at home, I always purposely tried to display absent-mindedness, capriciousness, etc. so that you would think I had acquired little polish and was little pressed by evil. But there is probably not anyone who suffered so many ingratitudes, stupid injustices, ridiculous pretensions, cold disdain, etc. I bore everything without reproaches, without grumbling; no one heard my complaints; I always even praised those who caused me grief. Truly, I am considered a riddle by everyone; no one has found me out completely. There at home I am considered capricious, some kind of unbearable pedant who thinks that he is more intelligent than anyone, that he is created in another way than most people. Do you believe it, inside I laughed at myself along with you. Here they call me a humble one, an ideal of modesty and patience. In one place I am the quietest, the most modest and polite; in another I am gloomy, pensive, uncouth, etc.—in a third garrulous and annoying in the extreme. Some think I am smart; others think I am stupid. Consider me what you like, but with my real career you will discover my real character; believe only that noble feelings always fill me, that I have never debased myself in my soul, and that I have destined my entire life to Good. You call me a dreamer, rash, as if inside I didn't laugh at them myself. No, I know people too well to be a dreamer. The lessons I have learned from them will remain ineffaceable forever, and they are the true guarantee of my happiness.

You will see that with time I will be able to repay all of their bad deeds with good deeds, because in me their evil turned into good. This is an inevitable truth: that if someone has really had the edges pounded off in the school of hard knocks, if he has constantly been made to feel the powerful oppression of misfortunes—he will be the happiest. . . .

*Peter P. Kosyarovsky. September 8, 1828. Vasilevka.*[1]

. . . . I am going to Petersburg without fail at the beginning of winter, and from there God knows where things will take me; it is very possible that I will end up in foreign parts and that nothing will be heard of me for several years. . . .

As for me, if I find my happiness, if I become able to help my relatives and sisters—I will come. If not—I will bear poverty; and who is it that poverty does not improve and make rich? But I will not get too poor. If I don't have all the means for the constant acquisition of knowledge, I can fall back on something else—you still do not know all of my abilities. I know a few crafts. I'm a good tailor, I'm not bad at painting frescoes on walls, I work in the kitchen—and I already know very much about the art of cooking (you think that I am joking—make a point of asking mother); and moreover, what I always thank God for is my perseverance and patience, of which formerly I possessed little; but now I don't give up anything I have begun until I finish it completely. I don't say this to praise myself, but to reassure you with regard to my future fate. . . .

*M. I. Gogol. January 3, 1829. St. Petersburg.*

Most respected mama, I am very guilty before you for not having written you immediately after my arrival in the capital. The spleen or some such thing fell upon me, and for almost a week already I have been sitting with my hands folded doing nothing. This must be from my failures which have made me absolutely indifferent to everything. . . .

I will say only that Petersburg does not seem to me at all what I thought—I imagined it much more beautiful, magnificent—and the rumors which others have spread about it are also false. To live here not exactly à la pig—i.e., to have cabbage soup and porridge once a day—costs incomparably more than we thought. For the

apartment we pay eighty rubles a month—just for the walls, fire-
wood, and water. It consists of two small rooms with the right to
use the landlady's kitchen. Foodstuffs aren't cheap either. . . . All
this makes me live as if in a desert; I am forced to deny myself my
best pleasure—going to the theater. If I go once, I'll go often; and for
me that would be a pretty penny—for my thin pocketbook that is. On
the road alone I used up more than 300; and the purchase of a frock-
coat and trousers here cost me 200; and 100 went on a hat, boots,
gloves, cab-drivers, and other rubbishy but necessary trifles—and
eighty rubles went for the repair of my overcoat and purchase of a
new collar for it. . . .[1]

*M. I. Gogol. April 30, 1829. St. Petersburg.*

. . . . Now I will give you a few words about Petersburg. It seems
to me you were always interested in knowing about it and were enraptured by it. Petersburg is not at all like other European capitals
or Moscow. In general each capital is characterized by its people,
who throw their stamp of nationality on it; but Petersburg has no
such character-stamp: the foreigners who settled here have made
themselves at home and aren't like foreigners at all, and the Russians in their turn have turned into foreigners—they aren't one thing
or the other. Its quietness is extraordinary; no spirit glitters among
the people; all the civil servants and functionaries constantly talk
about their departments and colleges; everything is crushed, everything is sunk in the useless, insignificant tasks in which they fruitlessly expend their lives. A meeting with them on the boulevards or
sidewalks is very amusing; they are so occupied by their thoughts
that when you come up beside one of them you hear how he curses and
converses with himself, another spices this with gesticulation and
waving of the arms. Petersburg is a rather large city; if you wanted
to walk through its streets, squares, and islands in various directions,
you would probably cover more than 100 versts[1] and in spite of its
hugeness, you can have at hand everything you need—without sending far—even in the same house. The houses here are big, especially
in the main parts of town, but they aren't high, for the most part
three or four stories, very rarely—five; there are only four or five in
the whole capital six stories high; on many houses there are very
many signs. The house in which I abide contains two tailors, one
modiste, a shoemaker, a stocking-maker, a man who repairs broken
crockery, a sponger and dyer, a confectioner, a small grocery store,

a storage for winter clothes, a tobacco shop, and, finally, a high-class midwife. It is natural that this house should be pasted all over with gold signs. I live on the fourth floor, but I feel that even here it is not very profitable for me. When I was still staying with Danilevsky[2] it was not bad at all; but now my pocketbook perceives this very much; what we paid for by halves I now pay alone. But, by the way, my works are progressing and, taking care of them attentively, I hope to achieve something in a short time; if I have real and doubtless success, I will write you about it in more detail.

There is a great deal of strolling in Petersburg. In the winter all the idlers stroll along Nevsky Prospect from twelve to two (all the civil servants are at work at this time). But in the spring (if one can call this time spring, because the trees are still not dressed in green) they stroll in Ekaterinhof, in the Summer Garden, and on Admiralty Boulevard. However, all this promenading is unbearable, especially that in Ekaterinhof the first of May; all the pleasure consists in the promenaders getting in carriages—which stretch out in a row for more than ten versts, not only that, but so close to each other that the noses of the horses of the carriage behind amiably kiss the richly garbed, lanky heydukes. These carriages are constantly kept in rows by policemen, and occasionally they halt for whole hours to keep in order—and all this is for the purpose of driving around Ekaterinhof and returning in a ceremonious row without getting out of the carriage. I too was going to direct my humble footsteps thither, but, enveloped by a cloud of dust and barely breathing from the closeness, I returned. Now Petersburg is beginning to empty—everyone is dispersing to summer cottages and estates for the spring and summer. The nights do not last more than an hour now, and in the summer there won't be any at all—just an interval between the setting and rising of the sun occupied by two colliding glows, the sunset and dawn, and it doesn't look like either evening or morning.

That's enough about Petersburg for the first time. In another letter I will talk some more about it. Now, most respected mama, my good guardian angel, now I ask you in your turn to do me the greatest of favors. You have a subtle, perspicacious mind: you know a great deal about the customs and mores of our Ukrainians, and therefore I know that you won't refuse to inform me about them in our correspondence. This is very, very necessary for me.[3] In the next letter I expect from you a description of the full dress of a village deacon from the coat to the very boots, with the names that all were given by those most steeped in the spirit of the Ukraine, the most ancient and least changed Ukrainians; likewise the names of the articles of clothing worn by our serf girls—to the last ribbon—also those of the married women and the male serfs.

Item the Second: the exact and accurate name of the dress worn before the time of the Hetmans. You recall once in our church we saw a girl dressed that way. You can question the old-timers about that; I think Anna Matveevna or Agafya Matveevna know a lot of things about years long past.

Also a circumstantial description of a wedding, not omitting the smallest details; you can question Demyan about that (I think that's his name, I don't recall his nickname), the one whom we saw as the arranger of weddings and who apparently knew all possible superstitions and customs. Also a few words about carols, about St. John the Baptist, and water nymphs. If there are other spirits or house goblins besides these—then about them in detail with their names and what they do; the simple folk have a multitude of superstitions, terrifying tales, legends, various anecdotes etc. etc. etc. All this will be extremely entertaining for me. . . .

Also I would like you to send me two of papa's Ukrainian comedies: *The Sheepdog* and *Roman and Paraska*.[4] Everything Ukrainian interests everybody here so much that I will make an effort to try to see if one of them can't be put on at a local theater. For this I might at least make a little collection—in my opinion nothing should be neglected; it is necessary to consider everything. . . .

## M. I. Gogol. July 24, 1829. St. Petersburg.

I do not know what feelings will agitate you on reading my letter; I know only that you will not be at peace. Speaking frankly, it seems that I have still not given you one completely true consolation. My rare, magnanimous mother, forgive a son who is still unworthy of you.

Now, gathering my strength to write you, I cannot understand why the pen trembles in my hand; thoughts lie upon each other like clouds, not giving each other room, and an incomprehensible power at once forces them to pour out and prevents them from pouring out before you and expressing all the depth of a tormented soul. I feel the heavy right hand of the Almighty laid upon me as a just punishment; but how terrible this punishment is! Madman! I wanted to resist those eternal, those never-silent desires of my soul which God alone put in me, changed me into a thirst which cannot be quenched by the empty indifference of the world. He has pointed out to me the road to a foreign land, so that there I would bring up my passions in silence, in seclusion, in the din of eternal work and activity, so that I myself would ascend the slippery steps to the highest one from

which I would be in a position to sow good and work for the benefit of the world. And I dared to cast aside these divine designs and grovel in this capital among these civil servants who squander their lives so fruitlessly. It is another matter to grovel where every minute of life is not wasted in vain, where every minute is a rich store of experience and knowledge. But to live out one's life where there is absolutely nothing ahead, where all the years spent at insignificant tasks will sound like a painful reproach to the soul—that is murderous! What kind of happiness is it to reach your fiftieth birthday in service and be made some kind of State Councillor and have a salary barely sufficient to keep yourself decent, and not to have the power to bring a kopek's worth of good to humanity? I think the young people here are very ridiculous; they incessantly shout that they definitely do not serve to attain high rank or make a career. Ask them why they serve. They won't be able to tell you themselves: just so—so as not to sit at home and twiddle their thumbs. Still more stupid are those who leave the remote provinces where they have estates where they might be good landlords and bring incomparably more good; and if nobles absolutely must work in the civil service, let them do it in their provinces; but no, they have to drag themselves to Petersburg where that they earn next to nothing is not as bad as the money they carry away from home and unnoticingly annihilate in a terrifying quantity here.

In spite of all this I decided, mostly to please you, to serve here no matter what; but this did not please God. Absolutely everywhere I met only failure—and, what is stranger still, where one could not expect it at all.[1] Absolutely incapable persons without any protection easily received what I could not achieve with the help of my patrons; wasn't the obvious providence of God over me in this; didn't He obviously punish me with all these failures, intending to turn me onto the true path? And what? Still I was stubborn, I waited for entire months to see if I wouldn't get something. Finally—what a terrible punishment! Nothing in the world was more poisonous or cruel for me than this. I cannot, I do not have the strength to write . . . Mama! Dearest mama! I know you are my one true friend. But would you believe it, even now when my thoughts are no longer occupied by that, even now when I remember it an inexpressible melancholy cuts into my heart. Only to you alone can I tell it. . . . You know that I was gifted with firmness—for a young man even rare firmness. . . . Who would have expected such a weakness from me. But I saw her. . . . No, I will not give her name . . . she is too exalted for anyone, not only for me. I would call her an angel, but this expression is low and does not suit her. An angel is a being which has neither virtues

nor vices, which has no character (because it is not a human), whose thoughts live in heaven alone. But no, I am babbling trifles and cannot describe her. She is a divinity—but one to a certain extent invested with human passions. A face whose striking radiance engraves itself in the heart in one instant, eyes quickly piercing the soul. But no man of the human race will survive their radiance, burning, piercing through everything. . . . Oh, if you had looked at me then. . . . True, I was able to conceal myself from everyone; but could I hide from myself. Hellish anguish with all possible torments seethed in my breast. Oh, what a cruel state! I think that if hell is prepared for sinners it is not as tormenting. No, this was not love . . . at least I have never heard of such a love. In a burst of madness and terrible mental torments, I thirsted, I seethed just to stare, I was greedy only for one look . . . To glance at her one more time—that was my one single desire growing stronger and stronger with inexpressibly cutting yearning. With terror I looked around and discerned my terrible state; absolutely everything in the world was alien to me then, life and death were equally unbearable, and my soul could not give an account of its actions. I saw that I had to run away from myself if I wanted to preserve my life, to return even a shadow of peace into my tortured soul. With tender emotion I recognized the Unseen Hand caring for me and I blessed the road so miraculously appointed to me. No, this being whom He sent to deprive me of peace and quiet, to upset my shakily created world was not a woman. Were she a woman, not with all the powers of her enchantment could she have produced such terrible, inexpressible impressions. This was a divinity created by Him, a part of Himself. But for the sake of God, don't ask her name. She is too exalted, exalted.[2]

And so I made my decision. But where, how should I begin? A trip abroad is so difficult; there are so many troubles involved. But no sooner had I undertaken it than to my surprise nothing could have gone better; why I even got permission easily. The one thing that finally stopped me was money. Here I was almost in utter despair. But suddenly I receive the money owed to the Court of Wards.[3] I immediately went there and found out how long a postponement they could give us on paying the interest; I learned that the postponement lasts four months after the due date with a payment of five rubles per 1000 per month as a penalty. Therefore they will wait until November. A decisive act, an unreasonable one—but what was I to do? I kept for myself all the money owed to the Court of Wards, and now I can say decisively: I will not demand anything more from you. Only my work and my own diligence will reward me. As for how to make up this sum, to pay it in full, you have a complete right

with the power of attorney I have executed and enclosed with this
to sell my share of the estate, in part or *in toto,* to mortgage it, to give
it as a gift etc. etc. You have complete control of it in all respects. I
had wanted to make out a deed of purchase or deed of gift, but I would
have had to pay 300 rubles just for the papers. However, even with
the power of attorney you will possess it as full and legal owner.

Don't be distressed, dear incomparable mama! This turning
point is essential for me. This school will certainly educate me; I
have a bad character, a spoiled and pampered temperament (I admit this frankly); laziness and my lifeless stay here would certainly
have made them a lifelong habit in me. No, I need to remake myself,
to be reborn, to come alive with a new life, to flower with the strength
of my soul in eternal work and activity; and if I cannot be happy (no,
I will never be happy for myself; that divine being tore peace from
my breast and went away from me), at least I will devote my entire
life to the happiness and good of my fellowmen.

But do not be terrified by the separation, I won't go far; now
my road leads to Lübeck. It is  a large German port city well
known for its trade relations with the entire world. It is four days
distant from Petersburg. I am going by steamer and therefore it will
take even less time. Your letters will take only four days to get to me.
Before this letter reaches you I will already have been able to write
to you from Lübeck and inform you of my address. . . .

Now I fall at the terrible feet of the Almighty with prayer and
supplication: let Him preserve the precious and sacred years of your
life, cast aside everything that causes you grief and displeasure and
give me strength to really earn your maternal blessing. Your most
devoted son, who loves you most of all,

                                              Nikolai Gogol-Yanovsky


*M. I. Gogol. August 13, 1829. (New Style). Lübeck.*

This morning at about three o'clock I arrived in Lübeck. I
was on the water for six days; that happened because the wind was
against us all during that time. Only now when I am alone amid the
infinite waves have I discovered what separation from you means,
my priceless mama. In those solemn, terrible hours of my life when
I ran away from myself, when I attempted to forget everything which
surrounded me, the thought of what I am causing you by this lay
upon my soul like a heavy stone; and in vain did I try to assure myself
that I was forced to submit to the will of the One who guides us from

above. . . . Forgive me, dear, magnanimous mama, forgive your un-happy son who today would wish only one thing—to throw himself into your arms and pour out before you his soul gutted and desolated by storms, to tell his whole painful story. I often think about myself: why did God, having created a heart which is perhaps unique—or at least uncommon—in the world, a pure soul flaming with a hot love for everything elevated and beautiful, why did He put all this under such a crude cover, why did He dress all this in such a terrible mix-ture of contradictions, stubbornness, insolent conceit, and the most humiliated humbleness? But my frail reason is not able to compre-hend the great decisions of the Almighty.

I ask only one thing of you: for the sake of God, don't imagine that our separation will be lengthy. I don't intend to stay here long in spite of the fact that life here is cheaper and more bearable than in Petersburg. Also, it seems I have forgotten to inform you of the main reason that made me come specifically to Lübeck. During almost the entire spring and summer in Petersburg I.was sick; now, although I am healthy, a large rash has spread all over my face and arms. The doctors said it was a result of scrofula, that my blood was badly con-taminated, that I needed to take a blood-purifying decoction and pre-scribed that I use the waters in Travemünde, a little town eighteen versts from Lübeck. I won't have to stay more than two weeks to take them. . . .

*M. I. Gogol. September 24, 1829. St. Petersburg.*

With horror I read your letter mailed September 6.[1] I expected everything from you: deserved rebukes which would still be too merciful for me, just indignation, and everything that my reckless action could bring down upon me. But this I could never have ex-pected. How, mama? You could even think that I am the prey of vile debauchery, that I am on the lowest level of human degradation! Finally, you dared attribute to me a disease the thought of which always made even my very thoughts tremble. It is the first time in my life, and I pray God that it be the last, I have received such a terri-fying letter. It seemed to me that I was hearing a curse. How could you think that the son of such angel-parents could be a monster in which not one speck of virtue remained! No, that could not happen in nature. Here is my confession to you: only the proud plans of youth (flowing, nevertheless, from a pure source, from a fiery desire to be useful) because they were not tempered with prudence, carried me

too far. But I am ready to answer in the presence of God if I have committed even one act of debauchery, and my morality has been incomparably purer here than during my life at school and at home. As for drunkenness, I have never had the habit. At home I sometimes drank wine; but I don't recall ever using it here. In no way can I understand how you concluded that I must certainly be ill with that disease. I don't think I said anything in my letter which could mark out this disease in particular. It seems to me I wrote you about my chest disease, due to which I could breathe only with great effort— and which, fortunately, has left me now. . . .

For the sake of God and the happiness of your children, do not worry about me. But one thing only I ask of you with tears in my eyes: do not consider me capable of debauchery; don't confuse mad recklessness with that; even if you hear that I am among the most debauched of the most debauched believe me: I will never transgress the sacred rules of virtue which have been ineffaceably engraved in my heart. . . .

*M. I. Gogol. February 2, 1830. St. Petersburg.*

. . . . My entire income consists in occasionally writing or translating some piece for Mssrs. the journalists, so don't be angry, my generous mama, if I often bother you with the request to send me information about the Ukraine or something like that. This is my bread.[1] And now I will ask you to collect some such information: if you hear an amusing anecdote somewhere among the peasants in our village or some other one, or among the landowners. And please, also include for me the customs, mores, and superstitions. And if no one else, at least question Anna Matveevna or Agafya Matveevna about the old days: what kind of clothes the small and large landowners and their wives or they themselves had; what kinds of material were known then, and all this with the most detailed details; what kind of anecdotes and stories—funny, amusing, sad, terrible—happened in their time. Don't scorn anything, everything has value for me. . . .

*M. I. Gogol. June 3, 1830. St. Petersburg.*

. . . . I gave up my literary activities and participation in journals long ago, although one of my essays got me the position I occupy at present.[1] Now I am just collecting materials and pondering

in quiet my vast work. I hope that you, most respected mama, occasionally in hours of leisure will not stop sending, as before, all information interesting to me which you have managed to collect. . . .

Every day at nine o'clock I set out for class at the academy of arts where I am studying painting which I am absolutely unable to give up—all the more that here there are all the means to perfect oneself in it, and none of these require anything except work and effort. Through my acquaintance with artists (many of them famous even) I have the opportunity to make use of means and advantages inaccessible to many. Without even saying anything about their talent, I cannot help being enraptured by their character and manners —what people they are! Having made their acquaintance, one can never get along without them—what modesty combined with the greatest talent! . . .

*M. I. Gogol. October 10, 1830. St. Petersburg.*

. . . . I am sending you, most precious mama, the last three issues of *Notes of the Fatherland,*[1] excluding, however, only a few essays of little interest. I forewarn you not to look for anything of mine there, because for a long time now I have not participated in this journal— as much, first, because my work at the civil-service office has increased as because the cursed laziness common to almost all Ukrainians possessed me in the rest of my free time—laziness with which until now I have been in irreconcilable hostility and which, it seems, at present is laughing at my effort to overcome it. . . .

*M. I. Gogol. February 10, 1831. St. Petersburg.*

. . . . Your letter made me happy because I saw from it that our estate, thank God, is in good condition. Have faith that God is preparing nothing for us in the future but well-being and happiness. Their source is in our own hearts. The better the heart is, the more right and claim to happiness it has. How I thank the hand of God for those unpleasantnesses and failures which I have had to suffer. I would not exchange them for all the treasures in the world. What haven't I experienced in that short time. Another wouldn't have happened to have such variety in a lifetime. That time was the best education for me, one which I think a Tsar would seldom have. But now what peace and quiet there is in my heart! What steadfast firmness and courage in my soul! Yearning burns inextinguishably in me—but this yearning is: to be useful. . . .

*A. S. Pushkin. August 21, 1831. St. Petersburg.*

.... In Petersburg it's unbearably dull. The cholera has chased
everyone off in all directions. ... I was at Pletnev's[1] and gave him
your package and letter in good condition. Most curious of all was my
meeting with the printers.[2] No sooner had I got in the door when
the type-setters, catching sight of me, each let loose snorting and
spitting in their hands turning away to the wall. This somewhat surprised me. I went to the foreman, and after several clever digres-
sions he finally said that: "The items that you deigned to send from
Pavlovsk for printing are to extremity amusing and brought the type-
setters great amusement." From this I concluded that I am a writer
completely to the taste of the rabble. Apropos of the rabble, do you
know that there is scarcely anyone who is able to express himself
to it better than our mutual friend, Alexander Anfimovich Orlov.[3]
In the foreword to his new novel, *The Ceremony of the Burial of Ivan
Vyzhigin, Son of Vanka Kain,* he said, addressing himself to the readers: "I have many, very many novels in my head [his own words],
but they are all still sitting in my head—but what lively little kiddies
these novels are; they fairly hop out of my head. But, no, I will not allow them out until it's time, and then, if you please, I will supply them
by the half-dozens. If you please, if you please! Oh, you my cordial
friends! Orthodox people!" The last salutation really touches the
heart of the Russian people. This is completely in his spirit, and just
here, not joking, is the decisive superiority of Alexander Anfimovich
to Thaddeus Benediktovich.[4] Another friend of ours, Bestuzhev-
Ryumin,[5] is thriving and not long ago said in his newspaper: "It
must be admitted that *The Northern Mercury* is a bit sharper than
other *Literary Supplements.*"[6] Still more about the rabble. Do you
know what a good idea it would be to write an aesthetic analysis of two
novels—let us suppose: *Peter Ivanovich Vyzhigin* and *The Falcon
Would be a Falcon But a Hen Ate Him.* To begin like they begin in
our journals nowadays: "Finally, it seems, the time has come when
romanticism has triumphed decisively over classicism; and the old
standard bearers of the French koran on stilts (something like
Nadezhdin)[7] have gone to the devil. In England Byron, in France
Victor Hugo (immense in his greatness), Ducange, and others have,
in a certain display of objective life, reproduced its new world of
indivisibly-individual phenomena. Neither could Russia, the wisdom
of the government of which amazes all the educated peoples of Europe et cetera et cetera, remain standing still. Soon two representa-
tives of its transfigured greatness arose. The readers will guess that
I am speaking of Mssrs Bulgarin and Orlov. One of them, that is,

Bulgarin, is marked by a purely Byronic tendency (indeed it is not a bad idea to compare Bulgarin to Byron). In our countryman we can see that same haughty pride, that same storm of strong indomitable passions which sharply outline the fiery and at the same time gloomy character of the British poet. The same selfless work and scorn for all that is base and mean appertain to them both. Even Bulgarin's life itself is nothing more than a repetition of Byron's life; even in their very portraits an extraordinary resemblance is noticeable. One may refute the opinion of Feofilakt Kosichkin[8] about Alexander Anfimovich—it is said that Orlov is more a philosopher, that Bulgarin is all poet." Here it would not be a bad idea to take the heroes of Bulgarin's novel—Napoleon and Peter Ivanovich—and examine them both as pure creations of the poet himself. Naturally here it is necessary to arm oneself with the glasses of a severe reviewer and cite passages (ones, it goes without saying, such as were not in the novel). It would not hurt to add: "Mr. Bulgarin, why did you make Peter Ivanovich confess his love to so-and-so so early, and why didn't you continue the conversation of Peter Ivanovich with Napoleon, and why did you involve the Pole (could you even think up a name for him) in the very place where the denouement occurs?" All this is so that the readers should see the complete impartiality of the critic. But the main thing is—one must agree with the complaints of our journalists that, really, party spirit has rent our literature in a terrible manner; and because of this one cannot overhear a just evaluation. All opinions are divided into two parties, some on Bulgarin's side, the others on Orlov's side. While their adherents attack each other with such violence, they know absolutely no enmity between themselves; and inside, like all great geniuses, they respect each other. . . .


*V. A. Zhukovsky.[1] September 10, 1831. St. Petersburg.*

I had difficulty with the arrangements for my book,[2] and only now have I received copies to send to you. One for you yourself, another for Pushkin, a third, with a sentimental inscription, for Rozetti,[3] and the rest for whom you decide at your discretion. How much trouble this book gave me. For three days I constantly gadded back and forth from the printing house to the Censorship Committee, from the Censorship Committee to the printing house; and only now, finally, have I caught my breath. My God! How many copies I would give up just to be able to see you for a minute. If, I often think to my-

self, there were to appear in the area around Petersburg some kind of
wandering nighttime bandit and he would steal this unbearable hunk
of land, this twenty-four versts from Petersburg to Tsarskoe Selo,
and would take to his heels toward the edge of the world with them—
or that some starved bear would hide them in his bearish belly instead of his breakfast. Oh! With what ecstasy would I then brush off
the dust of the earth from your boots with my hair, with what ecstasy would I fall on my knees at the feet of Your Poetic Excellency
and with greedy ear catch from your lips the supersweet nectar prepared by the gods themselves from an infinite quantity of witches,
devils, and all that is dear to our heart. But not such is vexatious reality and material actuality; quarantines have turned this twenty-four
versts into the road from Petersburg to Kamchatka. Do you know
what I found out only the other day? That, er . . . But you won't believe
me, you will call me superstitious. That the cause of all this is none
other than the enemy of the honorable cross of the churches of our
Lord and all that is protected by the holy sign. This was the devil who
put on himself a green uniform with crested buttons, hung at his
side a sharp-edged sword, and became a quarantine observer. But
Pushkin, like a holy angel, was not frightened by this horned civil
servant; like a spirit he floated past him and in a twinkling of an eye
turned up in Petersburg on Voznesensky Prospect and called out in
a trumpet-like voice to me as I was scuffling along a low sidewalk
past high houses. This was a joyous moment. It has already past.
That happened on August 8. And towards evening of the same day
everything again became boring, dark, as in an empty house:

> The windows with chalk
> Are whitened; the mistress is gone,
> But where? God knows, there's not a trace.[4]

The memory remained—and there are still a lot of other things which
will sufficiently sweeten the loneliness here: the news that your
"Folktale" is already finished and another has been started—just
the fine beginning of which nearly made me go crazy. And Pushkin
completed his folktale![5] My God, what will come next? It seems
to me that now the huge edifice of purely Russian poetry is being
raised; the terrible granite blocks have already been set as the foundation, and the same architects will raise the walls and the cupola to
the praise of the ages; and let our descendents worship and have a
place to raise their prayers of adoration. How beautiful is your lot,
Great Architects! And how terrible is the Hell prepared for the pa-
gans, renegades, and other rabble: they do not understand you, and
do not know how to pray. . . .

## A. S. Danilevsky. November 2, 1831. St. Petersburg.

. . . . I have spent the entire summer in Pavlovsk and Tsarskoe Selo. Therefore I was not a witness to the times of terror in the capital. Almost every evening we met: Zhukovsky, Pushkin, and I. Oh, if only you knew how many beauties have come out from under the pens of these men. Pushkin has a tale written in octaves, *The Cook*,[1] in which all Kolomna and Petersburg nature is alive. —Besides that: Russian folktales—not like *Ruslan and Ludmila*,[2] but completely Russian. One is even written without meter, just with rhymes—unimaginable charm![3] Zhukovsky also has Russian folktales,[4] some in hexameters, others simply in tetrameter—and a strange thing: it is impossible to recognize Zhukovsky! It seems that a new great poet has appeared—and a purely Russian one. There's nothing left of the former one, nothing German. And what a heap of new ballads! They will appear in a few days. . . .

## A. S. Danilevsky. March 30, 1832. St. Petersburg.

. . . . Now a few words about your letter. On what grounds did you start talking about the jokes with which my letter was supposedly filled? And what did you find that was senseless in my writing you that you talk only about the poetic side, not making reference to the prosaic? Don't you understand what the poetic side means? The poetic side: "She is incomparable, unique" etc. The prosaic: "She is Anna Andreevna so-and-so." The poetic: "She belongs to me, her soul is mine." The prosaic: "Aren't there perhaps some obstacles to her belonging to me not only in soul, but in body and all, in a word—*ensemble*." Beautiful, fiery, exhausting, and inexplicable is love before marriage; but he who has loved before marriage has displayed only one burst, one effort to love. This love is not complete; it is only a beginning, momentary, but it is a strong and fierce enthusiasm which shakes the organism of a man for a long time. But the second part, or better, the book itself—because the first is only the advance announcement of it—is calm, an entire sea of quiet pleasures which open up more and more each day; and you are amazed by them with all the more pleasure because they seemed absolutely insignificant and ordinary. This is the artist in love with the work of a great master —from which he can never tear his eyes; and every day he discovers in it new and still more new enchanting features full of a vast genius, amazed at himself because he could not see them before. Love before marriage is the poetry of Yazykov[1]: it is effective, fiery; and

already in the first moment it possesses all one's feelings. But love after marriage is the poetry of Pushkin: it does not grasp you suddenly, but the more you look into it, the more it opens up, unveils itself, and finally turns into a vast and majestic ocean—and the more you look into this ocean, the more infinite it seems; and then the very poetry of Yazykov seems only a part, a small river falling into the ocean. See how beautifully I tell a story! Oh, I would make a fine novelist if I started writing novels! By the way, I will prove this very thing to you with an example, for without an example no proof is proof, and the ancients acted very well in putting one into every dissertation. I think you have already read "Ivan F. Shponka."[2] Before marriage he is amazingly like Yazykov's poetry, while after marriage he becomes absolutely the poetry of Pushkin.

Do you want to know what is going on here in this water city? The Elevated One arrived with Mr. Plato and Pelikan.[3] All this troupe will stay here until May and perhaps longer. The Elevated One is the same as ever. His *Tasso* which he has written for the sixth time already is extraordinarily fat, taking up quarter of a ream of paper. The characters are all extraordinarily noble, full of self-sacrifice, and to boot he leads out on the stage a thirteen-year old lad, a poet up to his ears in love with Tasso. He plays with similes like balls, shakes Heaven, Hell, and Earth like a feather. It's enough to say that the former: "his lips were blue like the color of the sea" or "the reed whispered like chains whisper in the darkness" are nothing compared to the ones he uses now. As before he still doesn't like Pushkin. Boris Godunov doesn't please him. . . .[4]

*A. S. Danilevsky. December 20, 1832. St. Petersburg.*

I have finally received a letter from you. I already thought that you had bolted for Odessa or some other place. I understand and feel the state of your soul very much, although thanks to fate I have not managed to experience it.[1] I say "thanks" because that flame would turn me into ashes in one instant. I would not find pleasure for myself in the past, I would strive to turn it into the present and I myself would be the victim of this effort; and therefore, for my salvation I have a firm will which has twice led me away from the desire to glance into the abyss.[2] You are a lucky fellow—it is your lot to taste the greatest good in life—love. And I . . . but it seems we have turned onto Byronism. And why do you attack Pushkin for pretending? It seems to me that it is Byron rather than he.[3] Byron is too ardent, he

talks too much about love—and almost always in a frenzy. There is something suspicious about it. Strong lasting love is as simple as a dove, that is, it is expressed simply without any defining and picturesque adjectives; it does not express, but it is apparent that it wants to express something which, however, it is impossible to express—and by this it speaks more powerfully than any fiery eloquent tirades. And as proof that I am right, read the very same lines which you command me to kiss.[4] It's a pity you aren't coming to Petersburg, but if you find it profitable in Odessa there's nothing to be done—just don't forget to write. It's a pity we got to live together so little at home. It still seems to me that I hardly saw you.—I'll tell you only that Krasnenkoy[5] is clamoring (and not kidding) about marrying some actress who, it is said, has extraordinary talent, better than Bryansky[6] (however, I haven't seen her); and he insists very strongly that it is essential for him to marry. However, it seems to me that this enthusiasm will grow cold for a while. The dragoon is here too.[7] Such a handsome lad! With terrifying side-whiskers and spectacles, but an extraordinary phlegmatic. His little brother, in order to show him all the curiosities of the city, took him to a bordello the other day; only the whole time that his little brother was sweating away behind the screen, he read a book with extreme coolness and went out, as if from a pastry shop, without having touched anything, without even having made a significant face at his brother. . . .

*M. P. Pogodin.[1] February 1, 1833. St. Petersburg.*

. . . . You ask about Dikanka Evenings. To Hell with them! I won't publish them. And although monetary acquisitions would not be superfluous for me, I cannot write, add tales, for that. I have absolutely no talent for speculations. I had even forgotten that I was the creator of these Evenings, and only you reminded me about it. However, Smirdin[2] printed 150 copies of the first part, because without the first no one was buying the second from him. I'm glad there weren't any more. And let them be doomed to obscurity until something weighty, great, artistic comes out of me. . . .

I don't want anything shallow and can't invent anything great. In a word—mental constipation! Pity me and wish me well! Let your word be more effective than an enema. Do you see what a prosaist I have become and how nastily I express myself? It's all from inactivity.

*A. Danilevsky. February 8, 1833. St. Petersburg.*

. . . . My mind is in a strange state of inaction. My thoughts are so confused that I can't gather them in one whole; and it seems it is not just
I—but everything is drowsing. Literature is not moving: only a pair
of rubbishy anthologies have come out—*Alcion* and *Bela's Comet.*
There is perhaps a teaspoon of honey in them, and all the rest is tar.
You don't meet Pushkin anywhere except at balls. He will waste his
whole life there unless some chance event or greater necessity drags
him off to the country. Only Prince Odoevsky is more active. In a
few days he is printing fantastic scenes with the title *Motley Tales.*[1]
I recommend it; it will be a very fanciful edition, because it is being
executed under my supervision. Are you reading the *Iliad?* Poor
Gnedich no longer exists.[2] People and poets die like flies. . . .


*M. Pogodin. February 20, 1833. St. Petersburg.*

. . . . I don't know why I thirst so much for contemporary fame now.
The entire depth of my soul fairly bursts out. But I have still written
absolutely nothing. I didn't write you: I am possessed with the idea
of a comedy. When I was in Moscow, on the road, and when I arrived
here I couldn't get it out of my head; but I still haven't written anything. The other day I was even about to begin to form the plot; the
title was already written on a thick white notebook: *Vladimir of the
Third Degree.*[1] And how much malice! laughter! salt! But suddenly I stopped, seeing how my pen kept knocking against points
which the censorship wouldn't pass for anything. And what does it
mean if the play would not be performed? Drama lives only on the
stage. Without the stage it is like a soul without a body. What master
painter will exhibit an unfinished work to the people? Nothing is left
for me to do but invent the most innocent plot, something which
couldn't even offend a policeman. But what is comedy without truth
and malice? So I can't begin a comedy. I take up History—and the
stage moves before me, the applause rings out, mugs stick out of the
loges, gallery, parterre and bare their teeth, and—to hell with history. And that's why I'm sitting with my thoughts inactive. . . .


*M. I. Gogol. October 2, 1833. St. Petersburg.*

. . . . Do me a favor, my priceless mama, don't bring up Olya
as Liza was brought up.[1] Keep her away from the maid's room so
that she never goes in there. Order her to be in your presence con-

tinually. There is no better bringing-up of a girl than under her mother's eyes, especially one like you. Let her sleep in your room. Can't you arrange it so that in the evening everyone is together at one table—you, sister, Pavel Osipovich,[2] and she—and each one would do his own work. Give her a few more chores, let her do the same work grown-ups do; give her necessary household things to sew, not scraps. Assign the pouring of tea to her. For the sake of God do not neglect these trifles. Do you know how important the impressions of childhood years are? What is just a good habit and inclination in childhood turns into virtue in mature years.

Inspire her with the rules of religion. It is the foundation of everything. If religion had power over Liza, one could do anything with her. Don't teach her any catechism—which is gibberish for a child. And also, it will do her little good if she goes to church constantly. Nothing there is comprehensible to a child either—neither the language nor the rites. She will become accustomed to viewing all this as a comedy. But instead of all this tell her that God sees everything, knows everything that she does. Tell her more about the future life; with all possible colors which children like describe the joys and pleasures which await the righteous, and what horrible, cruel torments wait the sinful. For God's sake tell her about this more often, at every good or bad deed of hers. You will see what beneficial results this will produce. One must shake children's feelings strongly, and then they will preserve all that is fine for a long time. I experienced this on myself. I remember very well how I was brought up.

To this day I often imagine my childhood before me. You employed every effort to bring me up as well as possible. But, unfortunately, parents are rarely good educators of their children. You were still young then, you had children for the first time; for the first time you had dealings with them, and so could you know exactly how you ought to proceed and exactly what was necessary? I remember I didn't feel anything strongly, I viewed everything as things which were created to please me. I didn't especially love anyone—except only you, and that only because nature itself instilled this feeling. I viewed everything with dispassionate eyes; I went to church only because I was ordered or I was taken; but standing in it I didn't see anything except the priests' robes, the priest, and the repulsive howling of the sextons. I crossed myself because I saw that everyone was crossing himself. But one time—I remember that instance vividly, as if it were now. I asked you to tell me about the last judgment; and so well, so comprehensively, so touchingly did you tell me, a child, about the blessings which await people for a virtuous life—and so

strikingly, so terrifyingly did you describe the eternal torments of the sinful—that this shook and awakened all sensitivity within me. That sparked and subsequently produced the most elevated thoughts in me.—But enough about religion; now let us turn to the science of life. She should even play with her toys in your presence in the living room or wherever you are sitting.—If guests arrive, make her be in the guests' presence continually. Let her even talk and mix in the general conversation if the conversation is comprehensible to her. If not, let her bring her toys or do some chore—sew or work right there in the presence of the guests. That alone will destroy the wildness which children who stay in the maids' room get.—By that alone she will acquire the poise which is so nice and always enchants us. By that alone she will acquire and learn ahead of time how to talk pleasantly and interest others with her conversations. Can you find at least one girl in our neighborhood who knows how to entertain, with whom it would not be boring? But how many there are who absolutely don't know how to say a word! And why? Because of the maids' rooms, because of the lack of common sense of mothers who only take their daughters under their care and get them away from the maids' rooms when they are already becoming of age, and they protect them when there is no longer anything to protect, when foolishness and prejudices have already put their roots too deep.[3]— There is much which I see better and more clearly than others. In a few years I learned a great deal, especially in this regard; I studied man from his cradle to his end and am not a bit happier for it. My heart aches when I see how people go astray. They discuss virtue and God; however, they do nothing. I think I would like to help them, but rare ones of them possess the bright natural mind to see the truth of my words. You are different, priceless mama, you understand me in this respect. . . .

*M. A. Maximovich.[1] November 9, 1833. St. Petersburg.*

My very amiable fellow countryman, I received your letter through Smirdin. I'm devilishly mad at myself that I don't have anything to send you for your *Morning-Star.*[2] I have a hundred different beginnings and not one story, not even one complete excerpt suitable for an almanac. From someone else's hands Smirdin got one ancient story[3] of mine—about which I had almost completely forgotten and which I am ashamed to call my own; however it is so big and clumsy that it's not at all suitable for your almanac. My dear fellow countryman, I love you with all my heart and soul; don't be

out fail. But not now. If you knew what terrible upheavals have happened inside me, how violently everything within me has been torn to pieces. God, how many things I have burned, how many things I have suffered through![4] But now I hope that everything will calm down and I will again be active, in motion. Now I have taken up the history of our one and only, poor Ukraine. Nothing so calms one as history. My thoughts are beginning to flow more quietly and harmoniously. It seems to me that I will write it, that I will say much which has not been said before me.[5]

I was made very happy hearing from you about the rich accumulation of songs and Chodakowski's collection.[6] How I would like to be with you now and examine them together by a flickering candle, between walls crammed with books, book-dust, with the greed of a Jew counting gold pieces. My joy, my life! Songs! How I love you! What are all the chronicles I am now digging through next to these sonorous, living chronicles!

I have received many new ones myself now, and what charms there are among them.[7] I'll copy them for you. Not so soon, because there are very many of them. Oh yes, I'll ask you, do a favor and copy all the songs which you have, excluding the printed ones and the ones I communicated to you. Do a favor and send a copy to me. I cannot live without songs. You do not understand what a torture it is. I know that there are so many songs, and at the same time I don't know. It's the same as if someone told a woman he knew a secret and wouldn't inform her. Order a scribe with handsome legible handwriting to copy it in a notebook *in quarto* at my expense. I don't have the patience to wait for the printed one; besides, then I will know what songs to send you so that you don't have two like duplicates. You can't imagine how songs help me in history. Even the nonhistorical ones, even the dirty ones; each one provides a new feature for my history, they all reveal more clearly and clearly a life which, alas, has passed and people who, alas, have passed . . . Order this done as soon as possible. In return I will send you the ones I have, of which there are almost two hundred. . . .

*M. Pogodin. January 11, 1834. Petersburg.*

Ehe, he, he he! Half a month of the 1834th has been swallowed already! Yes, a long time! A lot of rubbish has floated past in the world since we exchanged scant little letters the last time, and even more since we've shown each other our figures!

I would send you New Year's greetings and wish you . . . but I don't want to—in the first place because it's too late, and in the second because our good wishes aren't worth a damn. It seems to me that fate doesn't do anything with them except wipe itself when it goes to the john.

To this day all my wishes haven't got me a penny.

You are lucky, golden grasshopper, that you're sitting in your newly built house—which is, without doubt, cold. (N. B. But he who has a warm soul is not cold inside.) Your hand flies along the paper, your field marshal keeps vigil over it, and under your feet lies a fat fool, i. e., the first issue of Smirdin's *Library* . . . . Apropos of *The Library:* that is a rather amusing story. Senkovsky[1] is much like an old drunkard and debauchée whom the barkeeper himself did not dare let in the pub for some time. But who, nevertheless, bursts in and, screaming drunk, smashes the flasks, bottles, cups, and all the noble apparatus.

The class standing above Brambeus's is indignant with the shamelessness and insolence of the pub carouser; this class, loving decorum, loathes it—but reads it. The heads of divisions and directors of departments read and overstrain their sides from laughter. Officers read it and say, "Son of a bitch, how well he writes!" Landowners buy, subscribe, and, no doubt, will read it. Only we sinners set it aside for housekeeping. Smirdin's capital grows. But that's nothing. Here's what's good. Senkovsky authorized himself the power to decide what is good or bad, to put things together the way he likes; he takes the plays sent to the journal, crosses out passages, redoes them, cuts off the ends, and pins on different ones. Of course, if everyone is going to be as humble as the highly respectable Thaddeus Benediktovich[2] (whose face strongly resembles Lord Byron's, as one officer of the Kirasirsky regiment of the Light-Guards expressed himself in all seriousness) who has declared that he always considers it a great honor for himself when his essays are corrected by such an elevated editor—whose *Fantastic Journeys* are even better than his own.[3] But it is doubtful that all writers are as timid as this respectable statesman.

But here's what is bad—we have all been made fools! All of our literary bigwigs have suddenly realized this—but too late. The respectable editors have begun to ring bells with our names, have collected subscribers, made the people stand openmouthed, and now they are riding around on our backs. They have set another cornerstone for their power. That's another *Bee!*[4] And now our literature is without a voice. Meanwhile, these horsemen are influencing all Russia. . . .

At present I'm completely engrossed in a History of the Ukraine and a World History; both are starting to move. This imparts a certain calmness to me and indifference to everyday affairs, and without this I would be terribly angry at all these circumstances.

Oh, my brother, how many thoughts are coming to me now! And what immense, full, fresh thoughts! I think I will do something unique in my Universal History. My Ukrainian History is extremely wild, but it couldn't be otherwise. I am reproached because the style is a little too fiery—burning and lively in a manner unlike histories—but what kind of history is it that is boring? . . .

### A. S. Pushkin. May 13, 1834. St. Petersburg.

. . . . Now I'm going to trouble you with the following request: if when you talk to Uvarov,[1] the conversation gets around to me, tell him you visited me and found me barely alive.[2] On this point curse me roundly for living here and not getting out of the city immediately; say that the doctors ordered me to go immediately and try to catch the season in Kiev. And having said that within a month I could very easily give up the ghost altogether, start talking about something else—the weather or something like that. It seems to me that this won't be completely useless.

### A. S. Pushkin. (End of December 1834, beginning of January 1835.) St. Petersburg.

"Notes of a Madman" hit a rather unpleasant snag during the censorship yesterday. But, thank God, things are a little better today. At best I'll have to limit myself to throwing out the best passages! Well, forget about them! If it hadn't been for this delay, my book might have come out tomorrow.[1] But I am sorry that I didn't get to see you. I am sending you the foreword. Do me a favor—look it over and if you find anything, correct and change it with ink immediately. As you know I haven't yet written any serious forewords, and therefore am completely inexperienced in this matter.

### A. S. Pushkin. (About January 22, 1835.) St. Petersburg.

I'm still sick. I would like to see you very much. Drop in around two or three; at that hour you'll probably be somewhere nearby. I'm

sending you two copies of *Arabesques*[1] which, to the surprise of everyone, appeared in two parts. One copy is for you and the other, cut, is for me. Read mine and do me a favor: take a pencil in your little hands and in no way stop your indignation at the sight of errors, but mark them all out immediately. —I need this very much.

God send you enough patience to read it!


## M. A. Maximovich. March 22, 1835. St. Petersburg.

. . . . I am sending you *Mirgorod*.[1] I hope you will like it. At least I would like it to drive away your splenetic mood which, as far as I can notice, occasionally takes possession of you even in Kiev. I swear, we have all gotten terribly far away from our primitive elements. We, especially you, just can't get accustomed to looking at life with a to-hell-with-everything attitude as the Cossack always did. Have you ever tried dancing a trepak all over the room in nothing but your nightshirt when you get up from bed?

Listen, my brother: in our soul there is so much that is sad and doleful that if you allow all of it to come out to the outside, then the devil alone knows what will happen. The stronger the old sadness which approaches the heart, the louder the new external gaiety should be. There is a wonderful thing in the world—a bottle of good wine. When your soul demands another soul to tell all of its half-sad story, get into your room, uncork the bottle, and when you have drunk a glass, you will feel how your feelings become animated. This means that I, separated from you by 1500 versts, am drinking and remembering you. . . .


## M. Pogodin. March 23, 1835. St. Petersburg.

Since *The Moscow Observer* will not exist, send me my nose back, because I need it very much.[1] And please print an announcement for *Arabesques* in *The Moscow News*.[2] Do me a favor in words like: "Now everyone everywhere is doing nothing except talk about *Arabesques*. This book has aroused universal curiosity, and it is selling at a fearful rate" (N. B. I haven't received so much as a half-kopek profit yet), etc. . . .

## M. I. Gogol. April 12, 1835. St. Petersburg.

. . . . You give way to your dreams too much. Speaking of my works you call me a genius. Whatever else that may be, it is very strange. To call me a genius—me, a good, ordinary, simple person, perhaps not entirely stupid and having common sense. No, mama, these qualities are too little to make genius—otherwise we would have so many geniuses that it would be impossible to get through the crowd. Therefore, mama, I request you not to call me this—especially in conversation with anyone. Don't express any opinion about my works and don't expatiate on my virtues. Just simply say that he's a good son; add nothing more, and don't repeat it several times. This will be the best praise for me.

If you only knew how unpleasant, how disgusting it is to hear parents talk incessantly about their children and praise them! I tell you that I have never felt respect for such parents, and I have always considered them pitiful little braggarts; and as far as I have been able to hear from others, all this praise seemed disgusting to them too. One more request: my good and intelligent mama, never express opinions about literature. You are greatly mistaken. You imagine that an intelligent person must without fail understand and express opinions about literature—not at all so.

I know very many intelligent people who pay absolutely no attention to literature, and I respect them nonetheless. Literature is not at all a result of the intellect; it is a result of feeling—just like music and painting. For example, I have no ear for music, and I don't talk about it; but no one despises me because of this. I don't know a smidgin about mathematics, and no one laughs at me. But if, not knowing mathematics, I start to talk about it, everyone will laugh at me.

Do you know what kind of scrape one can get into. Now you, for instance, have ascribed to me the works of an author who is repugnant to good taste, an author who has absolutely nothing in common with me, who sends only those people who live on farms into rapture, who enjoys the disdain even of readers who do not entirely comprehend things; you attributed his things to me, and when I assured you in my letter, swore to you—you stubbornly held on to your idea.[1] When I read this part of your letter to a man who has taste (however, I didn't say a word about the letter being yours), he burst out laughing. I myself was amused when I read it, but at the same time I was vexed to see how a fine intelligent lady filled with true nobility of spirit could compromise and abase herself. Do you see how much subtlety and special sensitivity for literature is necessary in order to judge it correctly—even few literary people possess it. . . . This art

is very difficult. Do you realize that in Petersburg, in all Petersburg there are perhaps only five persons who understand art deeply and correctly, and at the same time there are many truly fine, noble, educated people in Petersburg. I myself, having wallowed in and devoted myself to this craft, I myself never make so bold as to say that I can judge and completely understand such and such a work. No, I may understand only a tenth of it. Therefore, don't talk about it. If you are asked, answer—but answer in a monosyllable and immediately shift the conversation to something else. . . .


*A. S. Pushkin. October 7, 1835. St. Petersburg.*

I have decided to write you myself; I asked Natalya Nikolaevna before, but I still haven't received any news. I earnestly request you to send me my comedy—if you took it with you (it's not in your study)—the one which I gave to you for your comments.[1] I'm sitting here without money and absolutely without any means; I have to give it to the actors for performance—which is usually done at least two months in advance. Do me a favor and send it as soon as possible and hastily make at least a few general comments. I have begun to write *Dead Souls*.[2] The plot has stretched out into a very long novel, and it will, I think, be extremely amusing. But now I've stopped it on the third chapter. I'm hunting for a good slanderer with whom one can become intimate. I want to show all Russia—at least from one side—in this novel.

Do me a favor and give me some plot; whether it's amusing or not amusing doesn't matter as long as its a purely Russian anecdote.[3] In the meantime my hand trembles to write comedy. If this doesn't happen, my time will be wasted for nothing, and I don't know what I will do with my financial circumstances then. Besides my stinking university salary of 600 rubles I have no other sources now. Please, give me a plot, in a jiffy it will be a comedy in five acts; and, I swear, it will be funnier than hell. For the sake of God. My mind and stomach are both starving. And send *The Marriage*. I embrace you, and wish to kiss and embrace you personally soon.

Your Gogol.

Neither my *Arabesques* nor my *Mirgorod* are moving at all. The devil knows what this means. Booksellers are people such as one can hang on the nearest tree without feeling any pangs of conscience.

## M. P. Pogodin. January 18, 1836. St. Petersburg.

Hey brother, you have completely forgotten me! I was waiting for a letter from you in answer to mine, but I gave up waiting. Forgive me for not sending you my comedy yet.[1] It was all ready and copied; but, as I see now, I must certainly rework several scenes. It won't be delayed, because I have decided that in any case it will certainly be performed at Easter. Towards Lent it will be all ready, and during Lent the actors will have time to memorize their roles completely. And please tell me (you didn't inform me) what arrangements you made for the ninety copies of *Mirgorod* which were sent to you back in the month of May. If they still haven't been sold, and if you need the 500 rubles that I took, I will try to send them to you, because I should get something for the comedy. And do me a favor—send me my "Nose." I have extreme need of it now. I want to re-do it a little and place it in a small collection which I am getting ready to publish.[2] Thank you very much for your gifts: *The Pretender*, the Russian history, and the lectures on Heeren. . . .[3]

## M. P. Pogodin. February 21, 1836. St. Petersburg.

. . . . Now I'm busy with the staging of the play. I am not sending you a copy because I am constantly making corrections. I don't even want to send it to the actors before my arrival, because if they just read it without me, it will be difficult to re-instruct them in my way. I expect to be in Moscow in May if not in April. Can't you send me a catalogue of the books about Slavistics, history, and literature which you have acquired or have not acquired—you'll greatly oblige me— and, if possible, note in two or three words the merit of each and in what respect it can be useful.

There is no special news here. Undoubtedly you already know about Pushkin's journal.[1] I know only that there will be many good essays in it, because Zhukovsky, Prince Vyazemsky,[2] and Odoevsky have taken lively interest in it. Incidentally, you will find out about it in more detail from him personally, because I think he is going to your Moscow in a day or two. . . .

## A. S. Pushkin. March 2, 1836. Petersburg.

I am sending you "A Civil Servant's Morning."[1] If possible, submit it to the censor today or tomorrow morning, because he can

take it to the Censorship Committee together with "The Carriage,"[2] because it meets tomorrow morning. And get the essay about journalistic literature[3] from the printing house. You and I are most negligent people and forgot that much of the tail-end which I still have must be included in it. I would like you to arrange it so that this scene comes first and about literature after it.

*M. S. Shchepkin.[1] April 29, 1836. St. Petersburg.*

. . . . I'm sending you *The Inspector-General.* Perhaps rumors about it have already reached you. I wrote that lazybones of the first guild and the most dissolute person on earth, Pogodin, to inform you. I even wanted to send it to you, but changed my mind, wanting to take it to you myself and read it with my own voice so that distorted ideas about some of the characters would not be formed in advance, ideas which I know are extremely difficult to eradicate later. But having met the management of the theater here, I have conceived such repugnance for the theater that even the thought of those pleasures which are being prepared for me in the Moscow theater as well is enough to keep me from both the trip to Moscow and the attempt to fuss over anything. . . . Do what you want with my play, but I am not going to trouble about it. The play itself has begun to bore me as much as the troubles connected with it. The reaction that it produced was big and noisy. Everyone is against me. Respectable middle-aged civil servants shout that there is nothing holy for me if I dare to talk this way about those who serve the government. The police are against me, the merchants are against me, the literary people are against me. They curse and go to the play: it is impossible to get tickets for the fourth performance. Were it not for the lofty intercession of the Emperor[2] my play would not have appeared on the stage at all; there were already people trying to have it forbidden. Now I see what it means to be a comic writer. The slightest phantom of truth, and not one man, but entire classes will rise up against you. I can imagine what it would have been like if I had taken something from Petersburg life—which I know much better and more completely than provincial life now. It is vexing to see people whom you love with brotherly love against you. I have now re-done and corrected my comedy (which I read to you in Moscow) entitled *The Marriage,* and now it is a little more like something sensible. . . .[3]

## M. S. Shchepkin. May 10, 1836. St. Petersburg.

Dear Mikhail Semenovich, I forgot to inform you of a few pre-
liminary remarks about *The Inspector-General*. First, out of friendship for me you must without fail take the whole task of staging it
upon yourself. I don't know any of your actors, which one and how
each one of them is good. But you can know this better than anyone
else. You yourself, without doubt, should take the role of the Mayor;
otherwise, without you, it will be lost. That leaves the most difficult
role in the whole play—the role of Khlestakov. I don't know whether
you will choose the actor for it. God forbid it be played with the usual
farcicalness—as braggarts and theatrical scapegraces are played. He
is simply stupid; he babbles only because he sees that they are
disposed to listen; he lies because he had a hearty dinner and drank
a considerable quantity of wine. He is frivolous only when he approaches the ladies. The scene in which he starts lying at random
should receive special attention. His every word, i.e., sentence or
utterance, is a completely unexpected impromptu, and therefore
should be expressed abruptly. One shouldn't lose sight of the fact
that towards the end of the scene the wine begins to have an effect on
him, little by little. But he absolutely should not totter on the chair;
he should only turn red and express himself more unexpectedly and
more and more loudly the further he goes. I am extremely worried
about this role. It was performed poorly here, too, because decisive
talent is necessary for it. I am sorry, very sorry, that there is no way
I can be with you; many of the roles can be completely comprehended only when I read them. But there's nothing to be done. I am
so little tranquil in spirit now, that I could hardly be very useful. But
on my return from abroad I intend to stay with you in Moscow. . . .
I am completely at odds with the local climate. I will stay abroad
until spring, and in the spring—to you. . . .


## M. P. Pogodin. May 10, 1836. St. Petersburg.

. . . . After various anxieties, vexations, and such, my thoughts
are so confused that I cannot gather them into harmony and order.
I had wanted to go to Moscow without fail and to talk with you to our
hearts' content. But it didn't turn out that way. I feel that Moscow
will not bring me peace of mind now, and I don't want to arrive in a
disturbed state such as I am in presently. I am going abroad; there
I will shake off the melancholy which my countrymen are inflicting
on me every day. The contemporary writer, the comic writer, the

writer of morals and manners should be farther away from his fatherland. The prophet finds no glory in his homeland. I am not disturbed
by the fact that now every class has already risen up against me
resolutely, but it is somehow painful and saddening when you see
your own countrymen whom you love from the depths of your soul
unjustly risen against you, when you see how wrongly, in what a
false perspective, everything is perceived by them, how the particular is taken for the general, and chance for the rule. That which is said
accurately and with vivid realism immediately seems a pasquinade.
Bring two or three scoundrels out on the stage, and a thousand honorable people get angry saying: "We aren't scoundrels." But forget about
them. I am not going abroad because I could not bear these dissatisfactions. I want to improve my health, to divert and distract myself,
and then, having chosen a more or less permanent residence, think
my future works over thoroughly. It is high time for me to create
with greater reflection. In the summer I will be at the waters, August
on the Rhine, fall in Switzerland; I will go into seclusion and get busy.
If things turn out well I plan to spend the winter in Rome or Naples.
. . .

*M. P. Pogodin. May 15, 1836. St. Petersburg.*

. . . . I am not angry at what people are saying as you write; I
am not angry that those who find their own characteristics in my ec-
centrics get angry, turn away, and curse me. I am not angry because
my literary enemies, whose talents are for sale, curse me. But I am
sad to see the universal ignorance which moves the capital; it is sad
when you see how the stupidest opinion of a writer shamed and spat
upon by them has an effect on them and leads them by the nose. It is
sad when you see what a pitiful condition a writer is in in our country.
Everyone is against him, and there is no force even nearly equivalent
on his side. "He's a rabble-rouser! He's a revolutionary!" and who
says this? Government men, men who have served well, experienced men who should have enough sense to understand a thing as it
actually is, people who consider themselves educated and whom society, Russian society at least, call educated—they say this. Scoundrels are brought out on the stage and everyone gets enraged—why
bring scoundrels out on the stage. Well, let the scoundrels get angry;
but those whom I by no means know as scoundrels get angry. I find
this stupid irritability deplorable, a sign of deep and stubborn ignorance spread among our classes. The capital is so sensitive it is of-

fended by having the customs of six provincial officials shown on stage; what would the capital say if even a few of its own customs were shown. I am not embittered by the present violence against my play; my sad future concerns me. Provincial life is already held weakly in my memory, its features are already pale; but Petersburg life is bright before my eyes, its colors are vivid and sharp in my memory. Its slightest characteristic—and then how will my countrymen start to talk? And the same thing which enlightened people would take with loud laughter and interest stirs up the bile of ignorance, and the ignorance is universal. They consider it an undermining of the government mechanism if you say that a scoundrel is a scoundrel; to mention only one realistic and correct characteristic means, in translation, to disgrace a whole class and to arm all others or its subordinates against it. Examine the position of a poor author who all this while loves his country and his countrymen earnestly and tell him that there is a small circle which understands him, which looks at him with other eyes—will this console him? . . .

Goodbye. I am going to drive away my melancholy, to ponder deeply my duties as an author, my future creations; and I will surely return to you, refreshed and renewed. Everything that has happened to me has been salutary for me. All the insults, all the unpleasantnesses were sent to me by high Providence for my education. And I feel that now it is not a will of this earth which is guiding my path. Surely it is essential for me.

## V. Zhukovsky. June 28, 1836. Hamburg.

. . . . With what elevated, what triumphant feelings unseen and unnoticed by the world my life is filled! I swear I will do something that the ordinary person does not do. I feel leonine strength in my soul, and I perceive clearly my transition from childhood spent in school exercises to a young age.

If in fact one examines it rigorously and correctly, what is everything that I have written so far? It seems to me as if I am turning the pages of a student's old notebook in which carelessness and laziness are visible on one page, impatience and haste on another, the shaky hand of a beginner and the daring flourish of a mischievous boy who in place of letters has painstakingly traced out little hooks for which teachers beat one on the hands. Occasionally, perhaps, there manages to appear a page which may be praised only by the teacher who foresees in it an embryo of the future. It is time, it is

time at last to do something serious. Oh, what an incomprehensibly amazing significance all the incidents and circumstances of my life have had! How salutary all the unpleasantness and disappointments were for me. They had something elastic in them; touching them, it seemed to me, I bounced higher—at least I felt the rebuff more strongly in my soul. I can say that I never sacrificed my talent to society. No amusement, no passion was strong enough to possess my soul and distract me from my duty for a minute. For me there is no life outside my life. And my present moving away from the fatherland is sent from above by that same Providence which sent down everything for my education. This is a great turning point, a great epoch in my life. I know that I will encounter much that is unpleasant, but I am going to endure want and poverty, and not for anything in the world will I soon return. Longer, longer—as long as possible I will be in an alien world. And although my thoughts, my name, and my works will belong to Russia, I myself, my frail body, will be far removed from it. . . .

## M. P. Pogodin. September 22/10, 1836. Geneva.

. . . . I'm sorry, extremely sorry, I didn't see you before my departure. I deprived myself of many pleasant minutes. . . . But there is such a fine collection of nasty mugs in Russia that I couldn't stand to have to look at them any longer. Even now when I remember them I feel like spitting. Now there is foreign land ahead of me, foreign land around me; but Russia[1] is in my heart, not the nasty Russia, just the beautiful Russia—you and a few others who are close, and the small number of those who have beautiful souls and true taste. I am not writing you anything about my journey. My impressions have already passed. I have already become accustomed to the surroundings, and therefore I doubt that a description of them would be interesting. Only two things struck me and made me stop to take notice: the Alps and the old Gothic churches. Autumn has set in, and I ought to put my traveling cane in the corner and get to work. I plan to stay either in Geneva or in Lausanne or in Vevey where it will be warmer (here they have no warm houses like ours). I am beginning to reread all of Walter Scott again, and perhaps then I will take up the pen again.

Address letters to me in Lausanne. . . .

## N. Ya. Prokopovich. September 27, 1836. Geneva.

. . . . I'm not writing you anything about all the cities and lands through which I've traveled. . . . Of all my memories there remains only the memory of the endless dinners with which gluttonous Europe pursues me, and that's probably because the stomach preserves it, not the head. Oh, these dinners; I have had more than enough! Damned custom! I eat a little bit of every other dish, but I feel awful crap in my stomach. As if someone had driven a whole herd of horned cattle in there. I'm very sorry I didn't take the waters. Next spring or maybe summer I'll wash it all clean.

Europe strikes you from the first moment you go through the gates into the first town. Picturesque little houses, now at your feet, now overhead, dark blue mountains, spreading lindens, ivy together with grapevines covering the walls and fences; all this is fine, it pleases, it's new because the whole expanse of our Russia doesn't have this; but then when you see the same thing as you go farther, you get used to it and forget that it's fine. Of the German cities the best one after Hamburg is Frankfurt. This city is a fop. A very fine garden surrounds the entire city and serves it as a wall. They say that life is gay there, especially in the winter. But I have an antipathy for Jewish cities. . . . Now I am going to the little town of Vevey which is located on this same lake not far from the castle of Chillon which is known to you. There the climate is completely different, because a mountain protects it from the north. This morning I visited old man Voltaire. I was in Ferney. The old man lived well. A fine long avenue of three rows of chestnut trees leads to his house. The house has two floors of grayish stone and is still rather sturdy. I [. . .] into his chamber where he dined and received; everything is arranged the same way, the same pictures hang there. From the chamber there is a door to his bedroom which was also his office. The portraits of all his friends are on the wall—Diderot, Frederick, Catherine. The bed is made, an ancient muslin blanket barely holds together; and it seemed to me that in a moment the doors would open and the old man would walk in wearing the familiar wig with an untied bow, like old Chromis, and ask: "What can I do for you?" The garden is very fine and large. The old man knew how to do it. . . . I sighed and scratched my name in Russian letters [on a tree], not knowing why myself. . . .

## M. P. Balabina.[1] October 12, 1836. (New Style). Vevey.

JOURNEY FROM LAUSANNE TO VEVEY

Although you, dear Madam Maria Petrovna, have not deigned

to describe your journey to Antwerp and Brussels for me, and although I on my side ought to do the same thing, nevertheless I have decided to describe my journey to Vevey for you—first because I am a very well-mannered cavalier, and second because the subjects are so interesting that it would be a sin for me not to describe them. Having said good-bye to you, which, as you recall, was just before one o'clock, I set out for the *hôtel du faucon* to have dinner. Three of us had dinner. I was in the middle, on one side a respectable old Frenchman with a bandaged hand, with a medal, and on the other side a respectable lady, his wife. We were served vermicelli soup. When all three of us had finished eating the soup we were served the following dishes: boiled beef, lamb chops, boiled potatoes, spinach with larded veal, and medium-sized fish in white sauce. When I had finished eating the potatoes, which I love extremely, particularly when they are well cooked, the Frenchman who was sitting beside me, turning to me, said: "Dear sir," or, no, I forgot, he didn't say: "Dear sir," he said: *Monsieur, je vous servis* this beef. This is very good beef," to which I said: "Yes, really, this is very good beef." Then, when the beef had been taken away I said: "Monsieur, allow me to treat you to a lamb chop." To which he said with great pleasure: "I will take a chop, all the more willingly that it seems to be a good chop." Then the chops were taken away too, and the following dishes were set down: roast chicken, then another roast—leg of lamb, then suckling pig, then a dessert, compote with pears, then another dessert, with rice and apples. No sooner had my plate been changed and I wiped it off with the napkin than the Frenchman, my neighbor, treated me to chicken, saying: *"Puis-je vous offrir* chicken?" To which I answered: *"Je vous demande pardon, monsieur.* I don't want chicken, I am very disappointed that I cannot take the chicken. I would rather take a slice of leg of lamb, because I prefer leg of lamb to chicken," To which he said that, to be sure, he knew many people who preferred leg of lamb to chicken. Then, when we finished eating the roast the Frenchman, my neighbor, offered me pear compote, saying: "I advise you, Monsieur, to take this compote. It is very good compote." "Yes," said I, "it really is very good compote. But I have eaten (I continued) compote prepared by Princess Varvara Nikolaevna Repnina with her own hands and which can be called the king of compotes and the commander-in-chief of all desserts." To which he said: "I haven't eaten that compote, but from everything I judge it must be good, for my grandfather was also a commander-in-chief." To which I said: "I am very sorry that I was not personally acquainted with your grandfather." To which he said: "That's all right." Then the dishes were taken away and dessert was served,

but I, afraid of being late to the stagecoach, asked permission to leave the table—to which the Frenchman, my neighbor, answered very politely that for his part he could see no obstacle. Then I, having hung my overcoat on my left arm and taken in my right my traveling briefcase containing white paper and all sorts of personal junk, set off on the road. The road from the Faucon to the post station is completely well known to you, and therefore I will not undertake to describe it. Besides that you know yourself that there are very few things on it which would strike the imagination very much. When I walked up to the stagecoach I saw, to my extreme amazement, that inside the carriage almost everything was occupied; only one seat in the center remained. The ladies and gentlemen sitting there were extremely respectable people, but somewhat fat, and therefore I devoted myself to meditation for a moment. Although, thought I, I will not be cold here if I sit myself in the middle; it is extremely possible, since I am a skinny and puny man, that they will make a wafer out of me before I get to Vevey. This circumstance made me take a seat on top of the carriage. My seat was so wide and comfortable that I found it suitable to put my feet with me, for which, to my very great surprise, I was not charged anything and no fare was added, which made me think that my feet are very light. Thus, having settled on the coach in a recumbent position, I began to examine all the sights which were on either side. The mountains are extremely pretty and hardly a one of them went down, but rather all went up. This alone so surprised me that I stopped looking at the other sights; but most of all I was struck by the pea-colored frock coat of the conductor sitting beside me. I was so deep in meditation about why one half of it was darker and the other lighter, that I didn't notice that we had arrived in Vevey. I liked my seat so much that I wanted to lie on the roof of the carriage still longer, but the conductor said that it was time to get down. To which I said that I was ready, with great pleasure. "So please give me your hand!" said he. "If you please," answered I. I got down from the carriage with my left foot first and then the right one. But to your very great regret (because I know that you love details) I don't remember onto which spoke of the wheel I stepped with my foot—the third or the fourth. If I recall all of the circumstances well, I think it was on the third; but again, if I examine it from another aspect, it seems to have been as if on the fourth. However, I advise you to send for the conductor immediately now; he surely should know—and the sooner the better, because if he has a good sleep he will forget. After the descent from the carriage I set out along the quay to meet a steamer. This journey could be of very great usefulness especially for young people, and would probably develop their

abilities in a fine manner if it were not too short; for in no way did it last for longer than a minute and a half. Of the passengers who were on the steamer not a single Russian physiognomy turned up, not even one on which a German city could be built.[2] Three ladies of God knows what origin, two Krauts, and three Englishers with such long legs that they could get out of the boat only with great effort. Having gotten out of the boat they said gosh and went off to look for the *table d'hôte*. Then I went to my room where first I sat on one divan, then changed seats to another; but I found that it was all the same and if there are two divans alike then sitting on them is absolutely identical. Here ends the journey. Everything else that happened, was not worth mentioning. Do as you wish, but you must without fail write me an answer. If you have a hard time figuring out how to write, I can give you a small sample. You can write in the following vein:

"Dear sir, most respected Nikolai Vasilevich! I had the honor to receive your most respectable letter this October, on such-and-such a date. I cannot express to you, dear sir, all of the feelings which agitated my soul. I poured forth tears in heartfelt emotion. Where did you acquire the great art of speaking so comprehensibly to the soul and heart? A hundred times, a hundred times I would desire to possess an artful pen like yours in order to have the chance to utter grateful and touched gratitude in just such words." Then you may write: your humble servant or obedient servant or something like that. . . . And the letter, I assure you, will be good. Now allow me to wish you everything that is good in the world and remain your most devoted and most humble servant.

N. Gogol

*V. A. Zhukovsky. November 12, 1836. Paris.*

. . . . Having roamed around the spas during the summer, I moved over to Switzerland for the fall. I wanted to settle down some place faster and get to work; for this I lodged in a little house outside of Geneva. There I undertook to reread Molière, Shakespeare, and Walter Scott. I read until it got so cold that all desire to read disappeared. The cold spells and winds in Geneva drove me to Vevey. . . .

At last a fine autumn set in in Vevey, almost summer. It became warm in my room, and I took up *Dead Souls* which I had just begun in Petersburg. I re-did anew everything that had been started, considered the whole plan more thoroughly; and now I am carrying it forward calmly, like a chronicle. Switzerland has become more

agreeable to me since then; its grey-lilac-light-and-dark-blue-pink mountains are lighter and airier. If I accomplish this work as it should be accomplished then . . . what a huge, what an original topic! What a varied heap! All of Russia will appear in it! This will be my first decent thing, something which will make my name endure. Every morning, in addition to my breakfast, I added three pages to my epic poem, and I had enough laughter from these pages to sweeten my solitary day. But finally it got very cold in Vevey too. My room was not warm at all; I couldn't find a better one. Then I imagined Petersburg, our warm houses; then I imagined you more vividly—just as you met me when I came to see you and you took me by the hand and were glad of my arrival . . . and I felt terrible melancholy, my *Dead Souls* didn't cheer me up; I didn't even have enough cheer in reserve to continue it. My doctor found symptoms of hypochondria in me, resulting from the hemorrhoids; and he advised me to amuse myself; but seeing that I was in no condition to do that, he advised me to move somewhere else. Until then my intention had been to spend the winter in Italy. But the cholera was raging in Italy in a terrible way; quarantines covered it like locusts. With no hope of amusing myself in Italy, I set off for Paris where I had had no intention at all of going. . . .

Paris is not as bad as I imagined; and what is best of all for me, there is a multitude of places for walks—just the Tuileries gardens and the Elysée fields are enough for a whole day's walking. Without noticing it I get a very decent amount of exercise—which is essential to me now. Here God has stretched his protection over me and He performed a miracle: He pointed out to me a warm apartment in the sun, with a stove; and I am blissful, again I am happy. The Dead Ones flow in a lively way, more freshly and briskly than in Vevey; and it seems to me exactly as if I were in Russia; before me are all our people, our landowners, our civil servants, our officers, our peasants, our huts, in a word—all Orthodox Russia. It even amuses me when I think that I am writing *Dead Souls* in Paris. Another leviathan is being undertaken. A holy trembling runs through me beforehand when I just think about it; from it I perceive something. . . . I will experience divine moments . . . but . . . now I am completely engrossed in *Dead Souls*. Vastly great is my creation, and not soon will it be finished. Still new classes and many people of all kinds will rise up against me, but what am I to do! It is my fate to be at war with my countrymen. *Patience!* Someone invisible writes before me with a mighty rod. I know that after my death my name will be luckier than I am, and that the descendants of these same countrymen of mine, perhaps with moist eyes, will pronounce reconciliation for my shade.. . .

Can you imagine any tangles that might result from the purchase of dead souls. This would be a fine thing for me; because, whatever it is like, your imagination will surely see that which mine will not. Inform Pushkin about this, maybe he will find something on his part. I want terribly much to exhaust this plot from all sides. I have many things that I would on no account have imagined formerly, but nevertheless you can still tell me much that is new, for each head has its own intellect. Don't tell anyone what *Dead Souls* is about. You may announce the title to everyone. Only three people—Pushkin, Pletnev, and you—should know the real thing. . . .

*M. P. Pogodin. November 28, 1836. (New Style). Paris.*

. . . . Of course, the stories[1] could provide a small amusement for those who are yawning, but where does one collect these stories? I do not have one, and my hand will no longer rise to write them. Let him who has nothing more to write write them. When I wrote my immature and unpolished experiments—which I called stories only because it was necessary to call them something—I wrote them only to test my powers and discover whether my quill was sharpened the way I needed it in order to take up the real task. Seeing its unsuitability, I sharpened again, and again made a test. These were pale snatches of those images with which my head was filled and from which a full picture should one day be created. But one cannot go on making tests forever. It is time finally to take up the real task. We ought to have posterity in mind, not base contemporaneity.

The thing over which I am now sitting and toiling and which I have long pondered, and which I will be pondering for a long time yet, does not resemble either a novella, or a novel; it is long, long in several tomes; its name is *Dead Souls*—for the present that is all you should learn about it. If God helps me complete my epic poem in the manner that I should, it will be my first respectable creation. All Russia will echo in it.

My lot is cast. Abandoning the fatherland I abandoned all current desires with it. An insurmountable wall has risen between it and me. Finally, the pride which only poets know, which grew up in the cradle with me, could no longer stand it. Oh, what a contemptible, what a base condition . . . my hair stands on end. People born for a slap in the face, for pandering . . . and before these people . . . on past them, past them! Even today I don't have the strength to call them angry with me. The next time I will prepare whatever you want with-

by name. Don't bother me with trivial requests for little articles. I cannot, I do not have the strength to busy myself with them. No criticisms, no good or bad talk interests me. I am dead for what is current. Don't start talking about the theater; nothing is connected with it except nastinesses. I am even happy that the rubbishy comedy that I wanted to give to the theater was appropriated here by one of my countrymen who, taking it for two days, disappeared with it as if he drowned, and to this time I don't know its present whereabouts.[2] God Himself prompted him to do this. This stupidity should not be published. If I were to hear that something of mine was being played or printed, it would only be unpleasant for me—nothing more. I see only an awesome and truthful posterity pursuing me with the irresistible question: "Where is the real thing by which it is possible to judge you?" And in order to prepare the answer to it I am prepared to condemn myself to anything, to a mendicant, wandering life, to the deep and uninterrupted isolation which from this time forth I am bearing everywhere with myself—whether it is in Paris or in the African steppe. Write to me. There are a few friends whose letters are like a redolent wind from my native land. The stench doesn't fly to me. Everything that concerns you personally, literary and not literary, is dear to me; and you will oblige me by doing this. I'm not writing you anything about Paris. The local sphere is completely political, and I have always avoided politics. It isn't the poet's business to worm his way into the world's marketplace. Like a silent monk he lives in the world without belonging to it, and his pure unspoiled soul can converse only with God. —Farewell! I embrace you!

*N. Ya. Prokopovich. January 25, 1837. (New Style). Paris.*

. . . . I landed in Paris almost by accident. In Italy there's cholera, in Switzerland it's cold. The spleen attacked me; and besides that, the doctor ordered a change of locale because of my illness. I received a letter from Danilevsky that he was sitting bored in Paris and decided to go and share his boredom. Paris is a good city for one who is headed specifically for Paris to immerse himself in its entire life. . . . Political life, a life completely opposite to the humble artistic one, cannot please such lucky idlers as you and I.[1] Here everything is politics; in every back street and alley there's a bookshop with magazines. You stop on the street to clean your boots and they jam a magazine into your hands; they give you a magazine in the john. Everyone is more concerned with Spanish affairs than with

his own. . . . Not so long ago I was in the *Théâtre Français* where
Molière's *Tartuffe* and *Le Malade imaginaire* were being given. Both
were played very well, at least in comparison with the way they are
played in our country. Every year the *Théâtre Français* celebrates
Molière's birthday. There was something touching in it. When the
play was over, the curtain rose; a bust of Molière appeared. All the
actors of the theater, in pairs and with the accompaniment of music,
went up to crown the bust. A heap of wreaths rose on his head. Some
strange feeling took hold of me. Does he perceive this, and where
does he perceive this? . . . . In Molière's plays the old men, uncles,
guardians, and fathers are played very well—the rascal-servants
also excellently. If one were to gather the first three actors from
each of the theaters here, one could in this way stage a play as one
writer of comedy or tragedy could imagine. All the theaters are organized excellently. They do not have splendid outer façades, but inside everything is as it ought to be. From the first to the last word all
is audible and visible to everyone. Ballets are staged with luxury such
as one finds in fairy-tales; the costumes especially are extraordinarily good, with frightening historical accuracy. The French now look
after minute details to the same extent that they formerly ignored
the spirit of an age; it goes without saying that in this situation much
that is important slips away. There is a lot of gold, satin, and velvet
on the stage. Here everyone to the last figurante is dressed like the
prima ballerinas on the stage in our country. . . . Ask Jules how,
really, he's not ashamed to live with Mademoiselle George.[2] Why
she's sixty-seven. And besides it's apparent that she succeeded only
because of her beauty. Her acting is rather a monotone and often
pompous. But they say one must see her only in the old tragedies
which, however, are never played in the theater where she is now.
She plays in the theater Porte St. Martin where only the newest
dramas and melodramas are played, and where the spectators
make more noise than at any of the other theaters. Almost every
time there's a comedy in the parterre, or even a vaudeville if the
spectator's voice is good. Then the actors become the spectators:
at first they listen, then they walk off the stage; the curtain de-
scends, the music starts to play, and they begin the play again. The
people love dramas very much, especially the republican party.
They are a gloomy people; they rarely applaud. Others go to the
vaudeville; the middle class to the theater *Variété* or the theater
*Palais royale* (the best vaudeville theaters!). The *nobility,* as is always the case, make the faces of music lovers and go to the Italian or
the Grand Opera (in the French dialect), where they are still whack-
ing out *The Huguenots* and *Robert,* pounding on copper pots and

plates³ for all they're worth; and sometimes to *l'Opéra Comique* (the French opera). But forget about all of them, all these operas, vaudevilles, and comedies! . . . Your Petersburg literary news is meager. And tell me please why you all write about *The Inspector General?* In your letter and in Pashchenko's letter which Danilevsky received yesterday it says that *The Inspector General* is played every week, the theater is full, etc. . . . and for this to be brought to my knowledge. What kind of comedy is it? Really, I absolutely cannot understand this riddle. In the first place I spit on *The Inspector General,* and in the second . . . what good is it? If this were true, no one in Russia could play a nastier trick on me. But, praise God, this is false; I see Russian newspapers every three days. Do you want to make something like a rattle out of this and amuse me with it like a baby? And you! Shame on you! You supposed so much petty ambition in me. If there was anything in me that could easily appear to be ambition to one who knew me, it no longer exists. The spaces which separate you and me have swallowed *everything* for which a poet hears reproaches in the bottom of his soul. It terrifies me to recall all of my scribblings. Like threatening accusors they appear to my eyes. The soul begs oblivion, long oblivion. And if there were to appear a moth that would suddenly eat all the copies of *The Inspector General* and along with them *Arabesques, Evenings,* and all the other nonsense, and in the course of a long time no one would utter a word about me either in print or orally—I would thank fate. Only glory after death (for which, alas, I have done nothing so far!) is familiar to the soul of the true poet. But contemporary glory is not worth a kopek. . . . Apropos of literary news, it really isn't meager. Where would one manage to find a six-month period in the course of which two things like "The Field Commander" and *The Captain's Daughter* appeared at once?⁴ Has such charm ever been seen anywhere! I'm glad that *The Captain's Daughter* produced a general effect. . . .

*P. A. Pletnev. March 28/16, 1837. Rome.*

Each month, each week—and a new loss; but it would have been impossible to receive any worse news from Russia. All the pleasure of my life, all my highest pleasure disappeared together with him. I didn't undertake anything without his advice. Not one line was written without my imagining him before myself. What will he say, what will he notice, what will he laugh at; for what will he ut-

ter his indestructible and eternal approval—that is the only thing that interested me and animated my powers. My soul was embraced by the secret trembling of a pleasure which cannot be experienced on earth. . . . God! My present work, inspired by him, is his creation. . . . I do not have strength to continue it. I took up the pen several times —and the pen fell from my hands. Inexpressible melancholy! . . . Write me at least a line, what you are doing, or say a few words to Prokopovich about it. He will write to me. I was very sick; now I am beginning to get a little better. Send me the money that Smirdin owes me around the first of April. Entrust it to Shtiglitz[1] in the same way, for him to send it to one of the bankers in Rome for delivery to me. It would be better if he transfers it to Valentini; he, they say, is more honest than the other local bankers. If possible, speed it up as much as possible. . . .

*M. P. Pogodin. March 30, 1837. (New Style). Rome.*

I received your letter in Rome. It is full of the same thing that all of our thoughts are full of now. I will not say anything about the magnitude of this loss.[1] My loss is greatest of all. You grieve as a Russian, as a writer, I. . . . I cannot express a hundredth part of my grief. My life, my highest pleasure died with him. My bright moments of my life were the moments during which I was creating. When I was creating I saw only Pushkin before me. All the criticisms were nothing to me; I spat upon the contemptible mob which is known under the name of the public; his immortal and immutable word was dear to me. I did not undertake anything, I did not write anything without his advice. Anything good that I have written, I am obliged to him for all of it. And my present work is his creation.[2] He made me take an oath to write it, and not a word of it has been written without him appearing to my eyes at the time. I used to comfort myself with the thought of how satisfied he would be, I used to guess what would please him; and this was my highest and first reward. Now there is no such reward in front of me! What is my life now? You invite me to come to your house. For what purpose. Wouldn't it be to repeat the eternal fate of poets in our native land? Or did you purposely make such a conclusion after the powerful example which you cited in order to make the example itself even more striking? Why would I come? Haven't I seen the rich collection of our enlightened morons. Or don't I know what Councillors are, beginning with the Titular up to the Actual Secret ones?[3] You write that all

people, even the cold ones, were touched by this loss. But what were these people ready to do for him in life? Wasn't I a witness to the bitter moments which Pushkin was forced to experience? In spite of the fact that the monarch himself (may his name be blessed for it) honored his talent.[4] Oh, when I remember our judges, patrons of art, learned wits, our noble aristocracy. . . . My heart shudders just at the thought. There must be powerful reasons when they made me decide on what I would have wished not to decide. Or do you think that it is nothing to me that my friends, that you, are separated from me by mountains? Or don't I love our boundless, our native Russian land?

I have lived for almost a year in an alien land; I see beautiful skies, a world rich in arts and man. But did my pen rise to describe things capable of striking everyone? I could not devote a single line to what is alien. With an insuperable chain I am linked to what is my own; and I preferred our poor, our dim world, our smoky huts, the bare expanses, to the best skies which look down on me more amiably. And after this is it I who cannot love his fatherland? But to come, to suffer the arrogant pride of a brainless class of people who will swell with pride before me and even do me dirt. No, I am your obedient servant, but excuse me. I am ready to suffer anything in an alien land, ready to stretch out a beggar's hand if it comes to that. But in my own—never. My sufferings cannot be completely comprehensible to you. You are tied up at the dock; you can bear it like a sage and be amused. I am homeless, the waves beat and rock me; and I can rely only on the anchor of pride which higher powers have placed in my breast. It is not in my native land that I am to die.

If you have a desire to travel to refresh and renew your strength, to see me—come to Rome. My constant residence is here. In June and July I go to Germany to the waters and having returned spend the fall, winter, and spring here. The sky is marvelous. I drink of its air and forget the whole world. Write me something about your nasty things in Moscow. You see how strong my love is; I am even ready to listen to the nasty things from my native land.

*V. A. Zhukovsky. April 18/6, 1837. Rome.*

This time I am writing you with the intention of dispiriting you with my petition. You are the only one in the world who is interested in my fate. You will, I know you will do everything within the limits of possibility. My future terrifies me. It seems that with each year

my health gets worse and worse. Not long ago I was very ill; now I have gotten a little better. If even Italy does not help me, I no longer know what to do. I sent to Petersburg for my last money, and there is not a kopek more; I see absolutely no means of getting any in the future. I could not busy myself with any trivial journalistic foolishness even if I were dying of hunger. I must continue the large work which I have begun, which Pushkin made me promise to write, the idea of which is his creation, and which since that time has turned into a sacred testament for me. Now I value the minutes of my life, because I do not think that it will be long, and meanwhile. . . . I am beginning to believe what I used to think was a fable—that writers can starve to death in our time. But that is almost true. I would be provided for if I were a painter, even a bad one; here in Rome there are about fifteen of our painters who were recently sent from the academy (some of whom draw worse than I do) ; they all get 3000 a year each. Were I to become an actor I would be provided for; actors each get 10,000 in silver and more, and you know yourself that I would not be a bad actor. But I am a writer—and therefore I have to starve to death. Sad thoughts often visit me—whether as a result of hypochondria or something else. The doctors ascribe it more to the former. I am ready to agree with them myself, but you can see that in their way my words are accurate too. Examine the position I am in (my sickly state, my inability to do anything extraneous) and give me salutory advice as to what I should do to prolong my life on earth until I do some of what I have to do. I thought and thought, and could not think of anything better than to have recourse to the sovereign. He is gracious; I will remember to the grave the consideration which he gave to my *Inspector General*. I wrote a letter which I am enclosing; if you find it written as it ought to be, be my intercessor, submit it; if, however, it is not written as it ought to be—he is gracious, he will forgive his poor subject. Say that I am an ignoramus who doesn't know how to write to his high person, but that I am all full of love for him such as only a Russian subject can be filled with, and that I only dared trouble him with the petition because I knew that we are all as dear as children to him. But I know that you will say it better and more properly than I. It is not for the first time that I am obliged to you for much, for much which my heart cannot express; and I would feel conscience-stricken to trouble you if you were not you. But all this to the side; I am talking with you simply, and I would blush to the ears if I paid you some ingenious compliment. If I had a pension such as is given to the wards of the Academy of Arts who live in Italy, or even one such as is given to the deacons who are attached to our church here, my life would be prolonged—all the more so because it is cheaper to live in

Italy. Somehow find an opportunity and way to point out my stories "Old World Landowners" and *Taras Bulba*[1] to the sovereign. These were the two lucky stories which pleased absolutely all tastes and all different temperaments. All the shortcomings with which they teem were completely unnoticed by everyone except Pushkin, you, and me. I saw that people were more considerate after reading them. If only the sovereign would read them. He has such a proclivity for everything that has warmth of feeling and which is written straight from the soul. . . . Oh, something assures me that he would increase his interest in me.[2] But may everything be as God pleases. My hope is in Him and you. . . .

## *N. Ya. Prokopovich. September 19, 1837. (New Style). Geneva.*

. . . . The cholera which is now decimating Rome upset all my plans and proposals now. I had almost arranged and contrived my affairs so that I could live in Rome as if at home—far more cheaply than I lived in Petersburg. Now I am dragging myself about without shelter. In Switzerland everything is twice as expensive as in Rome. On top of that the state of my illness is such that now I cannot take myself into the deepest backwoods, and I have to seek amusement against my will; I am afraid of the hypochondria which is chasing me and is right on my heels. The death of Pushkin seems to have removed half of what could have amused me in anything that I look at. My stomach is nasty to an impossible degree; and although I eat very moderately now, it absolutely refuses to digest. After the departure from Rome my hemorrhoidal constipation began again, and would you believe it, if I have no bowel movement during the whole day I feel as if my brain had some kind of cap pulled over it, which befogs my thoughts and prevents me from thinking. The waters didn't help me at all, and now I see that they are terrible rubbish, I just feel worse my pockets are light and my stomach heavy. . . .

## *V. A. Zhukovsky. October 30, 1837. (New Style). Rome.*

I received the assistance which has been given me by our magnanimous sovereign.[1] Gratitude is strong in my breast, but its effusion will not reach his throne. With a full hand he pours out good deeds like some god, and he does not desire to hear our speeches of gratitude. But perhaps the word of a poet who is poor in lifetime will

reach posterity and add a touch of tender emotion to his valorous royal deeds. But my gratitude can reach you. You, always you! Your glance, full of love, keeps vigil over me. As if fate had purposely given me a thorny path and crushing need had twined around my life so that I could be the witness of the most beautiful things on earth. The letter of notification and the note of credit came to me in Rome in the month of August, but because of the cholera I couldn't return there for a long time. Finally, I broke away. If you knew with what joy I abandoned Switzerland and flew to my dear soul, my beauty— Italy. She is mine! No one in the world will take her from me! I was born here.—Russia, Petersburg, the snows, the scoundrels, the civil-service department, the professorship, the theater—I dreamed all that.[2] I have awakened in my native land again, and I regret only that the poetic part of the dream—you and the three or four who have left the eternal joy of memory in my soul—was not carried over into reality. There is one more irretrievable thing. . . . Oh Pushkin, Pushkin! What a beautiful dream I was lucky to see in life, and how sad my awakening was. What would my life be in Petersburg after this? But as if with a purpose the almighty hand of providence cast me beneath the sparkling sky of Italy so that I would forget about grief, about people, about everything—and would fix my eyes only on its luxurious beauties. It has replaced everything for me. I look at everything like someone in a frenzy, and I still haven't had my fill of looking. You told me about Switzerland, about Germany, and you always recalled them with rapture. My soul also accepted them animatedly and I was enraptured by them, perhaps with even more animation than when I entered Italy for the first time. But now when I have visited them after Italy, with all their mountains and views they seemed low, vulgar, nasty, gray, and cold to me; and it seems to me that I have been in Olenetz Province and heard the bearish breathing of the northern ocean. But can it be you will not come here, and will not look at it, and will not give it that bow which everyone who burns incense for the beautiful owes to that beauty nature. Here is her throne. Only the hem of her chasuble flashes in other places, but here she looks straight into one's eyes with her piercing eyes.—I am gay; my soul is bright. I am hurrying and laboring with all my strength to complete my work. Life, life, I want more life! I still haven't done anything that would merit your touching approbation. But perhaps that which I am writing now will merit it. At least the thought that you would read it some day has been one of a few which has animated me during my vigil over it. God preserve your beautiful life for a long long time!

*A. S. Danilevsky. February 2, 1838. (New Style). Rome.*

.... I am very sorry that you are bored. As for me, I have never felt so immersed in such peaceful bliss. Oh, Rome, Rome! Oh, Italy! Whose hand will tear me away from here? How is your Grisi?[1] They seem 500 times better to me than before.[2] (Apropos of Grisi: I had a dream that you came to Rome together with Grisi in the same carriage and introduced her to me as your wife or lover, I don't recall exactly, and the carriage was gilded.) What a sky! What days! It is neither summer nor spring, but better than either the spring or the summer that other corners of the world have. What air! I look and I drink it in, but still I can't satisfy myself. Heaven and paradise are in my soul. I have few acquaintances in Rome now, or, more accurately, almost no one (the Repnins[3] are in Florence). But I have never been as gay, as satisfied with life. . . .

*A. S. Danilevsky. April 23, 1838. (New Style). Rome.*

.... You ask where I am going this summer. Nowhere, nowhere but Rome. My wanderer's staff no longer exists. You recall that my stick was carried away by the waves of Lake Geneva. Now I'm sitting home. I have no tormenting desires leading off into the distance except perhaps to make a trip to Semerenki, i.e., Naples, and to Tolstoe, i.e., to Frascati or to Albani. I would advise you to put off any idea of Germany where you will get so God-awful tired of the vile waters which only upset the stomach and get our filet parts into such condition that as a result there isn't anything to sit on. I'm quite vexed with you—you didn't think of copying either "Egyptian Nights" or "Galub"—neither is available here.[1] No one gets *The Contemporary* in Rome—or anything contemporary for that matter. If Turgenev[2] has *The Contemporary* ask him to bring all of it for me if possible, and if not to copy the poetry. Also, please buy Mickiewicz's new poem for me, a wonderful thing, *Pan Tadeusz*.[3] It is sold at the Polish shop; you can find out where the Polish shop is from other booksellers. Also, can you find the first volume of Shakespeare in the edition that has two volumes and two columns; I think it's extremely easy to find it in the shops on the Palais royal. . . .

*M. P. Balabina. End of April, 1838. Rome.*

. . . . How abominable the Germans seemed to me after the Italians, the Germans with all their petty uprightness and egotism! But I think I have already written you about that. I think you yourself sensed many features of the wit of the people in Rome, a wit for which the ancient Romans were sometimes famous—even more the Attic taste of the Greeks. Not one event takes place here without some witticism or epigram being made up by the people. . . . But probably you haven't happened to read the sonnets of the present-day Roman poet Belli, which, however, one must hear when he reads himself.[1] In them, in these sonnets there is so much salt, so much totally unexpected wit, and the life of present-day Transeverines is so faithfully reflected in them that you will laugh, and the heavy cloud which so often floats down on your head will float away together with your tiresome and annoying headache. They are written *in Lengua romanesca;* they haven't been published, but I'll send them to you later. Pertinently, we have begun to talk about literature. Only the epic literature of the Italians is well known to us, that is, the literature of the XVth and XVIth centuries. But one should know that in the eighteenth century which has passed and even at the end of the seventeenth century, the Italians revealed a strong predilection for satire, for gaiety. And if you want to study the spirit of present-day Italians, you must study them in their heroic-comic poems. Imagine that the collection of *Autori burleschi italiani* consists of forty fat volumes.[2] Such humor, such original humor sparkles in many of them that it is amazing that no one talks about them. However, I should note that only Italian typographies can print them. In many of them there are a few immodest expressions which not everyone can be allowed to read. . . . What a spring! God, what a spring! But you know what a young fresh spring amid the crumbling ruins blossoming with ivy and wild flowers is. How beautiful the blue patches of sky are now—between the trees barely covered with a fresh almost yellow greenery, and even cypresses, dark as a raven's wing—and still further the mountains of Frascati, Albani, and Tivoli, blue and lusterless like turquoise. What air! It seems that when you inhale through your nose at least 700 angels will fly in your nasal nostrils. A wonderful spring! I look, but don't get my fill of looking. Roses have covered all Rome now, but the flowers which have just begun to blossom, and the name of which I really don't remember at the moment, are much sweeter to my smell. . . . We do not have them in our country. Do you believe that I often have a fierce desire to turn into nothing but a nose—so that there wouldn't be anything else—neither eyes, nor arms, nor legs,

just one super-tremendous nose the nostrils of which would be the size of big buckets so that I could inhale as much of the fragrance and the spring as possible. . . .

## A. S. Danilevsky. May 13, 1838. Rome.

I got your letter yesterday. In place of that it would have been much more pleasant for me to see your smiling face sticking itself out from behind the doors. But this suits the higher fates! Let it be as it ought to be for the best! Your thought about a wife and beetroot sugar struck me. If this is a solid, well-considered intention, then of course it is good; because any firm intention is good and attains its goal for sure. The creature that met you on the stairway made me become thoughtful, but on the other hand I absolutely cannot coordinate your meeting with the grisette and inviting her to spend the night on the same day. If it happened before, all right; but in your letter you say clearly: I will spend tonight gloriously. Well, what if she slaps you with a case of .. .. ..[1] Then both the marriage and the sugar factory will suffer strongly. But let's put these troubled thoughts aside. . . .

The other day I got a letter from Smirnov. Among other things he mentions a dinner given for Krylov on the occasion of his fiftieth year in literary life.[2] I think you already know that the sovereign, having learned about this dinner, sent an Order of Stanislav, second degree, on Krylov's plate. But it is noteworthy that Grech[3] and Bulgarin refused to be at this dinner, but when they found out that the sovereign himself was interested they immediately sent a request for tickets. But Odoevsky, one of the directors, refused them; then they came brazenly on their own, saying that they were ordered to be at the dinner; but there were no tickets left, and therefore they could not and did not attend. Smirnov adds that on the return trip to Dorpat Bulgarin was so thoroughly thrashed by someone, probably some of the Dorpat students, that he lay in bed about two weeks. In my opinion it would be just as repugnant to thrash Bulgarin as to kiss him. . . .

## A. S. Danilevsky. May 16, 1838. (New Style). Rome.

. . . . Incidentally, now you can send the things that I asked you for with Pavé;[1] he will bring them right to Rome for me. If you can, help him pick out a wig for me. I want to shave my head, not so that

my hair will grow this time, but for my head itself, to see if it will help the perspiration and along with it the inspiration to come out more intensely. My inspiration is clogged up; my head is often covered by a heavy cloud which I have to try constantly to dissipate, and meanwhile there is so much that I still have to do. A new kind of wig which fits any head has been invented; they are made not with iron springs but with gum-elastic ones. . . .

## M. P. Pogodin. August 14, 1838. (New Style). Naples.

. . . . I cannot say anything too comforting about myself. Alas, my health is bad! And my proud plans. . . . I hoped to accomplish much. . . .[1] My mind is still full—but my strength, strength—but God is merciful. Surely he will lengthen my days. I am sitting over the work about which you already know (I wrote to you about it); but my work is lackadaisical, it doesn't have its former liveliness. The ailment due to which I went away and which, it seemed, was starting to get better, has now worsened anew. My hemorrhoidal disease has turned all its force on my stomach. It is an unbearable disease. It is drying me up. It tells me about itself every minute and hinders my work. But I am going on with my work, and it will be finished—but other ones, other ones. . . . Oh, friend! What great plots exist! Have pity for me! But I will see you. Now I direct one very cold and prosaic request to you. You were so kind to offer a loan to me if I was in need. I didn't want to avail myself of your kindness. Now I have been brought to that point. If you are rich, send me a money-order for 2000 rubles. I will return it to you in a year or a year and a half at most.[2] My work[3] is large and in our country the goods are sold by size, and therefore I expect to get enough for it to be in a position to pay this debt at the end of next year. My financial circumstances are bad, and all of my relatives are suffering too—but to hell with money; if only I am healthy, the year can drag by somehow, maybe with your help or maybe with God's.

## M. P. Balabina. November 7, 1838. Rome.

. . . . Though at the sight (i.e., the thought) of Petersburg a shiver runs over my skin and my skin is pierced through with the terrible dampness and foggy atmosphere, I would like very much to ride on the railroad and hear this mixture of words and speeches of our

Babylonian population in the train cars. There you can find out much that you won't find out in the usual way. There perhaps I would get angry again—and very strongly—at my dear Russia, towards which my angry disposition is already beginning to weaken; and without anger, you know, you can say very little; one only tells the truth when one gets angry. When I was a youth in school, I was very ego-tistical (not egotistical in *that* sense); I wanted terribly to know what others were saying and thinking about me. It seemed to me that everything that they said to me was not what they thought about me. I purposely tried to start a quarrel with my comrade; and he, natu-rally, in his anger told me everything that was bad about me, and that was all that I needed; I was completely satisfied just having found out everything about myself. . . .

## *A. S. Danilevsky. December 31, 1838. Rome.*

. . . . I got a letter from mama. She writes that they waited in Poltava very long in order to wait until *The Inspector General* was given at some theater there, and that the peasant dolt who was sent to find out about it garbled and mixed things up, finding out nothing, and that instead of *The Inspector General* they got into *Hamlet* which they listened to until the end; and the next day, to their unutterable pleasure (that is, mama's and sister's), they learned that *The In-spector General* was going to be given and they set out that same evening. I imagine that *The Inspector General* must have been played in all respects in a barbarous manner, because even mama herself, a woman, as you know, who is very condescending, says that they played the servant pretty well and the others, according to their abilities, they played as they could—what wealth they had, they gave. From a few words dropped by chance in mama's letter I could also note that my countrymen, that is, Poltava Province, cannot stand me. . . .

## *A. S. Danilevsky. April 2, 1839. (New Style). Rome.*

. . . . I wouldn't even advise you to go to Petersburg. To hell with it! It's cold both for the body and for the soul. It seems to me it would be better for you to settle in Moscow. It's cheaper to live there, people are friendlier. My friends who love me genuinely and sincerely live there. They will love you too. It will be more amiable for you

there. We will talk a little about this in Marienbad, where I hope you will be too. I even think that you can sooner find some kind of service in Moscow or else—it's time for you to try yourself, don't be stubborn; perhaps God gave you a propensity and talent which you don't yet know yourself. Take up something—write! Out of love for me at least, if you don't want to out of love for yourself. Surely it is pleasant for you to carry out my order since it is pleasant for me to carry out yours. Write or translate. You know French very well now, and doubt-less Italian too—or simply start a notebook. You have compiled ma-terial for it. You've already seen and heard a lot—bustling Paris and Rome at carnival time. Really, a lot of everything and a Russian in the midst. Pogodin and Shevyrev[1] will seriously undertake to pub-lish a really sensible journal; you could work for it too. I think the first book is supposed to appear the first day of 1840. Apropos of the jour-nal *Notes of the Fatherland,* immediately after my arrival in Rome I received a very long letter from Kraevsky[2] which I didn't intend to answer at all; I admit I don't even know how to. Besides, the letter itself got around to some kind of religious ceremonies. Kraevsky simply howls and incites absolutely everyone to take up arms against satan; he says that in this we must move with universal efforts, that this is the last crusade and that if this [. . . .] then it will be abso-lutely necessary to give up everything and despair. In my mind's eye I imagine how this homunculus bustles about and very sedately scratches the side whiskers on his miniature face.

Pogodin saw the first book and says it's twice as big as *The Library for Reading,* but that he didn't glance into the middle of the book and didn't have time for that. He said further that one person had told him that Kraevsky was acting with very good intentions, was encouraging young writers, gathering them around, but that it was difficult to remember the names of these writers—but that they were good and highly educated writers. I think the same thing my-self. Pogodin and Shevyrev will deliver my next letter.


*M. P. Balabina. May 30, 1839. (New Style). Rome.*

.... If your letter had come a few months earlier I would have set off agreeing with you and contradicting you with readiness and lively loquacious willingness—giving my opinions and arguing about all topics about which you write; but now I feel that I'm going to be dull and flaccid and stupid. Ideas absolutely refuse to crawl out of my head; instead of the ones called for the wrong ones turn up, ones

not called for. Alas! I am also writing you under the influence of a book I am now reading, but it is different—and how completely opposite to yours! Sad and mournfully eloquent are its pages. I am now spending sleepless nights at the bedside of my sick and dying friend Iosif Vielgorsky.[1] Without doubt you have heard of him, perhaps you have even seen him sometime; but no doubt you did not know his beautiful soul or his beautiful feelings or his strong character (too firm for tender years),) or the extraordinary soundness of his mind, and all this is the prey of inexorable death; and neither his youthful age nor right to life (doubtless a beautiful and useful one) will save him. Now I live his dying days, catch his minutes. His smile or his expression when it brightens for a moment are epochs for me, an event in my day which passes monotonously. So don't blame me if I am stupid and am not able to write you a letter as intelligent as you wrote to me. My poor Iosif, the one singularly fine and elevatedly noble person out of all your young Petersburg people and he. . . . I swear, incomprehensibly strange is the fate of all that is good among us in Russia! It no sooner manages to manifest itself—and immediately death! Merciless, inexorable death! I don't believe in anything now, and if I come across anything beautiful I immediately shut my eyes and try not to look at it. It wafts the odor of the grave to me. A voice I can hear whispers tonelessly: "It is for a brief instant. It is given only so that the eternal melancholy of regret for it can exist, so that the soul will be deeply and painfully grieved by it." . . . Apropos of health and illnesses, since we have already started talking about them. It is said that a sick person can have no greater pleasure than to meet with another sick person and to talk to him to his heart's content about his illnesses. They talk about this with the same pleasure with which only gluttons talk about the dishes they have eaten. So because of this, I will tell you about my health too. My health *non vale un fico,* as the Italians say; it's worst than current Russian literature, about which you sent me news in your letter. In the summer I am going to Marienbad for one month. You won't believe how sad it will be to leave Rome for one month—and my clear, my pure skies, my beauty, my beloved land. Again I will see this mean Germany, nasty, begrimed, and smoke-blackened by the huge quantity of tobacco. . . . But I have forgotten that you love it so and I almost uttered a few more epithets which befit it. However, I absolutely cannot understand your passion. Or perhaps it is necessary to live in Petersburg to feel that Germany is good? And how is it you are not ashamed? You who were so ecstatic about Shakespeare in your letter, that deep, lucid man, who reflects the entire world and all that makes up man in himself as in a faithful mirror; and reading him

you can think about the smoky German confusion at the same time!
And can one say that every German is a Schiller?! I am agreed that
he is a Schiller, but only the Schiller whom you discover if you ever
have the patience to read my story, "Nevsky Avenue." In my opinion
Germany is nothing but the most vile-smelling belch of the nastiest
tobacco and most loathsome beer. Excuse the slight untidiness of this
expression. What can one do if the subject is untidy, in spite of the
fact that the Germans have long been noted for their tidiness? But I
know you will get mad at me for this is an awful way and perhaps
even possess a slight desire to grill me over a slow fire for it. But
enough! I'm not going to anger you any more. . . .

*A. S. Danilevsky. June 5, 1839. (New Style). Rome.*

Your letter smells of dejection, one can even say of desperation
and attacks of absolute hopelessness. Only it seems to me that it is
too early to surrender to the latter two things. Can it be that already
there is absolutely nothing left in the world to which you could be attached? At least wait until I die, then you can surrender to them; at
least find some excuse for them if you like them so much, but until
then God knows. Of course, I don't have any means of my own to help
you now. But I am still alive, so I must be necessary to you for something or other. However, I understand your position perfectly. Loneliness in that densely inhabited desert Paris, and at this time of year
besides, a time of exhausting heat waves which are exhausting everywhere except Italy. Of course that is terrible! If only you knew how
sad it is for me to leave Rome for two months, almost as sad as for you
to remain in Paris. Not long ago I felt intense sadness (sadness almost unknown to me these years,) a sharp sadness, sadness of the
fine years of youth—if not of the adolescence of the soul. The other
day I buried my friend whom fate gave to me at the time, during the
period of life when friends are no longer given. I am speaking of my
Iosif Vielgorsky. We had long been attached to each other, had long
esteemed each other; but we came together closely, inseparably, and
absolutely like brothers only, alas, during his illness. You cannot
imagine to what extent this was a nobly elevated, childlike, pure soul.
At times we often see upstarts of intellect and talent among people,
but intellect, talent, and taste joined with such solid soundness, with
such a firm, brave character is a phenomenon which is rarely repeated among men. And he had all this at the age of twenty-two. And
such virginal purity of feelings together with firmness of character,

with aspiration to act usefully and magnanimously. This was a man who alone would have adorned the future reign of Alexander Nikolae-vich.[1] None of the others surrounding him had even a grain of talent. And what was fine had to perish, as everything that is fine in our Russia has to perish. . . .

## E. G. Chertkova.[1] June 22, 1839. Vienna.

A strange thing. As soon as I drink tea, someone invisible tugs at my arm telling me to write to you; and Elizaveta Grigorievna doesn't leave my thoughts for a minute. Why would this be? If only this desire appeared during coffee, then at least it would be understandable. In my memory you are glued to coffee: you poured it yourself and put sugar in it for me; but during tea you performed no service. Why is this? I get mixed up and become like that respectable citizen and nobleman who all his life kept asking himself the question: why am I Khrisanfy and not Ivan and not Maxim, and not Onufry, and not even Kondrat and not Prokofy. Surely you know why you are more vivid in my thoughts after tea. Surely once having drunk it you imagined you were pouring it on my head and poured out your cup on the floor. Or wanting to hurl the saucer at my forehead, you hit the upper lip and front tooth of your doctor, who had just finished telling you how the whole town marvels at the patience of your Grisha; or perhaps your Liza, taking a cup of tea and getting ready to drink, shouted at the top of her voice: "Oh, mama, imagine it—Gogol is sitting here in the cup." You rushed from your place and cried: "Where is Gogol?" Liza undertook to catch him with a spoon in the glass and shouted anew: "Oh, it isn't Gogol, it's a fly!" And you saw that it was indeed a fly and perhaps at that moment said: "Oh, why is the fly which so bored me now already so far away from me." In a word, something must have happened or I wouldn't have felt such a strong desire to write to you specifically after tea. . . .

Do you know this letter is being written to you from Vienna? I could go to *post restante* this minute, get your letter there, and write an answer to it; but I didn't want to do that—so that until tomorrow I could have the sweet assurance that your letter is lying there for me. If on the other hand it is not there—God! How much malice will pour forth! Everybody will get it—the Germans, Vienna, my hat, gloves, the pavement, and my own nose—about which, it seems, I have already written. And I won't let a single German who is sitting with me in the diligence smoke a single cigar. Let him burst, damn him! Farewell, I kiss your little hands.

*M. P. Balabina. September 5, 1839. (New Style). Vienna.*

. . . . When I read your letter and folded it up I lowered my head, and a melancholy feeling took possession of my heart. I recalled my former, my beautiful years, my youth, my irretrievable youth; and I am ashamed to confess I almost burst out crying. That was the time of freshness [. . .] of youthful strength and excitement as pure as the sound produced by a perfectly tuned violin. Those were the years of poetry; at that time I loved Germans without knowing them, or perhaps I confused German erudition, German philosophy, and literature with the Germans. However that may be, German poetry transported me far into the distance then, and then I liked its total separation from life and actuality. And I viewed everything ordinary and mundane much more contemptuously then. To this day I love the Germans that my imagination then created. But let us leave this. I don't like it; it is painful for me to wake the strings which are rusting in the depth of my heart. I will tell you only that it is painful to turn out to be an old man during years that still belong to youth. It is terrible to find ashes in oneself instead of fire and to experience the helplessness of ecstasy. Gather all the unfortunate people into a cluster, pick out the most unfortunate of them, and that unfortunate fellow will be fortunate compared to him whom fate doomed to such a condition. From your letter (which stirred something of the old in me, for which I thank you) it is apparent that you took what I said[1] about the south and north in particular for a decisive position that there is poetry only in the south. No, perhaps it has flamed up more often and abundantly in the north. And for one whose powers are young and whose soul feels fresh—for him the north is revelry. But you will forgive the earlier words of that unfortunate whose soul, deprived of everything that elevated it (a terrible loss!), has kept only the sad ability of feeling this to be his condition. And now imagine this unfortunate wandering beneath the northern sky in sight of activity and everything that agitates the soul and moves it to create. Can you understand the terrible reproaches, the hellish, unbearable torments which he feels within himself? Now imagine that God in his great mercy took pity on this man (I don't know why) and threw him (why I really don't understand, he had done nothing worthy of this), threw him into a country, into a paradise where unbearable mental reproaches do not torment him, where peace embraced his soul, peace as clear as the sky which now surrounds him and about which he had dreams in the north during his poetic visions, where in place of that tempestuous fountain of poetry striving every minute to burst from his breast, a fountain of poetry which he had carried in himself in

the north and which had run dry, he saw poetry not in himself, but around himself [. . .], in the heavens, the sun, the transparent air, and in everything a quiet poetry bringing oblivion to his torments. There is nothing higher in the world for me now than nature. People, cities, nations, relations, and everything that crushes, agitates, and torments people has disappeared from before me. I see it alone, and I live by it. Here is why I am partial to it; it is my last treasure. He who has experienced deep spiritual losses will understand me. You didn't see Italy when you should have. Not during youth and freshness of powers must one see it, no! But when inexorable fate has taken much, very much away from you. But my letter has taken on an overly serious physiognomy. I make this request of you: When you have finished reading it tear it into pieces. No one should read this, and no one needs it either. . . .

## S. P. Shevyrev. September 10, 1839. (New Style). Vienna.

I received your letter the day before yesterday. I needn't say how pleasant it was for me. It would have been pleasant even without the important piece of news announced by you; but this news, this huge, weighty news—it is impossible to say how good it is. You are at Dante![1] Oh, ho, ho, ho, ho! And such a way you announce it, almost at the end of the letter. For this may God preserve Münich and the boredom that it engendered in your breast. But aren't you ashamed not to enclose two or three lines in the letter? I swear on my word of honor I have an insuperable desire to read them! Oh, how long it has been since I have read verse! And I believe in your translation unalterably, decisively, doubtlessly. It is a small thing that you know how to handle verse and that your verse has strength—this was so even before; but what is the main thing and what you had less of before is the deep inner poetry flowing from the heart, a note struck with amazing accuracy of tone and by a violinist whose violin has a soul. I conclude all of this from those memorable verses which you wrote in Rome on my birthday. Even now I read them and it seems to me I hear Pushkin. I don't know whether you know or feel how many times better a poet you have become in comparison to the poet you were before. That is why I was made so happy by your vast undertaking. And you didn't even send me a sample! Is that good? And do you know that that is essential? And surely you are tormented by a secret desire to read your beginning and hear an evaluation. No artist could exist without that. Because of this send me as

much as you can and want, without fail. I won't show anyone and won't tell anyone. Hurrah for Münich! You should engrave its name on the threshold of your house in gold letters.

As for me, I . . . it's a strange thing, I cannot, I am not able to work when I am devoted to seclusion, when I have no one to chat with, when I don't have other occupations at the same time, and when I possess an entire space of time, unbounded and unmeasured. I was always amazed by Pushkin who had to take himself off to the country alone and lock himself up in order to write. On the contrary, I could never do anything in the country; and in general I cannot do anything where I am alone and where I have experienced boredom. I wrote all of my currently printed sins in Petersburg and at precisely the time when I was busy with the civil-service job, when I had no time amid that bustle and change of occupations; and the more gaily I spent the eve before, the more inspired I was returning home and the fresher I was in the morning. . . . I am bored in Vienna. Pogodin still isn't here. I am acquainted with hardly anyone; however there is no one to get acquainted with. All Vienna makes merry, and the local Germans eternally make merry. But Germans, as is well-known, make merry boringly; they drink beer and sit at wooden tables beneath chestnut trees—that is all there is to it. The work which I have begun is not moving ahead, but I feel that it can be a glorious thing. Or maybe for dramatical creation one must work in the sight of the theater, in the whirlpool of spectator's faces and eyes fixed on you from all sides—as I worked. I will wait; we will see. I have much hope for the road. Content usually comes to my mind and develops on the road; I worked out almost all of my plots on the road. Can it be I am going to Russia? I can hardly believe it. I am afraid for my health. I have become completely unaccustomed to the cold now; how will I bear it? But my circumstances are such that I must go without fail: the graduation from the institute of my sisters—whose fate I must see to, and there is no chance of entrusting this to anyone else. In a word, I must go in spite of all my disinclination. But as soon as I fix up two things—one with regard to my sisters, the other to my drama[2] (if only I have the will of Almighty God who has helped me in this so far)—as soon as I arrange this, I will fly to Rome as early as February, and I think I will catch you there. Meanwhile, I am still sitting in Vienna. Pogodin is still not here. It is a beautiful season. It is warm and the weather is eternally good. . . .

## P. A. Pletnev. September 27, 1839. Moscow.

I am in Moscow. Don't tell anybody about it for a while. It's sad, I wanted so badly not to be here. But it is my duty and last obligation: my sisters. I must see to their fate. No matter how I shifted things I couldn't find any way without coming myself. I am here for a very short time, and as soon as I arrange things, I won't pay attention to any obstacles or season, and within a month and a half or two months I'll be on the road to Rome. I have a most urgent request for you to find out if I can take my sisters before the examination and thus gain time, or if it is essential for them to wait until graduation. Give me your answer and very soon if possible. Perhaps I will embrace you personally soon after that. I heard of and grieved over your loss. You were deprived of your kind and dear spouse who had walked so many years at your arm, the witness of your griefs and joys and all that stirs us in the beautiful years of our life. Do you know that I had a premonition of it. And when I was saying good-bye to you, something vaguely told me that the next time I would see you as a widower. There is another premonition; it has not yet been fulfilled, but it will be fulfilled because my premonitions are accurate, and I don't know why this gift of prophecy has been lodged within me now. But of one thing I could not have a premonition—the death of Pushkin, and I parted with him as if separating for two days.

How strange! God, how strange! Russia without Pushkin. I will arrive in Petersburg and Pushkin won't be there. I'll see you— and Pushkin won't be there. Why do you stay in Petersburg now? Why do you need your former dear customs, your former life now? Give it all up and let's go to Rome! Oh, if only you knew what a haven there is there for one whose heart has experienced a loss: How the inexhaustable expanses of emptiness in our life are filled there! How close it is to heaven there. God, God, God! Oh my Rome. My beautiful, wonderful Rome. Unhappy is he who has left you for two months, and happy is he for whom those two months have passed and who is returning to you. I swear that no matter how wondrous it is to travel to Rome, it is a thousand times more wonderful to return there. . . .

## M. N. Zagoskin. First Half of October 1839. Moscow.

I address my letter to you as a member of that elevated and enlightened circle which is the honor and pride of Moscow. It was painful to my heart, and I swear I still feel this pain when rumors

have reached me that my failure to appear in the theater[1] was ascribed to some contempt for the Moscow public which had met me so warmly, and which at another time would have produced grateful streams of tears. No one saw my inner state. No one could read in my face the blow of misfortune in my family circumstances which had shaken me, which I had received a few minutes before the presentation of my play. For all that, knowing that a warm reception awaited me from a public which until then had been so favorably inclined toward me without meeting me, I controlled myself and was at the theater in spite of my grief. I even collected all my presence of spirit in order to appear at the first call and express my deep appreciation. But when the thunder of unanimous applause, so flattering to an author, touched my ears, my heart contracted and my strength left me. I looked at my infamous fame with a kind of contempt, and I thought: now I am enjoying it, becoming intoxicated by it, but a sad and threatening future watches over those beings who are close and dear to me—for whom I would give up the best minutes of my life—my heart turned inside out! Through the shouts and applause I heard sufferings and cries of pain. I didn't have enough strength. I disappeared from the theater. There is the reason for my boorish act. I didn't want to announce it and I swear it has taken great efforts to do so, but I had to do it. In this I have overcome my own pride. I even request you to inform everyone who will add to my grief by rebuking me with the accusation of insensitivity and ungratefulness—an accusation which is so unjust and painful to my heart. Even show them my letter, to which, incidentally, I would never agree because feelings and sufferings should be kept holy, preserved in the heart and not entrusted to anyone; but I sacrifice this from a desire to show how much and how highly I value the public's goodwill toward me. It may not believe my words and this my heartfelt letter, it may even laugh at me. Let it add more contempt, more of the hate for me which many of my countrymen harbor; but I swear those momentary expressions of its warmth and goodwill will never leave my grateful breast. Again I will carry away into exile my beggar's pride and my soul crushed by calamity; but even amid the grief in my existence which has been darkened and troubled by mental and physical illness, in spite of all this, tears of gratitude will rush many times for that applause of approval which reaches me from my distant fatherland.

## V. A. Zhukovsky. About January 4, 1840. Moscow.

I don't even remember whether I thanked you for the haven in Petersburg and your love. God! How stupid I am, how worthlessly, unhappily stupid I am! And how strange my existence in Russia is! What an oppressive dream! Oh, if only I would awake as soon as possible! Nothing has the power to excite me, not even the people an encounter with whom would bring joy, nothing. Several times I have taken up my pen to write to you, and I stood in front of the table as if made of wood; it seemed as if all the nerves that are in contact with my brain had hardened and my head had turned to stone. I was given your letter just this minute; you worried about me and went to trouble for me, and at this very moment I imagined your animated eyes and the sympathy for me expressed in them . . . how can I thank you? I swear in my present condition I was consoled a thousand times more by this than by Smirdin's Jewish offer.[1] But let's talk about Smirdin's offer. I told you there would be no profit in publishing all my works together now. That although the copies of *The Inspector General* and *Mirgorod* have sold out, there are still plenty of *Arabesques* and especially *Evenings on a Farm,* and that except for *The Inspector General* they are not sought at all so eagerly that a new edition could be undertaken; the trifling sum offered by Smirdin serves as proof of this. But such is my fate; the booksellers have always made use of my critical situation and strained financial circumstances. If I wait a year until my new novel is published and draws the attention of 4,000 readers to itself, they will again go after my works which have been forgotten at present. And meanwhile the present difficult, hungry years of crop failure which have reduced the number of readers will pass. The booksellers say publicly that they don't have any money now, and that the people who bought books before have put this money aside to improve the estates which have been thrown into disorder by crop failure. . . .

I don't condemn Smirdin unconditionally; he has treated others well, but he has always been like a Jew with me. And after everything that he has done to me I have to humiliate myself before him again. I admit I thought you would make a proposal to another bookseller; it seems to me I told you I didn't want to have any relations with Smirdin. But perhaps you aren't aware what Smirdin's Jewishness can be like in this matter. Here is where it can be: I am given 6,000 for one-third—that is for the plays you assigned to the first volume of the collection—*The Inspector General, The Marriage,* and excerpts from an unfinished comedy. And I admit I was already prepared to agree in spite of the fact that I was awfully reluctant to

have my immature creations published (the *Bridegrooms* and the un-finished comedy).[2] But want forced me to agree to anything. I was all ready to give myself a couple of minutes of respite; I even cheered myself with the thought that I would finally somehow settle my onerous duties, and radiant, with a reanimated soul, I would set out for my promised paradise, to my Rome where I would again awaken and complete my work. But this was a daydream and made me happy only for a minute. I found only two fragments of the un-finished comedy; the whole thing was left in Rome. And I still cannot comprehend where *The Bridegrooms* got to. It seems to me I took it with me from Rome, but no matter how much I have rummaged through my papers, and underwear I haven't been able to find it any-where. Whether it was lost on the road or the customs inspectors who rummaged through my suitcase threw it out or it lies in Rome in my apartment in my trunk—I simply don't know. I know only that now I am again immersed in my terrible apathetic state. The last possi-bility has collapsed, and even if I were forced to accept Smirdin's of-fer, I could not fulfill its terms now. But agree yourself that I would really have to be stupid to agree. If they give 6,000 just for a third of the collection, surely they will give at least 3,000 for the other two thirds. That's 9,000 already. But by publishing them now I would lose a great deal—I am told this by both the booksellers and literary people who make frequent bargains—and finally by the difficult and hungry time which also threatens this year, if not even more. Shiryaev[3] would give me 16,000 for the same works with the sole condition that I give him the novel in advance—and he says perhaps even more; but he won't give me anything now because he doesn't want to proffer a small sum—so that people won't say he deceived me and used my lack of knowledge; but Smirdin was not ashamed. Besides, don't you see how I would fall into Smirdin's claws by ac-cepting his terms. Note what a small number of copies he is printing so that the bill for the copies won't be too big. But who can vouch that he will print only 1,500 and not three or four thousand—why you can't see this on Smirdin's face; and I'm not about to hire a spy to see what's going on in his house and the typography. And what good is it to me that he has the rights for two years if he supplies himself with enough copies for twenty years? Of course if these were new works it would be profitable to sell them for two years, knowing that these copies would all be sold in two years and a new edition could be undertaken. But in this case it is all over with—I won't see another edition in my lifetime. This is my last resource, and I cannot risk it like this now. Then I was alone. Now I have a bankrupt family.

And so I have decided not to sell my works, but to search out

and employ all means if not to stop at least somehow to put off the unfortunate course of my difficult circumstances for a year, to leave as soon as possible for Rome where my murdered soul will be resurrected again as it was resurrected last winter and spring, to take up my work zealously, and, if possible, to finish my novel in one year. But how am I to get the means and money for this. Here's what I have come up with: make a collection, make up a pool from all those who nurture true interest in me, put together a sum of 4,000 rubles, and loan it to me for a year.[4] I give you my word that in a year, if my powers do not deceive me and I don't die, I will repay it to you with interest. This will give me a way somehow to extricate myself from my circumstances to a certain extent and to return my own self to me to a certain extent.—Give me your answer, and, for the sake of God, quickly. I am waiting impatiently.


*M. I. Gogol. January 25, 1840. Moscow.*

 . . . . My sisters, praise the Lord, are well in spite of the fact that they don't have extremely strong constitutions. I have provided them with a society which is not noisy and flighty, but quiet and pleasant, which should have effect on their morality.[1] To my good fortune the archimandrite Makarius has arrived here, a man well known for his holy life, extraordinary virtues, fiery zeal for the faith. I asked him and he is so kind that in spite of his lack of time and a lot of business, he comes to our place and instructs my sisters in the great Christian truths. I myself stop and listen to him for several hours at a time; and I have never heard a priest speak so deeply, with such conviction, with such sagacity and simplicity. Firmness, patience, and unshakable hope in God. This is what we should take as our sacred motto now, dearest mama. Now we should show that we are Christians and that calamities are nothing to us and haven't the power to make us vacillate. Extremity threatens us. This means God is challenging us to battle. He wants to look at us, to see how we pass over this road, and if everything we have been saying up till now is correct —that we have faith in Him and place our hope upon Him. And so mama, you see that just here we must show presence of spirit. . . .


*N. D. Belozersky.[1] April 12, 1840. (New Style). Moscow.*

 . . . . I am leaving in two weeks. My health and I myself are no longer fit for the climate here, but the main thing is my poor soul;

there is no shelter for it here, or rather there is no shelter here where troubles do not reach to it. Now I am more suited for a monastery than for society life. In your letter you said, although casually and not otherwise than with conditions, that you would perhaps visit my home sometime (the country that is). Now I am going to make a serious request of you. For the sake of God, if you happen to be in Poltava go to my place in the village of Vasilevka thirty-five versts from Poltava. You will do me a great service and favor. Here is the point: examine it and the shape it is in and write 'me about it—and also how it is possible to improve conditions. I have neglected things. Mama is an extremely kind and extremely weak woman, she is deceived at every step. You are an intelligent and experienced man; you will immediately notice what I myself couldn't notice at all, for now, I confess, I can hardly even notice that I exist. Do me this favor. In Poltava you will learn where our village is and how to get to it from Ivan Vasilevich Kapnist[2] who lives in Poltava permanently. Mama has heard of you from me several times and will be inexpressibly happy to have you. My sisters, two of whom graduated from the institute the other day and whom you know slightly, are very good girls and without doubt still haven't had time yet to learn anything bad. Please stay on two or three days—they will certainly force you to do that. If you don't want to show that you are examining the estate or it seems to you awkward to let mama know, please tell her that I asked you especially to make a study of the soil and its suitability for an orchard; and mama knows that I always wanted to plant an orchard. This will make mama happy because she will take it as a sure sign that I intend to live in the country myself soon. . . .

## S. T. Aksakov.[1] June 10, 1840. (New Style). Warsaw.

Hello, Sergei Timofeevich, my good friend, friend close to my heart. It would be sinful if I didn't respond to you from the road. But what kind of foolishness am I uttering: "sinful." I wouldn't pay any attention to whether it was sinful or not, proper or improper and probably wouldn't have written you a word, especially now. If a sincere impulse hadn't been acting here. I embrace you and kiss you several times. It doesn't seem to me that I have parted with you. I see you beside me every moment and even in such a way that it seems you have just said a few words to me and I have to reply to them. Separation doesn't exist for me, and that is why I part more easily than

other people. And for the same reason none of my friends can die, because he lives with me forever. We got to Warsaw safely—that is all that can interest you for the present. There were no delays anywhere, not at any station; in a word, it is impossible to travel here any better. Even the weather was good; there was rain where needed, sun where needed. I found a few acquaintances here, but in two days we will leave for Krakow and from there, if we manage, to Vienna the same day. I kiss and embrace Konstantin Sergeevich[2] several times and supply him with the following rather dull chores: to bring with him a few books for me, to be specific, the miniature edition of *Onegin*,[3] *Woe from Wit*,[4] and Dmitriev's fables,[5] and, if a compact edition of Saxarov's *Russian Songs*[6] has come out bring it too. . . .

*P. I. Raevsky.[1] June 25, 1840. (New Style). Vienna.*

If you knew how sad I am that I have discovered you and grown close to you so late, Praskovya Ivanovna! There is a strange feeling of incompleteness in my soul; now I somewhat resemble the traveler whom chance, which plays with men, ordained to meet unexpectedly an old friend, a long-time comrade on the road. They cried out, raised their hats, and passed by each other quickly without managing to say one word to each other. Only afterwards one of them came to his senses, and full of sadness he utters reproaches to himself: Why didn't he stop his traveling cart? Why didn't he sacrifice the time? Why didn't he cast his important business aside? The state of my soul is almost like this now. You will believe my sincere feelings won't you, I am not capable of lying. And I wouldn't forgive myself for a century if I lied to you about anything. But is the love of a person you barely know interesting to you? In order to know and fall in love with a person much, too much time is necessary, and not everyone is given the gift of being able to know a person at once. How many people there have been who have deceived themselves! But how many, perhaps, have disappeared from the face of the earth who had hidden beautiful feelings in their souls; but they did not know how to display them, these feelings were not expressed on their faces and their lot was to die unrecognized. For me there is much that is sad in this truth. And I feel more at ease only when I imagine your quiet, bright gaze completely filled with sincere goodness. I won't say a word to you about my gratitude. Here we understand each other completely and you can know how great it is. My sister's situation

was an unbearable burden for me, and no matter how much I mulled over in my mind where I could find her a spot where her character would find a good road and be strengthened on it, I could not, however, and was almost completely at my wits' end. And suddenly God sent down to me more than I expected. I found everything in your home. First and most important—you; second, and what is an unheard-of rarity, everything surrounding you. Really, I found no one around you who was not a completely good person or on whose face a soul was not reflected. In any case it is amazing, whether this was communicated from you or whether they had all this in themselves. I congratulated myself internally and my soul found repose. That is why when you asked me how I wanted my sister to be guided and what I wanted her prepared for, I didn't say anything to you, because the main thing had been found. If she firmly establishes herself in just what is good and her soul acquires even a part of that which is in the society surrounding her, no matter where she is afterward, no matter where fate casts her, she will be happy everywhere. Besides, what could I tell you? You are a woman, you know better than I what a woman needs. For my part I would want my sister to learn the following:

    1) to know how to be satisfied with absolutely everything,

    2) to be more familiar with need than with abundance,

    3) to learn what patience is and find pleasure in labor.

I didn't worry about exactly what calling to prepare her for—that is temporary; I thought more about what is eternal. Besides all that about whether to be a governess or something else is one-sided and can teach only one thing. I have seen many governesses who got married who seemed as if they had just gotten out of a girls' institute; they were just as innocent and just as little acquainted with what we call the prose of life, prose without which, however, it is impossible to live. Family life is woman's assignment, and there are many heterogeneous duties in it. Here a woman is governess and nursemaid, slave and mistress. In a word, duties all of which at first glance it would seem impossible to learn, but which are learned imperceptibly of themselves, without any system. You have all of the means for this. For example, sometimes you can assign her some separate parts of the household work, especially something that would at the same time give her some exercise, because of their own accord young girls don't like to stroll about just to stroll about; this is, however, for the best. You will probably spend the summer in the country, and there are so many domestic chores that demand hustling and bustling about in the country! I have always wished for her to have some regular job which would occupy for about an hour and a

half, but absolutely every day at the same time. I mean translation, a task which can be very useful to her in the future and even provide her with a livelihood if other ways are not found. And with my literary connections I can to a certain extent provide her with a profitable market and proper price. It does not matter that she still translates badly now; it is necessary for her to translate and translate absolutely every day. Translation does not demand great talent; it is a matter of habit and practice. He who translates poorly in the beginning will translate well later on. It is also essential to vary the occupations. This enlivens work and leaves no place for boredom, and at the same time it is very good for the health. For example, having finished her translating, she should not occupy herself with work which also requires sitting down. On the contrary, after this she should be given a task for which she has to get up from her seat, run somewhere and again return and again run off—in a word, remain on her feet constantly. Then, after this, work which demands sitting down will seem pleasant to her and will no longer be work to her, but leisure. Apart from the one part of domestic work placed upon her, it wouldn't hurt to give her various commissions—to buy something, to pay off and settle accounts, to keep records of the income and expenditures. She is a poor girl and she has nothing. If she gets married, this will take the place of a dowry and surely her husband, if he is not a stupid man, will be more thankful for it than for financial capital. But even if my sister were not a poor girl and if a brilliant lot stood before her, even then (though perhaps I would add one or two extra languages and something for drawing rooms) I would certainly not exclude any of the points outlined for her education. They are just as necessary for a rich position as for a poor one, and it is almost more difficult to preserve what one has acquired than to acquire it.

But I feel ridiculous that I have launched into such long instructions, telling you what you know twenty times better than I. But I know this won't chagrin you. You will hear me out with the same indulgence with which your humble soul is so full. You won't reproach me because I have too little knowledge, but will correct me magnanimously where I have erred, for a man is fated to err and perfection is given to him only so that he can see his imperfection better. . . .


*S. T. Aksakov. July 7, 1840. (New Style). Vienna.*

. . . . I hope to spend another month and a half in Vienna, to drink the waters and rest. It is more peaceful here than at the watering

places where a society which is too boring for me gathers together. Here everything is closer, right at hand; and there is freedom in everything. You should know that the latter long ago ran away from the villages and small towns of Europe where waters and gatherings exist. Parades of people—it's unbearable! On top of that I have such a vile nature that one glance at this crowd that has come from all directions to be treated rather clogs me up, and that is no good at the waters; on the contrary, one's bowels should loosen. How I remember Marienbad and the faces, each of which crawled into my memory forcibly and impertinently by coming my way about forty times a day, and the insufferable Russians with the eternal and immutable question: "And what glass are you drinking?" a question from which I took to my heels along country roads. At that time the question struck me as the blood-brother of another familiar question: "What news do you have for us?" For by itself every word is innocent, but repeated twenty times it becomes more banal than the beneficent Tsinsky[1] or Bulgarin's novels which are all the same. . . . I notice that I haven't, it seems, finished the period. But to hell with it! Was there ever any sense in periods? I only see and hear sense in the feelings and the soul. So I am at the waters in Vienna; it's cheaper and more peaceful and gayer. I'm here alone; no one disturbs me. I view the Germans as the unavoidable insects in every Russian hut. They run and crawl around me, but they don't bother me; and if one of them crawls out on my nose—a little flick and he's had it! . . . .

I embrace Konstantin Sergeevich[2] with all my heart, though doubtlessly not as strongly as he does me (but that's not without profit, it's a little easier on the sides), and at the same time I ask him to add to the commissions I loaded on him a few more, to be specific: ask Pogodin if the second volume of my Shakespeare was found, which he should bring with him, and add to that both editions of Maximovich's songs,[3] and perhaps the third if it has come out. And what is the main thing: buy or commission Mikhail Semenovich[4] to buy some Petersburg tanned leather from the best bootmaker—the softest kind for boots, that is only the upper leather (it is already cut out so that it doesn't take up space and is easy to carry); two or three pairs. A misfortune happened; all the boots that Také made for me turned out too short. The stubborn German! I tried to tell him they'd be short, but he, the boot-tree, didn't want to listen to me! And they are so wide that my feet have swollen up. It would be good if this leather could be gotten to me: they make rather good boots here.

. . .

## M. P. Pogodin. October 17, 1840. (New Style). Rome.

Well, give me your hand! I forgive you for grieving me. My friend! . . . . God! Aren't you ashamed . . . there is much that you did not understand in me in certain instances. You met me with the severe rebuke of a man when my disturbed soul expected tender, almost feminine sympathy. My soul was ill then. Now perhaps a lot will be explained to you, and perhaps you will see yourself that you are sometimes hasty with your conclusions. But your last conclusion is the most hasty. At one stroke you wanted to deny me depth of emotions and heart and soul and to assign me a place lower even than that of the most ordinary people. As if that were easy, as if that can happen in nature. And in knowledge of the human heart you fell from Shakespeare to Kotzebue. But you probably have already made this reproach to yourself as soon as our relations to each other came to your mind. That's enough—I kiss you. . . .

I am very happy about your good fortune, i.e., the rare finds you made.[1] You treat me to one of them as it is the one that lies closest of all to me, but you do it like the crane who once invited his buddy the wolf (as I recall) to dinner—he ordered the dishes served in containers with such long necks that only the crane's beak could reach through, while his buddy just sniffed and flicked his tail, cursing his fat snout. If only I had some odorous excerpts from it to use, i.e., those where it smells more of ancientry and the customs of ancient times. I am even happier about the freshness of your powers, the health and pleasure which is visiting you in your good works. Lucky fellow. May God make this mental condition last until you are ninety years of age.

But I—would like not . . . oh, how I would like not to reveal my condition! And in my letter to you from Vienna I tried to keep my spirits up, and I didn't let you know a word. But know everything. I departed from Moscow in good shape, and the road through our steppes to Vienna immediately worked a miracle on me. Freshness and briskness such as I had never known took control of me. Incidentally, I began to drink Marienbad water in Vienna—in order to free my stomach some more from various old discomforts and the remains of Moscow dinners which had lodged here and there. This time it helped me surprisingly, I began to feel some of the briskness of youth; but the main thing was that I felt that my nerves were awakening and I was getting out of that lethargic mental inaction which I have been in during recent years and the cause of which was somnolence of my nerves. . . . I felt that ideas were stirring in my mind like an awakened swarm of bees; my imagination was becom-

ing more sensitive. Oh, what joy that was, if only you knew. The plot which I had of late carried lazily in my head not even daring to take it up, unfolded before me in such majesty that everything within me felt a sweet tremulousness. And forgetting everything I was suddenly transported into that world which I had not been in for a long time, and at that same moment I sat down to work forgetting that that was not at all suitable while drinking the waters and that precisely at this time peace of mind and ideas were necessary.

But how was I to restrain myself? Will it occur to someone who has sat in a dungeon for several years without sunlight to squint his eyes when he goes out of it for fear of being blinded—and not to look at that which is joy and life for him? And besides I thought, "Perhaps this is only a moment, perhaps this will again disappear from me, and then I will forever regret that I didn't utilize the time that my powers were awakened." Even if I had at least stopped drinking the waters at the time, but I wanted to finish the course of treatment and I thought, "When I am already in such a radiant condition, everything in me will be in even better order after finishing the course of treatment." This was still during the summer heat, and the awakening of my nerves suddenly turned into irritation of my nerves. Everything in me threw itself into my chest at once. I was terrified. I didn't understand my condition myself. I gave up my work, I thought it was a result of a sedentary life and the insufficiency of exercise while at the waters. I started walking and moving about until I got tired—and I made it still worse. The nervous disorder and irritation increased terribly; a heaviness and pressure in the chest which I had never before experienced grew strong. Fortunately, the doctors found that I didn't have consumption, that this was an extreme irritation of the nerves and a stomach disorder which stopped digestion. This didn't make me feel any better, because my treatment was rather dangerous and that which could help my stomach worked destructively on my nerves and my nerves back on my stomach. A painful anguish which has no description was combined with this. I was brought to such a state that I absolutely didn't know where to turn, where to find support. I couldn't stay calm for two minutes in bed or in a chair or on my feet. Oh, it was terrible, it was the same anguish and the same uneasiness that I saw poor Vielgorsky in during the last minutes of his life. Imagine it, after this I got worse and worse every day. Finally, even the doctor himself could not predict anything reassuring for me. Only Botkin was with me, a very good fellow to whom I will always be thankful for this, who comforted me a little, but who himself told me afterwards that he couldn't imagine that I would get well. I understood my condition and gathering my

strength I quickly scratched out a meager will as best I could, so that at least my debts would be paid off immediately after my death. But it seemed to me terrible to die among the Germans. I ordered them to put me in a stagecoach and to be taken to Italy. When I got to Trieste I felt better. This time too the road, my sole medicine, produced its effect. I could already move about. Although at the time it was still unpleasant and hot, the air did refresh me. Oh, how I would have liked to take some long road then. I felt, I knew—and I know that I would have recovered completely then. But I didn't have the means to go anywhere. With what joy I would have become a government messenger, even a courier on a Russian post chaise, and I would have ventured even to Kamchatka, the further the better. I swear I would have been healthy. But for me the whole road to Rome was only three days. There was little change of air there. Nevertheless, even this had its effect on me, and I felt better the first days in Rome. At least I could already even take a little stroll, although after that I was as tired as if I had done ten versts. I still cannot understand how I stayed alive, and my health was in a doubtful condition such as I had never been in before. It seems the more time passes the worse I get again, and treatment and medications only exacerbate things. Neither Rome, nor the sky, nor that which could so enchant me— nothing has any influence on me now. I don't see or feel them. If only I could be on the road now, yes, the road in the rain, the muck, through forests, through the steppes, to the end of the world. Yesterday and today the weather was rotten, and during this rotten weather it is as if I came to life. So I kept wanting to throw myself either into a stagecoach or even a post chaise. I couldn't sit in the room for two minutes; it got so painful for me that I set off wandering in the rain. I got tired after a few steps, but I really seemed to feel better. Friend! There is my condition for you. I didn't want to reveal it, I wanted terribly not to; and I have spent a long time writing this letter, I kept stopping and beginning to write again, and I wanted to tear it all up and hide everything from you. But it would have been a sin on my soul.

I look at myself with terror. I rode off to work and labor fresh and cheerful. Now . . . God. How many sacrifices have been made for me by my friends—when will I repay them. And I thought that the thing which would redeem me at one stroke, remove the burdens which lie on my conscience-less conscience would be ready this year. What faces me in the future? God, I do not fear a short life, but from such a fresh, brisk beginning I was sure that I would be given two years of fruitful life. And now this sweet assurance has disappeared from me. Without hope, without means to recover my health. No news from Petersburg whether I am to hope for a position with

Krivtsov. Judging by Krivtsov's intentions, about which I learned
here, I have nothing to hope for, because Krivtsov has been searching
for some European celebrity in the arts for the post. He wanted to
have the German Schadow, the director of the Dusseldorf Academy
of Arts who also wanted it, but then he even wanted to offer it to Overbeck[2] in order to cover up his natural ignorance in this field and
lend more weight to his position. But forget him and all this. I am indifferent to it now. What good would it do me. Perhaps provide medicine and an apartment? Two things of equal insignificance and use-
lessness if they aren't joined to a third which crowns everything
that languishes on earth.

In my present condition the question often comes to me why I
went to Russia, at least then less would lie on my conscience. But as
soon as I remember my sisters.—No my coming was not without
use. I swear I did a great deal for my sisters. They will see this later.
Going to Russia I thought: "You crazy fellow!—Well, it is good that
I am going to Russia, already the slight malice—so essential to an
author—against this and that, all kinds of various weeds, is beginning
to grow cold in me; now I will renew it and all of this will stand before
my eyes more vividly." And what did I take away instead of that?
All of the bad things, even the former ones, were erased from my
memory, and in place of them I have with me only what is beautiful
and pure, everything that I succeeded in discovering even more of in
my friends; and in my state of illness I constantly make myself the
reproach, "And why did I go to Russia?" Now I can't look at the
Coliseum or the eternal cupola, or the air, or anything; I can't look
at them with all my attention, only at them; my eyes see something
else, my thought is distracted. It is with you. God! How painful it is
for me to write these lines, I no longer have the strength. Farewell!
. . . .


*S. T. Aksakov. December 28, 1840. (New Style). Rome.*

Sergei Timofeevich, friend of my soul, I am very guilty before
you for not writing to you right after your letter, which is always so
pleasant for me. I was sick then. I didn't want to write you about my
sickness, because it would have grieved you. As I learned at the time
even without that you learned of a great loss; I didn't want to lie
either, so I decided to wait for a while. Now I am writing you because
I am well, thanks to the miraculous power of God who has resurrected me from the sickness from which, I confess, I did not expect to

rise. Much that is miraculous has taken place in my thoughts and life! In your letter you said you believed we would see each other again. As it may please the Almighty power! Perhaps this desire will be fulfilled, a desire of our hearts which are strong mutually. At least circumstances seem to be moving towards that.

It seems I won't get the post about which—do you recall?—we fussed and which could have provided for my stay in Rome. I admit that I almost foresaw this, because almost from the first glance I saw through Krivtsov who fooled everyone. He is a man who loves only himself too much and who pretended to love one thing or another only by means of this to further gratify his passion, i.e., his love for himself. He values me as much as a rag. He must without fail have with him some European celebrity in the world of art, in whose inner merit he himself doesn't believe—but in whose spreading fame he does believe, because with all of this glitter he wants (which is extremely natural) to play the role which he understands very well. But forget him! Everything, everything that happens to me in life makes me happy, and when I see to what wonderful usefulness and good I have been led by what are called failures in society, my touched soul cannot find words to thank the invisible hand which is guiding me.

Another circumstance which can give hope for my return is my work. I am now preparing the first volume of *Dead Souls* for the final revision. I am changing, polishing, and completely reworking many things, and I see that its publication cannot get by without my presence. Meanwhile, its further continuation is being elucidated more clearly and majestically in my mind, and now I see that with time it can be something colossal if only my weak powers permit. At least, surely, a few people know to what powerful thoughts and deep phenomena an insignificant plot, the first innocent and modest chapters of which you already know, can lead. My sickness took a lot of time away from me; but now, praise God, at times I even feel the freshness which is very necessary to me. I ascribe this partly to the cold water which I have begun to drink on the advice of the doctor, whom God bless for this and who thinks this cold treatment should help me. The air is wonderful in Rome now, clear. But the summer (this I have already experienced), I must certainly spend the summer on the road. I hurt myself very much by prolonging my stay in suffocating Vienna. But what was I to do? I confess I did not then have the means to undertake a journey; everything I had was too closely budgeted. Oh, if only I had the opportunity to take some distant road every summer! The road is amazingly salubrious for me. . . . But let's turn to the beginning. In my trip to see you, the significance of

which even I didn't understand in the beginning, there was much, much for me. Yes, I perceive the feeling of love for Russia is strong within me. Much that formerly seemed unpleasant and unbearable to me, now seems to have sunk into its triviality and insignificance; and I, calm and steady, am surprised that I could ever have taken them close to heart. And you know what I acquired on my present trip to Moscow! What I mean is there is no reason for you to go far to discover what this acquisition was. And I don't know how and by what means I am to thank God. But when I think about you and the young man so full of strength and every gift who became so attached to me—I feel something sweet in this.

But enough; treasured feelings somehow become banal when they are clothed in words. I had wanted to wait a while with this letter and send with it the altered pages of *The Inspector General* and request you to have a second edition printed—but I didn't manage. I just don't feel like working on what is needed in a hurry, but I keep on wanting to work on what is not to be hurried. But at the same time it would be very necessary as soon as possible. My hair almost stands on end when I remember what debts I have gotten into. I know that at times money is extremely necessary to you too; but in a week I hope to send you the corrections and supplements to *The Inspector General* which will perhaps make it sell better. It would be good if it made the money owed to you first and then the thousand borrowed from Panov which I promised to repay in February.

Panov[1] is a fine young fellow in all respects, and Italy did him a lot of good which Germany wouldn't have done—of which he is completely convinced. Incidentally, it won't hurt to inform others of this. And by the way, if one reasons correctly, I don't know why young people in general do not develop the fullness of their powers in the Russian land. But why—that could carry one away into lengthy cogitations. Farewell for now. . . .


*M. Pogodin. December 28, 1840. Rome.*

Be comforted! Miraculously merciful and great is God: I am healthy. I even feel a certain freshness, I am busy with corrections and emendations and even the continuation of *Dead Souls;*[1] I see that the subject is becoming deeper and deeper. I even intend to print the first volume in the coming year, if only it pleases the wonderful power of God who has resurrected me. Much has happened within me in a short time, but now I don't have strength enough to write about

it—I don't know why, perhaps for the same reason that in Moscow I didn't have strength enough to tell you anything which would have justified me before you in many respects.

Perhaps sometime when we meet together I will be in a mood such that my words will flow, and with the pure candor of a child I will tell you the state of my soul which has caused so much, both voluntarily and involuntarily. Oh! You should know that he who is created to create in the depth of his soul, to live and breathe his creations, must be strange in many respects. God! Another man needs only two words to justify himself—but he needs whole pages. How painful this is sometimes! But enough. . . .

## V. A. Zhukovsky. January-April, 1841. Rome.

. . . . Are you well? Happy? Do you think about me? I hear nothing and know nothing about you—and that is sad. I won't say that I am healthy. No, my health is perhaps even worse, but I am more than healthy. Often I experience miraculous moments; I live a miraculous life, a huge inner life enclosed within myself; and I wouldn't accept any health or comfort. From now on my entire life is one hymn of thankfulness. Don't reproach me because I haven't yet repaid the money I borrowed from you.[1] Everything will be paid, perhaps this winter. At last I will present myself to you without lowered eyes; but now I see and am surprised how I live on nothing in all respects, and I don't worry about life and I am not ashamed to be a beggar.

## S. T. Aksakov. March 5, 1841. (Old Style). Rome.

. . . . Now I must talk to you about an important matter. But Pogodin will inform you about this. Have a conference with him about how to arrange it best. Now I am directly and honestly asking help, for I have a right to, and I feel this in my soul. Yes my friend! I am deeply fortunate. In spite of my state of illness which has again become a little worse, I know and experience wonderous moments. A wonderful creation is being formed and created in my soul, and now my eyes are often filled with grateful tears. The radiant will of God is clearly apparent to me in this; such inspiration does not come from man, he could never invent such a plot! Oh, if only I have three more years with such fresh moments! I ask just as much life as is

necessary for the completion of my work; I don't need an hour more. Now the road and a journey are absolutely essential for me; they alone, as I have already said, restore me. All of my resources were exhausted several months ago. It is necessary for me to get a loan. Pogodin will tell you. At the beginning of forty-two I will repay everything because just that which I already have prepared and which, if God grants, I will publish at the end of the current year is enough for the payment.

Now I am yours; Moscow is my native place. At the start of fall I will press you to my Russian breast. Everything was wonderously and wisely arranged by the higher will; my arrival in Moscow and my present journey to Rome—all was good. Don't tell anyone I will be to see you or that I am at work, in a word, nothing. But I feel a certain timidity about returning alone. It is painful and now it is almost impossible for me to busy myself with the trifles and bother of traveling. I must have tranquility and the happiest, the gayest mood possible; you must preserve and cherish me now. Here's what I have thought up: let Mikhail Semenovich and Konstantin Sergeevich[1] come after me; they need this—Mikhail Semenovich for his health, Konstantin Sergeevich for the harvest it is already time he should make. And it would be impossible to find anyone dearer to my soul than these two who could come after me. Then I would ride along with the same youthful feeling that a schoolboy has at vacation time when he rides from the school which has bored him toward home, his native roof, and the free air. You must cherish me now—not for myself, no! They will not do a useless chore. They will bring a clay vase with themselves. Of course this vase is all cracked now, rather old, and barely holds itself together; but there is a treasure enclosed in this vase now; therefore it is necessary to preserve it. I await your answer; the sooner the better. . . .


*S. T. Aksakov. March 13, 1841. (Old Style). Rome.*

. . . . You write that I should send something to Pogodin's journal.[1] God, if you knew how painful; how destructive this demand is for me—what an anguish and tormenting state it drove me into all of a sudden! It is a calamity just to tear my thoughts away from my sacred work[2] now. No one who could really know what he was depriving me of would ever address such a request to me again. I swear that if I had the money I would give up however much money I had in place of submitting my essay! But so be it, I will hunt up some old scrap and, God, spend perhaps two or three weeks on its correc-

tion and finishing touches—because for me any small piece now requires almost as much consideration as a large one, because it will
be almost coercion and every minute I will remember the fruitless
magnitude of my sacrifice, my criminal sacrifice.[3] No, I swear it,
distracting me is a sin, a great sin, a burdensome sin! Only one who
does not believe my words and to whom my thoughts are inaccessible
can be allowed to do this. My work is great; my work is a way to salva-
t'on. I have died for everything trifling now; must I commit unfor-
givable crimes with daily rubbish for the contemptible vulgar business of a journal? And how will my essay help the journal? But the
essay will be ready and sent off in about three weeks. I will only be
sorry if it exacerbates my predisposition for illness. But I think not.
God is merciful. . . . The road, the road! I have strong hope for the
road. Now it will be doubly beautiful for me. I will see my friends,
my dear friends. Don't tell anyone about my arrival, and tell Pogodin
for him not to tell anyone either; if on the other hand you have already let the cat out of the bag, say that it is still not sure now. Don't
say anything about my work either. Embrace Pogodin and tell him
that I am crying because I cannot be useful to him with respect to
his journal, but that he, if a Russian feeling of love for the fatherland
beats in his heart, he should not demand that I give him anything. . . .

## A. S. Danilevsky. August 7, 1841. (New Style). Rome.

. . . . But listen, now you must heed my word, for my word is
doubly powerful over you, and woe unto anyone who does not heed
my word. Leave everything for a while, everything that occasionally stirs your thoughts during idle moments, no matter how entic-
ingly and pleasantly it stirs them. Give in and occupy yourself with
your estate for a year, for one year only. . . .

## N. M. Yazykov. September 27, 1841. (New Style). Dresden.

. . . . We have reached Dresden safely. . . . In general the trip
was good. I thought a lot about things; I thought about you and all the
thoughts about you were radiant ones. An unconquerable assurance
about you settled in my soul, and I was extremely joyful, because
the voice which flies out of my soul has not yet deceived me once. On
the road my tranquility was disturbed only by crawling out of the
carriage onto a train, where like a dream turning into reality I met

Bakunin[1] and extremely hard wooden benches. Both made things terribly uncomfortable . . . but we're in Dresden. Peter Mikhailovich[2] set off to see his family, and I remained alone and enjoyed the cool air after coffee, and many things are coming to me: that about which I speak to you comes, and finally once almost by accident there even glimmered a long Moscow house with a row of rooms, an even fifteen-degree warmness, and two impenetrable rooms. No, with its noise and irksomeness Moscow shouldn't seem terrible to you now; now you should remember that I am waiting for you there, and that you are going straight to your home and not visiting. Your path is firm, and it is not in vain that a staff has been left for you by the guarantee of these words. Oh believe my words! . . . . I don't have the strength to tell you anything more than just: Believe my words. I myself do not dare not to believe my words. There is something miraculous and incomprehensible . . . but the sobs and tears of a deeply agitated noble soul would keep me from ever finishing an explanation . . . and my lips would grow mute. No human thought has the power to imagine a hundredth part of the infinite love that God keeps for man. . . . That's all. Henceforth, your gaze should be radiantly and enthusiastically raised upwards—that is what our meeting was for. . . .

*V. A. Zhukovsky. First part of October 1841. Berlin.*

As you see I am still not in Russia and am now writing you from Berlin, I'm writing about Ivanov[1] with regard to the matter I already discussed with you. I'm sending you the letter to the Crown Prince which I wrote out in rough form for him. I already sent a copy of it to him. Within two or three weeks after this letter you will get a letter from him. He must be helped, otherwise it will be a sin on the soul; helping a talent means not just helping one friend, but twenty friends at once. When forwarding his letter to the heir, I think it will be enough for you to say that in imploring your intercession in presenting the letter Ivanov presented many reasons (which were, in all justice, convincing) for a decision to continue his pension for three more years, and that for your part you can witness: that Ivanov worked on his picture day and night; that to hurry its completion he refused all jobs and commissions, that he seeks nothing, no other rewards than the means and opportunity to complete it, that the most favorable comments about his picture echo from all sides, that Overbeck's picture,[2] half as large in the size of the canvas, nevertheless

took more than ten years of work, and that, finally, he is an artist adorned by a fierce love for art which reaches the point of self-sacrifice, a wise modesty and humility, one who fully deserves every attention and patronage. It is impossible for these words not to produce action, because they are pure truth. . . .

## P. A. Pletnev. January 7, 1842. Moscow.

Shattered both in body and in spirit I write to you. I would like very much to go to Petersburg now; it is necessary for me, I know, but nevertheless I cannot. Illness has never turned up in me as inopportunely as now. Now its attacks have assumed such strange forms . . . but forget about them; I must talk about the censorship now, not about illness. It is a blow which was in no way unexpected for me—the entire manuscript has been forbidden.[1] First I gave it to the censor Snegirev who is somewhat more sensible than the others so that if he found any passage leading to doubt in his mind, he would inform me straightaway, and then I would send it to Petersburg. In two days Snegirev solemnly informed me that he found the manuscript completely loyal both in relation to its purpose and in relation to the impression produced on the reader, and that except for one insignificant place—the change of two or three names (I immediately agreed and changed them)—there was nothing which could incur the suspicion of the strictest censorship. He declared the same thing to others as well. All of a sudden someone got him muddled, and I found out that he had presented my manuscript to the committee. The committee received it as if they had been prepared in advance and were all set to enact a comedy, for all the accusations without exception were comedy in the highest degree. No sooner had Golokhvastov, the acting president, heard the title than he shouted in the voice of an ancient Roman: "Dead Souls! No, I will never allow this—the soul is immortal, there cannot be any dead soul; the author is taking up arms against immortality." Only with some effort, finally, could the intelligent president understand that it was about serfs not yet taken from the tax rolls. No sooner had he understood and along with him the other censors understood that "dead" means souls not yet removed from the tax rolls than an ever greater mess was made. "No," cried the chairman and after him half of the censors, "even more that cannot be allowed, even if in the manuscript there were nothing else, but only the words 'tax-roll soul'—even this alone cannot be allowed; this means it is against serfdom." Finally, Snegirev

himself, seeing that things had already gone far afield, began to assure the censors that he had read the manuscript and there were not even any hints about serfdom, that there were not even any of the usual slaps in the face of serfs which resound in many stories, that this was about something completely different, that the main concern was based on the amusing misunderstanding of the sellers and subtle ruses of the buyer and on the general hodgepodge that this strange purchase caused, that this was a series of characters, the internal mode of life of Russia and a few ordinary inhabitants, a collection of scenes which were not at all scandalous. But nothing helped.

"Chichikov's undertaking," they all began to shout, "is in itself a criminal offense." "But nevertheless, the author does not justify him," observed my censor. "Yes, he doesn't justify him! But here he shows him off now, and others will go take his example and buy dead souls." That's the kind of views! Those are the views of the censor-Asians, i.e., of old people who have curried favor and are now sitting at home. Now follow the views of the censor-Europeans, young people who have just returned from abroad. "Whatever you say, the price that Chichikov gives (said one of these censors, to be specific, Krylov), the price of two and a half rubles which he gives for a soul makes the soul indignant. Human feeling cries out against this, although, of course, this price is given for the name alone, written on paper; but, nevertheless, this name is a soul, a human soul, it lived, existed. This couldn't be allowed in France, England, or anywhere. Why after that not one foreigner would come to our country." These are the central points upon which the prohibition of the manuscript was based. I won't tell you about the other minor observations —e.g.: in one place it is said that one landowner ruined himself decorating his Moscow house in the fashionable taste. "Why isn't it so that even the Tsar is building a palace in Moscow!" said a censor (Kachenovsky). A conversation unique in the world began among the censors about this. Then there were other observations which I'm ashamed even to repeat, and finally the affair ended by the manuscript being declared forbidden, even though the committee had read only three or four passages. There's the whole story for you. It's almost unbelievable, and besides that, for me it is suspicious. One couldn't suppose such stupidity existed in man. The censors are not all stupid to such a degree. I think that someone is against me. However, this matter is too important for me. I have a hangover from their comedies and intrigues. You yourself know that my entire existence and all my means are included in my poem.[2] The affair is coming to the point of taking away from me my last piece of bread, earned by seven years of selfless labor, seclusion from the world

and all its advantages; I cannot undertake anything else for my existence. My growing propensity for illness and my ailments even deprive me of the possibility of continuing further the work which has been begun. I don't have very many bright moments, but now my hands are simply paralysed. I no longer even remember what I have written you; I think you won't be able to make out my handwriting at all. Here's what must be done. Now you must act by joining forces and get the manuscript to His Majesty. I am writing to Alexandra Osipovna Smirnova about this. I asked her to act through the grand duchesses or by other means, that's your task, you have a conference about that together. Ask A. O. to read you my letter. Prince Odoevsky has my manuscript. Read it together, three or four people, no more. This case should not attract any publicity. Only those who really love me should know. I rely firmly on your friendship and on your soul, and we must not waste words any more! I embrace you firmly, and God bless you! If the manuscript is allowed to pass and it is necessary to give it to a censor only as a formality, I think it is better to give it to Ochkin to sign it, however, do as you find best. I have no more strength to write.

## N. M. Yazykov. February 10, 1842. Gastein.

I received a letter from you, written to me on the sixteenth of December and a week before I received a pair of your poems, wonderful poems which breathed their freshness and strength on everyone; everyone was enraptured by them.[1] However, all those who love you will probably not fail to inform you. I will say only that, aside from everything else, the power of the language in them is wonderful. It fairly sweeps you along and involuntarily you say: "Our language is a giant!" In my earlier letter I wrote you little, because I didn't feel like writing. I was sick and very upset; and, I confess, I didn't have strength to talk about anything. Society torments me, and melancholy burdens me; and no matter how solitarily I live here, everything weighs upon me—the local gossip, the rumors, and the tittle-tattle. I feel that the last bonds tying me to society have been broken. I need solitude, absolute solitude. Oh, how happily we would pass the time alone together with our marvelous coffee in the mornings, parting for easy, quiet work and getting together for quiet conversation at dinner and in the evening. I was not born for troubles and agitation, and I feel with each day and hour that there is no higher destiny on earth than the calling of a monk. . . .

## M. P. Balabina. February 17, 1842. Moscow.

Pletnev reprimanded me for you—for not answering your letter. But I wrote you. True, it was a small note, not a letter; but I didn't have strength to do more then, I was sick and too upset then. But the gentleman with whom I sent it to Petersburg probably dropped it on the street, after having a hearty dinner somewhere, and didn't dare appear before you with an apology. Otherwise I can't explain why you didn't get it. I was sick, very sick, and I am still sick internally; my sickness expresses itself in strange attacks such as I have never had. But the state which reminded me of my terrible sickness in Vienna[1] seemed most terrible of all to me, especially when I felt the agitation approaching my heart which turned every image that flew into my mind into a giant; it transformed every insignificantly pleasant emotion into a terrible joy such as man's nature cannot stand, and it transmuted every gloomy thought into sadness, painful, tormenting sadness, and then fainting spells followed, and finally a complete somnabulistic state. And to complete all this, when even without it my sickness was unbearable, I had to receive more unpleasantness which could be shattering even to a healthy man. How much presence of spirit I had to gather in myself to withstand it. And I withstood it. . . . But for the meantime I am still not well; everything, even the air itself torments and suffocates me. I was so well when I was coming to Russia, I thought now I would manage to live in her a little longer, find out about the sides of her with which I had not been so closely familiar till now—but, in the words of the proverb, everything went like a crooked wheel. . . . It's time for you to be healthy, and I want to find you not at Jean-Paul Richter,[2] but at Shakespeare and Pushkin who are read only when one is in a healthy disposition—but I think you hear this tune often even without me. I will pose one question for you. Have you ever had a desire, an insuperably strong desire to read the Gospel? I don't mean the desire which resembles duty and which everyone makes oneself have, no, a sincere impulse . . . but I will leave my speech unfinished. There are feelings about which one ought not to speak, and just uttering anything about them means profaning them.

Advise your brother Viktor Petrovich not to neglect painting. He has a definite talent. Talent is God's gift, and woe to him who neglects it! . . . .


## P. A. Pletnev. March 4, 1842. Moscow.

Although your letter (of February 24) which I received today (March 4) tempts me to expect the prompt receipt of the manuscript,

I am already so worn out by unexpected delays, and besides such wonders are happening to my manuscript that I expect only that some snag will turn up again.

Just in case anything happens I am enclosing a letter to Uvarov. Pogodin, to whom I showed it, says it is convincing, accurate, and surely will have an effect. It was written before the receipt of your letter, when I was exhausted from waiting for my poor manuscript. So if the necessity arises, deliver the letter to him; if not, keep it until my arrival. . . . And give my sincere thanks to Nikitenko,[1] especially if he is so kind and intelligent as to spare my poor expressions which do absolutely no evil to anyone.


## S. S. Uvarov.[1] Between February 24 and March 4, 1842. Moscow.

Not having received the permission of the censorship for the printing of my work, I am having recourse to your patronage.

All of my livelihood and my possessions are in my work. I sacrificed everything for it, condemned myself to severe poverty, to deep isolation; I was patient, I endured, as far as I could I mastered my painful ailments in the hope that when I completed it my fatherland would not deprive me of a piece of bread and my enlightened fellow countrymen would regard me with sympathy, value the gift which, as much as his strength allows, every Russian strives to bring to his fatherland. I thought I would receive rather approval and aid from the government which until now has nobly encouraged all noble impulses—but what. . . .

For five months now I have been tortured by the strange mystifications of the censorship, now beckoning with permission, now threatening with prohibition; and finally I myself can no longer understand what is going on and how my manuscript could attract ill will, and what the accusations by force of which it is being impeded can be. And meanwhile no one wants to glance at my position; no one cares that I am at the last extremity, that the time is passing when a book has a market and sells, and that therefore I am being deprived of the means of continuing my existence which is essential for the completion of my work for which alone I live in the world. Can it be you also will not be touched by my predicament? Can it be, you also refuse me your patronage? Think: I am not assuming the audacity to ask for assistance and alms; I ask justice, I ask for what is my own; my sole, my last piece of bread is being taken away from me.

How can we tell, perhaps in spite of my difficult and thorny

path in life my poor name is fated to reach posterity. And will it be pleasant for you if a just posterity, rendering you what you deserve for your fine deeds to help science, will at the same time say that you were indifferent to creations of the Russian word and were not touched by the predicament of a poor writer burdened with illnesses, unable to find himself a corner and shelter in the world when you could have been his first intercessor and patron? No, you will not do this; you will be generous. A Russian grandee should have a Russian soul. You will give me your decisive answer to this letter which has flowed straight from the depth of my heart.

With a feeling of absolute respect and similar devotion I have the honor to be a humble servant of your excellency, esteemed Sir,

Nikolai Gogol.

## P. A. Pletnev. March 17, 1842. Moscow.

Three weeks have already passed since I received the letter in which you informed me of the final completion of the matter, and the manuscript has still not turned up.[1] Constantly for two weeks already every day I send to inquire at the post office, at the university, and everywhere that it could have been addressed—and no word anywhere. God, how all this waiting and these anxieties have tortured and exhausted me! Meanwhile, time is passing, and the more it does, the less I see possibilities to succeed with its publication. For God's sake, inform me what has happened, so that at least I know that it hasn't been lost in the mail and what I should undertake to do.

I made an effort to write an essay for *The Contemporary,* one in many respects contemporary. I tortured and tormented myself every day, and couldn't write anything except three unintelligible pages which I immediately destroyed. But however that may be, you won't say that I didn't fulfill my promise. I am sending you my story, "The Portrait." It was printed in *Arabesques,* but don't let that worry you. Read it through and you will see that only the canvas of the former story remained, and everything is embroidered on it anew.[2] In Rome I reworked it completely, or, rather, I wrote it all over again on account of observations made as long ago as Petersburg.[3] Perhaps you will even see that, more than any other, it corresponds to the modest and pure direction of your journal.[4] Yes, your journal should not be occupied by that which occupies today's hurrying, noisy society. Its aim is different. It is the aroma of the

flowers growing solitarily on Pushkin's grave.[5] The crowd of the marketplace should not know the road to it; the glorious name of the poet is sufficient for it. Only cordial friends should come together there to press each other's hand silently and devote themselves to quiet reflection, even if only once a year. You say that I could pursue the profession of journalist in a fine manner, except that I have no patience for it. No, I have no abilities for it. Just as the theoretician and the practical man cannot be combined in one person, so the abstract writer and the journalist cannot be combined. Besides, each writer is already marked by a peculiar expression of his talent, and therefore there is no way that one can deduce a general rule for them. One is given a quick mind with which, in a second, he can seize all the phenomena of the world at the minute they are manifested. Another can say his word only when he has pondered it deeply; otherwise his word will be more stupid than any ordinary word pronounced by the most common of men. At the present time I do not have the strength to occupy myself with anything else except my one constant work. It is important, and it is great, and don't you judge it by the part which is now being prepared to appear (if only there is an end to its incomprehensible wandering through censorship committees). It is nothing more than the entrance porch to that palace which is now being built within me. My work has engaged my entire being, and just tearing myself away from it for a minute is unhappiness for me. Here, during my stay in Moscow, I thought I would busy myself with something apart from this work, that I could write one or two essays—because I cannot do anything of importance here. But the opposite happened; I cannot even collect my wits.

Besides, contained in my very nature is the ability to imagine a world graphically only when I have moved far away from it. That is why I can write about Russia only in Rome. Only there does it stand before me in all its hugeness. But here I've perished and got lost among others in the ranks. There is no open horizon before me. In addition, besides the external causes which are capable of disturbing me, I feel a physical obstacle to writing here. My head suffers in every way; if it is cold in the room, the nerves in my brain ache and grow cold, and you can't imagine what torment I experience every time that I attempt to overcome myself at a time like this, to get control of myself and force my mind to work. If on the other hand the room is heated, the artificial heat absolutely suffocates me, the slightest exertion produces such a strange clotting of everything in my head that it seems as if it wants to burst. In Rome I wrote in front of an open window, fanned by the salubrious air which does wonders

for me. But you yourself can feel in your soul how much I can suffer sometimes, while my sufferings can be seen by no one else. Having long ago grown cold and dead to mundane anxieties and passions, my own internal world is my life, and in this world anxiety can inflict misfortune much worse than all mundane misfortunes. Your concern is precious to me; don't leave my letter without an answer, write me a line right away. Don't divide the story[6] into two installments; put it all in one issue and print two copies for me. Tell me what you think of it (you must be frank with me). If you find stylistic errors, correct them. Right now I don't have strength enough to read it attentively. My head is stupid; my soul is uneasy. God, did I imagine I would endure so many torments on this arrival of mine in Russia! . . .

## *P. A. Pletnev. March 27, 1842. Moscow.*

My head has absolutely been spinning. Yesterday I received a letter from Prokopovich in which he informs me that you sent my manuscript back on March 4, on Wednesday in the first week of Lent. For God's sake, inform me whom you sent it with, and if it was really taken to the post office and by whom. God, what a strange fate! Did I think I would be left without anything like this? Time has passed, and I'm without a kopek, without a chance to collect anything for the road, unable to pay the most urgent debts which it would be dishonorable not to pay. An incomprehensible confluence of misfortunes! I don't even know where to look for traces of my manuscript. Resolve this at least, so that I know for sure whether or not it has been lost.

## *N. Ya. Prokopovich. April 9, 1842. Moscow.*

The manuscript was received April 5. The delay took place at the Censorship Committee, not at the post office. The Censorship Committee lied in telling Pletnev it was forwarded on March 7, because it wasn't signed by the censor until the ninth. They threw out my whole episode about Kopeikin, which is very necessary for me, even more than they think.[1] I have decided not to give it up no matter what. Now I have redone it so that no censorship could carp. I threw out the generals and all and am sending it to Pletnev for delivery to the censor. Please go to his place and find out about this. . . .

## A. V. Nikitenko. April 10, 1842. Moscow.

I thank you for your letter. In it one can see much concern, much honesty, much of everything that beautifully and nobly excites a man. Yes, I cannot complain about the censorship; it was condescending to me, and I know how to be grateful. But, I confess, the destruction of Kopeikin disturbed me a great deal. It is one of the best parts. There is no way I can patch up the hole which is visible in my poem. You yourself, gifted with aesthetic taste which is so well reflected in your letter, you yourself can see that this piece is essential, not for the connection of events, but in order to distract the reader for a moment, to replace one impression with another; and he who is an artist in his soul will understand that without it a large hole is left. It occurred to me that perhaps the censorship was afraid of the generals. I redid Kopeikin; I threw out everything, even the minister, even the word "excellency." In the absence of everyone a temporary committee remains in Petersburg. I drew out the character of Kopeikin more sharply, so that now it is clear that he himself is the cause of his actions—and not a lack of compassion in others. The Head of the Commission even treats him very well. In a word, now everything is in a form such as no strict censorship, in my opinion, can find anything reprehensible in any respect. I entreat you to return this passage to me—and as quickly as possible in order not to delay the printing. Get the manuscript from Pletnev and return it to him afterwards for forwarding to me. I will not say anything more to you, for you yourself said in your letter that you understand me, and therefore you will also understand my gratitude.

## A. S. Danilevsky. May 9, 1842. Moscow.

. . . . I don't expect to receive an answer to this letter in Moscow, because in a week and a half I am leaving. This will be my last and perhaps my most prolonged stay away from the fatherland: my return is possible only by way of Jerusalem.[1] That is all I can tell you. . . .

Within a week after this letter you will receive the printed *Dead Souls*—the rather pale threshold of the great poem which is being *formed* within me and which will finally solve the riddle of my existence. But enough. . . .

### N. Ya. Prokopovich. May 11, 1842. Moscow.

I imagine you are surprised that *Dead Souls* has still not come out. Nikitenko delayed the whole business. What an unbearable person! For more than a month and a half he's kept the sheets of Kopeikin and hasn't even given me a single word; and meanwhile all the sheets were already set up a week ago, and the printing house is waiting, and the time is so precious to me. But forget all of them! This whole story is a testing stone with which I must test what attitude many people have toward me. I will wait two more days and if I don't get it from Nikitenko, I'll turn to the censorship here again, all the more because now it feels repentance for having treated me in such a manner. I'm not writing you about anything, because in two weeks perhaps I will visit you myself; and we will talk about everything and the matter on which, as you'll see yourself, much of your position and your activity will depend. I received a letter from *Belinsky*.[1] Thank him. I'm not writing him, because as he knows himself, it is necessary to discuss and talk about all this personally, which we will do during my present trip through Petersburg. Farewell. Be healthy, sound, and firm in spirit, and hope for the future which will be good for you if you trust in me, the friendship, and the wisdom which is not given a man in vain.

### S. P. Shevyrev. June 4, 1842. St. Petersburg.

I'm writing you a few minutes before my departure. I bustled around madly and barely managed to fix up the main things in a kind of way. Prokopovich has zealously busied himself with an edition of my works in four volumes.[1] All the volumes will come out toward October. Prokopovich is writing you a report about *Dead Souls*. From him I took myself 500 rubles of the money advanced— I needed it badly. However, it will soon be made up by a gift from the Tsar which, it is said, is due after my departure. . . .

### V. Zhukovsky. June 26, 1842. (New Style). Berlin.

. . . . I wouldn't want our meeting to be like our meeting last year when you had many cares, distractions, and at the same time a life concentrated on you yourself, and you had no time for me—and when I too, crushed by many sensations, didn't have strength enough

to fly to you with a radiant soul. Then the desert and solitude were necessary for my soul. I recall how, desiring to convey to you something of the bliss of my soul, I didn't find words in conversation with you, I uttered only incoherent noises resembling the delirium of madness and perhaps until now perplexity has remained in your soul about whom to take me for and what strange thing took place within me. But even now I won't tell you anything—and what is there to talk about? I will say only that with each day and hour it becomes more radiant and triumphant in my soul, that my journeys, eloignments, and separations from the world were not without meaning or goal, that in them the education of my soul has taken place unseen, that I became far better than the man who was imprinted in the memory (which is sacred for me) of my friends, that my spiritual tears permit solemnity more and more often, and that in my soul there lives a deep and irresistible faith that the divine power will help me ascend the ladder which stands before me, although I am standing on its lowest and first steps. There is much labor and road and spiritual education ahead yet! My soul must be purer than the celestial snows and more radiant than the heavens, and only then will I acquire the strength to begin heroic deeds and the great pursuit, only then will the riddle of my existence be solved.

That is all that I can tell you! And also I bless you with the strength of my aspirations, the strength of tears, the strength of spiritual thirst to be worthy of this. This blessing is not powerless, therefore accept it with faith. About the everyday trifles of my life I say nothing to you; there are almost none of them, and incidentally, thank God I do not even feel or perceive them. I am sending you *Dead Souls*. This is the first part. By the assurance of the local postmaster you will receive it by mail along with a letter in three days. I have changed it in many ways since the time I read you the first chapters, but nevertheless I cannot help seeing its insignificance in comparison with the other parts which will follow it. In relation to them it still seems to me like an entrance portico attached to a palace planned to be constructed on a huge scale by a provincial architect—and without doubt now quite a few of the shortcomings which I still do not see have accumulated in it. For the sake of God, inform me of your observations. Be as severe and merciless as possible. You yourself know how essential this is for me. Don't even be seduced by a felicitous expression, although at first glance it seems enough to make up for a slip. Don't read without a pencil and paper, and immediately write your observations on little scraps of paper. Next, after reading each chapter, make two or three observations in general about the entire chapter. Next, about the interrelations of all the chapters, and then after

reading the whole book, in general about the whole book. Gather together all these observations, both the general and the specific,
seal them in a package, and send it to me. In no respect is it possible
to make a better gift to me now. . . .

*Addressee unknown. About July 20, 1842. (New Style).
Gastein.*

    . . . . In gratitude you must say a few words to me about *Dead
Souls.* I don't at all demand a definition of its merit and significance, but here is what I do demand of you: You imagine that I am an
innkeeper in some European hotel and I have a table for everyone or
a *table d'hôte.* There are twenty dishes on my table and perhaps
more. Naturally, not all these dishes are identically good or, at least,
it goes without saying that everyone will choose for himself and eat
only the dishes he likes—and concerning this he can tell the host
frankly, "You have such-and-such dishes, but I like these here;
they were more to my taste," and this will not offend the host in the
least. So I am only asking you to say this: "This is what is more to my
taste in your work, these places here." This you can say! . . . . Incidentally, here is one of my important character traits for you. I have
lived through the years of youth, gotten over the attraction to love of
fame, and moved far away from society in order to educate myself
for others in the depths of my soul; and it is still a long way to the end
of my education. I have long been indifferent to what tickles with
fame, I look at myself as at an outsider, and now there is no result
more desirable or beautiful to me than to see my mistakes, shortcomings, errors. When he has seen his shortcomings and errors, a
man is already above himself. There is no evil which cannot be corrected, but it is necessary to see just what this evil consists of. I tell
you this sincerely, right from the depth, and you will understand that
this cannot be insincere. My creations differ from other works in that
everyone can be a judge of them, all the readers from one to the next
—because the subjects are taken from the life which turns around
each person. I know many opinions in advance. I know in advance
what will be said about me in print in such-and-such a journal; but the
opinions of people who are deeply practical, who know life, who
have much experience and intelligence, who have turned everything
to their use, are more valuable to me than book theories which I
know by heart. That is why I have importuned you. . . .

## S. T. Aksakov. August 18/6, 1842. Gastein.

. . . . All of your news, everything included in your letter, every-thing to the last word and line was interesting and equally pleasant for me—beginning with the way you spend your time, the fishing in ponds and streams, down to your news about *Dead Souls.* Its first im-pression on the public was precisely that which I suspected before-hand. Indeterminate comments, quick haste to read, and dissatisfied emptiness after the reading. Annoyance at the continual triviality of the events of life, triviality which involuntarily becomes a sneer and a reproach. All this I knew in advance. The poor reader avidly grabbed the book in his hands to read it like an entertaining and fascinating novel and, exhausted, he dropped his head and hands, having encountered completely unforeseen boredom. I knew all this. . . .

Your opinion that there is no one who would understand *Dead Souls* the first time through is absolutely correct and should be spread around to everyone, because much can be comprehensible to me alone. Don't even be afraid of your first impression that the exaltation in many passages seemed to you to have reached the point of ridiculous excess. It is true, because the full meaning of the lyri-cal hints can only be elucidated when the last part is published. . . .

My long and difficult journey[1] frightens you. You say you cannot understand the reasons for it. . . .

How can you not want for there to be engendered in the breast of one who has experienced the elevated moments of a heavenly life, who has experienced love, the desire to look at the land where passed the steps of Him who first said the word of this love to men, the land whence it flowed into the world? We are moved by gratitude to a poet who, with his works, has gifted us with pleasures of the soul; we hurry to bring him the tribute of respect; we hurry to visit his grave, and no one is surprised by such an act, feeling that even his great ashes are worthy of respect. A son hurries to his father's grave, and no one asks him the reason why, feeling that the gifts of life and upbringing deserve gratitude. It is only considered somehow strange to worship at the very place of the earthly wanderings of the one who brought down the paradise of bliss to earth, who is the cause of all elevated aspirations. At least if anyone from our circle undertakes such a journey we somehow goggle at him, measure him from head to foot as if asking if he's a sanctimonious hypocrite, if he is crazy. Admit it, it seemed strange to you when I announced such an intention to you the first time. My character, appearance, way of thinking, the stamp of my intellect and what I say and my life—in a word, everything that

goes to make up my character seems unfitting for such a thing. For a man who bears neither cowl nor miter, who has made and is making people laugh, who until now has considered it an important matter to display unimportant matters and the emptiness of life—for such a person, isn't it so, it is strange to undertake such a journey? But aren't there strange things in nature? Wasn't it strange for you to meet lyrical exaltation in a work like *Dead Souls?* Didn't it seem amusing to you at first, and didn't you become reconciled to it afterwards, even though you still hadn't discovered its full significance? Thus, perhaps, you will become reconciled to this lyrical tendency of the author himself later. And how can we say that what seems to us a momentary inspiration, a revelation that has unexpectedly flown from the heavens, has not been put in our very nature by the omnipotent will of God and developed in us unseen by others? And can one know that there is not perhaps a secret connection between this distant journey and this work of mine which rattled out into the world through a dark low wicket and not through victorious triumphal gates accompanied by the thunder of horns and solemn sounds? And how can we know that there is not a deep and marvelous connection between all this and all my life and the future which approaches us unseen and which none of us perceives? Reverence to Providence! All the depth of my soul says this to you. Remember that at the time when the world becomes the shallowest, when life is emptiest, and all is enveloped in cold and egotism, and no one believes in miracles—at precisely that time a miracle can happen, the most miraculous of all miracles. Just as the most violent storm begins only when the sea's surface becomes more quiet than usual. My soul senses future bliss and knows that just our aspiration to it is sufficient for it to be sent into our soul by the almighty mercy of God. And so may your thoughts be more radiant and more radiant with each day and minute, and may your adamant faith in God be most radiant of all, and may you not dare to be saddened by anything which men insanely call misfortune. That is what a man who makes people laugh says to you.

Farewell. . . .

*A. V. Nikitenko. October 30, 1842. (New Style). Rome.*

I am writing to you dear and kind Alexander Vasilevich as a result of a sincere, heartfelt impulse. You see, I call you: dear and kind Alexander Vasilevich. Yes, we must be simple. You must feel

yourself that our ties have become warmer. I will tell you frankly: in spite of all the unpleasantness the strange delay in the publication of *Dead Souls* brought me much that was excellent; among other things it gave me you. Yes, before I just considered you an intelligent man, but I didn't know that you possessed such a loving, deeply sensitive soul. This discovery was a festive occasion for my soul. There is my sincere effusion for you. Repay me with the same. Write to me, even if only occasionally, and tell me about yourself. Don't forget to transmit your impressions, opinions, and judgments of my works—as candidly as possible. And just as you have made observations about their merits before, so now tell me everything about their shortcomings. I swear this is important to me, very important, and it will be a sin for you if you are silent about anything with me. Always remember that I have one virtue which is rarely found in the world and which no one wants to recognize in me. It is an absence of author's pride and irritability. No one knows that I read even the banal articles of *The Northern Bee* with pleasure, solely because they regard me from a hostile point of view there, and they try in all ways to see my shortcomings and vices. Apropos of my works. Please tell me how the printing is going. I don't get any news. Prokopovich doesn't write to me. Four days ago I sent him the last piece, *Departure from the Theater,* which closes my collected works.[1] Ask him if he received it safely and at the right time. I am not asking for special favor for my works in relation to the censorship. I firmly hope that you will do everything without my requests.

You yourself understand that I reached every sentence by means of careful reflection, long consideration, that it is more painful for me to part with it than for another writer whom it costs nothing to replace it with another in one minute. You also perceive that I cannot have so much imprudence as not to be aware of current circumstances and not take them into consideration with respect to the censorship, and that there is and has been no dissatisfaction with me from above. It comes from below—thanks to naive ignorance which is frightened only by what is expressed vividly and sharply, even if these are things that have already appeared in print twenty times. But you are aware of all this yourself and therefore I am untroubled. Farewell! Love me as I love you and don't forget to write. Give my sincere respects to your wife, though, perhaps, she doesn't remember me at all. Stay well.

Sincerely loving you,
Your Gogol.[2]

## P. A. Pletnev. November 28, 1942. (New Style). Rome.

. . . . Rumors have reached me that whole pages of *Dead Souls* are being dragged into the theater.[1] I could hardly believe it. It doesn't happen in any enlightened state that anyone would dare drag an author's works onto the stage without asking his permission. (And, as if on purpose, I have a thousand reasons for desiring that nothing from *Dead Souls* be transferred onto the stage.) Do me a favor and try to meet Gedeonov[2] somehow and explain to him that I gave no permission to this corsair whose name I don't even know. . . .

## M. S. Shchepkin. December 3, 1842. (New Style). Rome.

. . . . It is easy for you to attract the public to old plays now; you have bait—my fragments to be specific.[1] It's ridiculous to think you could be under anyone's control. In spite of everything, the director is ruled by the public, but the actor rules the public. Remember that the public is almost like a bashful and inexperienced kitten which, no matter what kind of instructions you give it, will not start to eat the sauce until, taking it by the ears, you poke its muzzle in the sauce and the sauce is smeared on its nose and lips. Finally, it's ridiculous to think that it is impossible to make it penetrate more deeply into the art of the comic actor, such a forceful art which speaks to everyone's eyes so sharply. The duty before you is to make them come to the theater not for the author of the play and not for the play, but for the actor-author. In the letter you ask about costumes. Why my frag-ments aren't from the middle ages—dress them properly, sensibly, and so that there isn't anything like a caricature—that's all. . . .

## S. P. Shevyrev. February 28, 1843. (New Style). Rome.

. . . . Prokopovich was completely free the whole summer; he could work on the printing tirelessly and constantly.[1] Part of my intent with this work was to arouse him to activity, which has been stifled somewhat by his stale and unproductive work. I could not ex-pect profits from this edition. Although, of course a few unknown plays[2] (which I had the good sense not to print in the journals) could have added some interest to the novelty of the book, neverthe-less it is not a novelty. It consists of four volumes, therefore it was ab-solutely impossible to set a high price. With the present scarcity of

money it is not as easy to take a large sum out of the pocket as to take out five or ten rubles. But besides that I don't have the spirit and the lack of conscience to raise the price, knowing that for the most part my readers are poor people and not rich ones, and someone would perhaps spend almost his last kopek. This vile cupidity is baser and nastier in this case than in some other circumstance. So in spite of the fact that the printing cost over 16,000 and there are 126 leaves in a book, I ordered it sold absolutely no higher than twenty-five rubles. Of course, the first copies will go more smartly and perhaps compensate for the expenses of the edition, but then more slowly. I wanted half or a third of the copies earmarked for dispatch to you in Moscow; but I don't know if this is convenient for you and how to do it—let me know about it. So there are all the reasons for the arrangement which I made with respect to this business; of course it could have been arranged more intelligently, but I didn't have strength for it, didn't have strength because I cannot and should not occupy myself with a lot of things that concern what is mundane—but there will be something to say about that later. It is quite possible that Prokopovich, as one who is still inexperienced, did many things not as they should have been done; and therefore please let me know about everything. Naturally, I won't tell Prokopovich that I heard it from you, but in a roundabout way I will let him know he should be more careful and sensible. But enough about that; let us talk about the second point of your letter.

You say it's time to print a second edition of *Dead Souls,* but that it should certainly come out together with the second volume. But if so, then it is necessary to wait for an extremely long time. I must repeat again that my work is much more important and significant than can be supposed from its beginning. And if over the first part, which encompassed hardly a tenth of that which the second part should encompass, I sat for nearly five years—which, naturally, no one noticed, only you noticed the long and painstaking revision of my passages. . . . And so, if I sat over the first part so long don't think that I was ever devoted to idle inaction; during the course of that time I was working with my mind even when it was thought that I was doing absolutely nothing, and living just for my own satisfaction. . . . And so, if I sat over the first part so long, judge for yourself how long I must sit over the second. It is true that now I can work more confidently, firmly, carefully, thanks to the great deeds which I undertook for my education—and which no one noticed either. For example, no one knew why I undertook revisions of my earlier pieces,[3] while I undertook them on the basis of an understanding of my own self, on the structure of my own mind. I saw that only on this basis

could I get accustomed to producing a solid creation which would
have substance, be strong, freed from excesses and immoderation,
completely lucid and perfect in its elevated sobriety of spirit. It goes
with saying that after these and other great deeds undertaken in the
depth of my soul, I can move the work far more rapidly and successfully now than before; but one must also know that through this my
horizon necessarily became wider and more spacious, that now I
have to embrace more things which probably would not have gone
into it before. And so if one presupposes the most constant work in-
terrupted by nothing, the shortest time limit is two years. But I don't
dare even to think of this, knowing my present insecure life and the
many mundane affairs which will sometimes have the power to dis-
turb me, even though I use all my efforts to keep myself far away
from them and to think and worry about them as little as possible.
Perhaps you told me the publication of the second volume as soon
as possible is compulsory because of the notice which was placed in
*The Muscovite* at one time, so here is the real truth for you: I have
never told anyone how much and what specifically I have ready; and
not even the first part was finished when, to my very great amazement, the announcement was printed in *The Muscovite* that two volumes were already written and a third was being written and that
the whole work would be published in the course of a year. That is
how difficult it is to create the things which on the surface do not seem
difficult to others at all. If by the word *necessity* of publishing the
second volume, you have in mind the necessity of destroying the unpleasant impression, the grumbling and indignation against me, believe me, I myself would like all too much to have my real meaning
understood and not a distorted one. But it is impossible to forestall
time; first it is necessary for everything to pour out of its own accord; and hate for me (extremely painful for one who would perhaps
want to repay it with all the power of love), hate for me must exist and
continue for some time, perhaps even a long time. And even though
I feel that the publication of the second volume would be bright and
extremely profitable for me, at the same time, having penetrated
more deeply into the course of everything happening before my eyes,
I see that everything, even the hate itself, is a good thing. And a man
can never think up anything more intelligent than what is created
from above and which in our blindness we sometimes cannot see,
which, it is more accurate to say, we do not even strive to comprehend. Believe me, I am not so careless and foolish in my important
affairs as I am careless and foolish in my everyday ones. Sometimes by the power of an inner eye and ear I see and hear a time and
place when my book should be published; sometimes for the very

same reasons that the function of a man's soul is clear to me, the way the masses function becomes clear to me too. Can't you see that to this time everyone still takes my book as satire and personalities, while there is not a shadow of satire or personalities in it—which can be noted fully only after several readings; but for the most part my book was read only once by all those who rise up against me. Also look how haughtily and contemptuously they look at all my heroes; it took a long time to write my book; it is necessary for them to devote some work to looking into it for a long time. It is necessary for opinion to become settled. I cannot act against the first impression. The critics should act against the first impression; and only when, with its help, the impressions take shape, will they emerge to some extent from the initial chaos and become clear and definite—only then can I act against them. Believe me, I am using all my strength to produce my work successfully; I do not live outside of it, and I died for other pleasures long ago. But as a result of the way my mind is organized, I can work only as a result of deep cogitations and reflections, and no power can make me produce (and all the less publish) a thing the immaturity and weakness of which I already see myself; I can die of hunger, but I will not give out an imprudent and ill-considered creation. Do not censure me. There are things which cannot be explained. There is a voice which commands us, before which our poor logic is insignificant; there is much that can only be felt in the depth of the soul at a moment of tears and prayers—and not in moments of mundane calculations!

But enough. Now I approach what I have long wanted to talk about and for which I somehow didn't have sufficient strength. But, after praying, I approach it firmly now. Read this letter together—Pogodin, Sergei Timofeevich, and you. My life is more closely tied to you; you have already showed me the elevated signs of sacred friendship which is not based on earthly relationships and bonds and from which tears have streamed forth many times in the depth of my soul. Now I will demand a sacrifice from you, and you must make this sacrifice for me. Take all my everyday affairs off my shoulders for three or even four years. There are thousands of reasons, deep and inner reasons, why I cannot and should not and do not have the power to think about them. I don't have the power to explain them to you; they are in interrelationships with my inner life such that I don't have the power to bring my soul into a cold and completely tranquil state in order to explain everything in a reasonably comprehensible language. I cannot tell you anything except that this is an extremely important matter. Believe my words—and nothing else. If a man with his full logic, in his years of maturity—and not at the time

of hasty youth—a man to a certain extent alien to the immoderation
and excesses which becloud the eyes, speaks (not having the strength
to explain with an impotent word), speaks only from the depth of
his deeply moved soul—believe me, it is necessary to believe the
words of such a man. I'm not going to tell you that my gratitude to you
for this will be infinite, as the love of our savior Christ for us is infinite. First of all I must be made financially secure for three years.
Arrange as you find best with regard to the second edition and others
if they follow, but arrange it so that I receive 6,000 each year for three
years. This is the most severe estimate; I could expend even less
if I stayed in one place, but travel and changes of scenery are as essential for me as daily bread. My mind is so strangely organized
that sometimes I need to rush along for several hundred versts and
fly some distance in order to substitute one impression for another,
to make my spiritual eyes clear and have strength to embrace what
I need and transform it into one thing. I'm not saying that my eyes
see new sides of Russia from every corner of Europe and that I can
embrace its full circumference perhaps only when I have looked at
all of Europe. A trip to England will be very essential for me though
inside I am not disposed to it and though I still don't know what funds
there will be for it. You, as a person who is more prompt than others,
must take the publication and forwarding of the money on yourself.
Divide the money and forward it (to wherever I write) on two dates,
the first towards the first of October, and the other the first of April
—3,000 each time; if for some reason this is inconvenient then on
three dates at 2,000 apiece. But for God's sake keep the dates punc-
tually. Sometimes it is extremely difficult in a foreign land. Now, for
example, I arrived in Rome sure that I would find money already
here—that earmarked by me for October first—and here it's already
the sixth month that I have been living without a kopek, not receiving from anywhere. The first month Yazykov and I even lived together in poverty; but, glory to God, he was sent more than he expected, and I was able to borrow a little more than 2,000 from him.
Now it is already time for me to repay him; I'm not sent money from
anywhere, I haven't received one of those gifts that I used to get from
Petersburg before, when Zhukovsky was there. It's already been
three months since I have even had a letter or news, and I don't know
what's happening with the printing. Sometimes such circumstances
are fatal to me not because of the earthly calamity and the extreme
poverty but because of my mental state. It is fatal when it happens
at a time when I must suddenly get under way and move from my
place; and when I feel a sincere necessity for this my condition is
extremely painful and sometimes ends in a serious illness. Two times

in my life already I had to go through extreme difficulties. . . . I don't know if you will give credence to my words, but my words are the sincere truth. And because of that I lost a great deal of time—for which I don't know what I wouldn't pay; I am as economical with it as I will be economical with the kopek I am asking for myself (for a long time now my belongings have consisted of the most miniscule traveling case and four pairs of underwear). So consider this and make up your mind about it. If there is not enough money from the earnings of my works for this, think up some other means. Judge for yourself: I think I have already done enough to be given an opportunity to complete my work without being made to rush about in all directions, to stoop to shady deals in order to provide myself, by this means, with an opportunity to work at my task—when every minute is valuable to me and when I see the necessity and essentiality of completing my work as soon as possible. If no other means are found, then openly beg for me; no matter how it is given to me I will accept it with gratitude, and perhaps every kopek thrown to me will pray for the salvation of the souls of those who have thrown that kopek to me. But do not take this kopek if this kopek be thrown as a result of a person denying himself something necessary. I should not cause anyone deprivation and do not yet have the right. Concerning the other part of my affairs, about my mother and sisters, I will write to Sergei Timofeevich and Pogodin and state how best to act with regard to the estate if such a necessity arises. I did everything I could by giving them half of the estate, one hundred souls; and I gave it away while I was a beggar myself and not getting enough for my own subsistence. Finally, I dressed and paid for my sisters, and I did not do this with profits and surpluses, but borrowing and contracting debts which I have to repay. Pogodin often reproached me for doing little for my mother and family. But how and from what source I could do more— no one showed me the means for that. I even suppose that in my mother's affairs intelligent advice will be much more important and useful than other aid. The estate is a good one, 200 souls; but, of course, not being a manager mother isn't able to handle it; but for help of this nature it is necessary to resort to radical measures, and I will write to Sergei Timofeevich and Pogodin about it, relying on their fine souls and their tender sympathy. And God only grant that I be able to write; but it seems to me that if they only try to understand it deeply, they can feel my position better. God! How often I lack the words and expressions when much of what my soul would like to express and say crowds into my soul, and how terribly onerous it is for me to write a letter. . . . There are a million reasons why I cannot be bothered with everyday affairs, even those which concern

me. I must say it again: take all of this off my shoulders for three or
four years. If Pogodin and Sergei Timofeevich actually find it essential
to help my mother financially occasionally, then of course take it out
of my money made from the sales—if there is any; but it is also necessary to keep my situation very well in mind, to weigh one against the
other as good sense commands.[4] They are in their own country,
on their own estate, and, praise God, can in no event be without a
piece of bread. I am in a foreign country and ask only daily subsistence so that I won't die for some three or four years. But God inspire
and give you counsel. In all respects you will do it more intelligently
and better than I. Write me whether I can hope to get anything in a
very short time, that is if any money has piled up in the treasury for
me. I need at least 3,500; I must repay Yazykov more than 2,000,
and I need more than a 1,000 in advance for living expenses and getting out of Rome. As for my trip to Moscow you see that there will be
no necessity for that; and having looked at everything with a pene-
trating eye, you will even see that I should not do that before the completion of my work. Perhaps it is even too painful a thought for my
heart, because, to tell the truth, everything that surrounds me here
died long ago; and most often my eyes look only at Russia, and there
is no measure of my love for it, as there is no measure of my love for
you—which I cannot, which I am unable to tell. Farewell, write me
at least a line, the most insignificant line. Your letters are very important for me and they will be even more important and significant
later when I remain alone and require seclusion and sequestration
from everything for the deep education, the education of my soul
which is being accomplished within me by the holy, miraculous will
of our Heavenly Father. Farewell. . . .


## S. P. Shevyrev. March 2, 1843. (New Style). Rome.

Last week I dispatched a letter[1] to you which I imagine you
have already received; if not I would be very sorry, because it cost
me a great deal of work. Oh, how difficult it is for me to explain anything that concerns me. There are many silent questions which await
answers and which I do not have the strength to answer. How onerous
it is during inner work to satisfy passersby (even those who are close
to the soul) with answers. Imagine an architect building an edifice
which is completely blocked off and obstructed by timber—what it
costs him to remove the timber and show the unfinished work—as if
brick in the rough and the first word that came to his mind could tell

about a façade which is still in the mind of the architect. And mean-while part of the time has already been lost, and the mind of the builder is enveloped by a strange chill. I will tell you that sometimes the silent and the spoken reproaches about secretiveness were very painful to me, because it resulted entirely from my impotent power to express many things . . . but I was silent. . . .


*M. I. Gogol. Second part of March-April, 1843. Rome.*

. . . . I cannot hide from you the fact that constantly in your own letters, as well as those of my sisters, there appears the most dis-torted conception not only of things and matters far from them but even of those which are close and by which they are surrounded. Let's begin with your letters, all the more so because there are points in them on which I must give you the most satisfactory explanation and about which I have wanted to speak seriously with you for a long time now. Here, incidentally, I am copying out the words just as they are in your letter: "I implore you, priceless son, take care of yourself, don't take risks in dangerous places" (i.e., in my journey to Jeru-salem). "Remember how many responsibilities lie upon you." To this remark I will again answer what I have already said to you many times in similar cases: it is time for you to learn at least a little about my character; if this is difficult for you, then at least simply get used to the thought that your son is not a twenty-year old hussar lieutenant and that there is some intelligence and common sense in his head, and, most of all, have more faith in God than in all the empty perplexities which come only at idle moments. If God wishes—I am dead this very hour in my own room without setting out on any dan-gerous road, if God wishes—and I am unharmed amid all the terrors in comparison with which the trip which seems so dangerous to you is nothing. And so let us stop talking about that once and for all. Now I turn to my sisters. One imagined that she can have no responsibility, no tasks, that she was born just so as not to do anything, that she is use-less and incapable of anything (as if anything created by God is use-less), and that her entire duty consists only in not doing anything evil. The other has devoted herself to daydreams and looks con-temptuously at reality and what surrounds her, senselessly thinking that she can only be happy somewhere else, not worrying about the acquisition of the tender nicety of manners without which one cannot be happy anywhere, all the less be liked by other people. The third imagined that she was stupid and capable only of things of little im-

portance, that she didn't know anything—when she might perhaps accomplish a great deed which would please God and save her family. Thus, they are all occupied with their responsibilities and think that he who lives beyond the seas should take care of them. But when a misfortune comes they all know how to be sad, all are masters at complaining about fate; have they ever devoted themselves to intelligent reasoning about the affairs which are close to them, about the ones by which they are surrounded? Has even one of them glanced at the state of these affairs? Why for the course of some fifteen years has agriculture on the estate gotten no better, but continually worse?—that it is impossible for failures and misfortunes to follow one after the other for fifteen years in a row, that man is given a mind in order to foresee, to stave off and repulse misfortunes, that failures and misfortunes are really teachers and are sent in order to guide one to intelligence and the real road? Has even one of them asked, even once in her life, has she asked God to make her understand how to comprehend the meaning and significance of the misfortune which has been sent, to see its good and constructive side? No, no one cares about that, but at the same minute and as fast as possible they even try to forget this misfortune; they don't even want to recall it and no one wants to look into it intently—why did it happen, were we ourselves to blame for it, wasn't it possible to foresee it somehow and fend it off ahead of time, and for what purpose did it happen, what does God want from us through this misfortune? No, they think it happened just so, without sense, that God does it foolishly. "God wants it that way" they usually say. "To test us" others add—and they don't even want to figure out for what kind of test, what does this test consist of. Know now that there are no misfortunes in the world, that our deep good fortunes are enclosed in these misfortunes. Every time, after every event that has happened to me and which other people call a misfortune, the eyes of my reason became clearer, and in sincere spiritual emotion I saw that they are really our wings and bring us closer to the goal from which it would apparently seem they were repelling us. They are really God's words to us and are all full of infinite wisdom. But people do not think, they do not wish to penetrate into their significance, they don't wish to recognize that God demands activity of our minds, and that misfortunes and difficulties are sent in order to awaken us, that through them He calls on us every minute to rouse ourselves from the laziness which embraces our souls, that every minute He says through them that we are not useless and were not created in the world in vain, that we should judge and weigh ourselves severely and learn what truly useful side we have, whether our eyes don't deceive us, as if

we really had no ability which we could use for Good. There is not a useless man in the world, and woe to him who does not discover what he is useful for and who doesn't pray God to open and make clear his eyes to see his usefulness. He who received talent from God and buried it in the ground was terribly punished, and there is no man who has not received some talent. Some men are given five, some two, some one, some little, some much—but each is given something as his share—and there will be equal retribution for all. Have they even once turned attention to the meaning of man's life? Man has been called into the world, therefore he is necessary to the world. Man has been put in this place and not another, therefore he is necessary in this place and not another. If he were not needed for anything, he would not stand on earth, but somewhere in the air where not one object around him would remind him that he should busy himself with it. . . . Has even one of them looked at how life in general goes on in the world? The peasant earns the means of life by toil and sweat; but we eat and wait for guests and figure out where we could go, where we could amuse ourselves better, and just how to amuse ourselves a little, and we read a pleasant book for a bit, and we yawn and complain of boredom when we ought to be amazed that this boredom doesn't suffocate us and make us sick to death. Is there even a shadow of fulfillment of duty in all that we do? If those under our power are created to work for us and carry out our commands, aren't we created to turn his work into good and know how to give him commands, to question our intellect constantly how to better the work of his hands and increase tenfold the fruits of the work of his hands? Didn't we receive a better education than he in order to be his guide and lead him to what is better? Or do they think only half of humanity was created for serious work and the other just for a joke, for the pleasant passing of time. Have they even once been astonished by the incomprehensible oddities that, for example, they, while living in the country, have the same comprehension about what is going on in the management of their estate as I have about what is going on in the Chinese state which is 15,000 versts away from me? Has their thought dwelt on the strange current condition of us all, how through our empty education we have gone away from, moved distant from the life amid which we live, and how finally we have gotten to the point that now it is difficult and even impossible to take up any task and overcome our incomprehensible laziness? . . . .

## N. Ya. Prokopovich. May 28, 1843. Munich.

Your letter surprised me even more than mine probably surprised you. From where, who is spreading all kinds of rumors about me? Did I ever tell you that I would be in Petersburg this summer? Or that I'm going to print the second volume this year? And what is the meaning of your words: "I don't want to offend you to such an extent with the suspicion that you haven't prepared the second volume of *Dead Souls* for print." As if *Dead Souls* were a pancake you could cook up all of a sudden. Look at the life story of any moderately illustrious author, or even of one who is just noteworthy. What did a large, well-planned work into which he had put his entire being cost him, and how much time did it take? His whole life—no more, no less. Where have you seen a person who has produced one epic who then produced five or six more? Shame on you for being such a child and not knowing this! Least of all can one who knows me a little demand speed from me. In the first place because I am more patient, inclined to rigorous preparatory cogitation, and besides, to a great degree I still bear all kinds of insanities from all kinds of painful attacks. The second volume of *Dead Souls* is not only prepared for print —it isn't even written. And it cannot appear in less than two years (and then only if my powers are constantly fresh during that time). And that the public wishes and demands the second volume is no reason. The public can be intelligent and just when it already has in its hands something which it is necessary to judge and on which they can show off their intelligence. There is always idiocy in the desires of the public, because it is guided only by the fleeting demand of the moment. And why should it know what is going to be in the second volume? Perhaps it is even something which it shouldn't know or read at the present time, and neither the public nor I are prepared for the second volume. You ought also to consider the fact that my works should not play the role of journal articles, it isn't necessary to hurry with them as soon as you notice the public has an appetite for them. They have been written over a long period of time; years have been spent on the careful planning of many of them, and wouldn't it therefore be suitable for my readers also to think about them at leisure and look into them more closely? An intelligent reason: because in the course of one year I suddenly published very much, therefore give just as much more. How am I guilty if the public has a stupid head and in its eyes I am the same thing as Paul de Kock.[1] Paul de Kock writes a novel per year, so why shouldn't I also write one: why that, they say, is a novel too and it's only called a poem as a joke. . . .

## N. M. Yazykov. June 10, 1843. Wiesbaden.

I'm writing you from Wiesbaden. In Frankfurt I met Zhukovsky who had been refreshed—in a word he is in the best of health. His wife is better, too. He has with him two books of the *Odyssey*[1] which, although I have not yet seen them, judging from everything, should be very good, because he says himself that he tried to simplify the hexameter still more so that even a child could read Homer. And he has two more tales in pentameter without rhyme.[2] And he has plans for still another long work.[3] In a word, Zhukovsky conducts himself as God grant all of us who are much younger than he should. . . .

I have been sent several criticisms of *Dead Souls* torn out of journals.[4] However, there is little that is noteworthy in them; mostly with regard to all kinds of. . . . The best criticisms are, for the most part, from the provinces. One from Ekaterinoslav[5] is more noteworthy than the others, but I cannot send it in a letter because of the size; and instead I am sending you the pages on cabbagestumps which immediately follow the analysis of *Dead Souls*. Though it's an unimportant subject, still and nevertheless it does show the contemporary trend of Russian literature. Farewell. . . .

## S. P. Shevryrev. September 1, 1843. (New Style). Dusseldorf.

. . . . I received various critiques of *Dead Souls* from the Petersburg journals. The most notable is in *The Contemporary*. Polevoi's review is partly notable in its own way. Unfortunately I don't have Senkovsky's, and I still haven't been able to get it no matter how I have tried. But in general I find that there is no middle ground between good-will and ill-will. Belinsky is ridiculous. His observation on "Rome" was the best of all. He wants a Roman prince to have the same view of Paris and the French that Belinsky has.[1] I would have been guilty even if I had inspired the Roman prince with the same kind of view that I have of Paris. Because in general even I cannot be of the same opinion as my hero, although occasionally our aesthetic sensibilities can overlap. I belong to a living and contemporary nation, but he to one which has been outlived. The idea of the novel was not bad at all. It consisted in showing the significance of a nation which has had its day and had it beautifully—in comparison to nations which are still alive. Although of course it is impossible to conclude anything from the beginning, nevertheless one can see that the point is what kind of impression the growing whirlwind of a new society produces on one for whom contemporaneity hardly exists any longer. . . .

*S. P. Shevyrev. September 20, 1843. (New Style). Dusseldorf.*

. . . . Of course it would have been better if all my business had been in Moscow and all of the obstacles about which I wrote could have been overcome, but I imagine that you noticed that in the same letter in which I enumerated the reasons which forced me to print my works in Petersburg there was something left as if unsaid. What is to be done, obviously it is preordained for me to be secretive. But nevertheless here is my word, everything to the last emotion will be apparent. There is much that I cannot say not because I don't want to say it, but I cannot say it because I still haven't found the words to say it. Sometimes a man is not understood by others not because they can't understand him, but because he is still stupid, uneducated, and isn't able to express himself so that they can understand him. It is better to keep silent about what you aren't able to explain. Well, what if I said, for example, that one of you,[1] innocently, was the reason that I firmly decided to publish my works in Petersburg. I can imagine what questions you and others would heap upon me, and I wouldn't answer them precisely because afterwards you yourselves would praise me for keeping silent. But let's leave all that, those are not important matters and they do not lead to the point. Thanks very much for your letter; although it talks only about business there are a few lines in it which are precious to me—ones which show your emotional state, the sadness of a man who has looked at the current condition of journal literature. Here is what I will tell you about this: the feeling is unpleasant and I am fully acquainted with it. But it appears when one pays more attention to that circle than one should. Then this evil seems huge, as if it embraced the whole sphere of literature. But as soon as you get yourself out of this circle even for a moment, and when you go into yourself, you will see that it is such an insignificant little corner that one shouldn't even think about it. Up close, when you are with them, there's little that one doesn't imagine. It even seems that this influence is terrible for the future, for youth, for education; but when you look from a place which is a little higher you will see that all of this is here for the moment, everything is under the influence of fashion. You look away—in place of one thing there is already another: today the Hegelists, tomorrow the Schellingists, then again some other "ists." What is to be done? Such is the aspiration of society—to be some "ists." Humanity rushes headlong, no one stands in place; let it run, it's necessary. But woe to those who have been placed to stand motionlessly at the fires of truth if they are carried away by the general motion, even if it be to make those who are rushing comprehend. This ring of dancers circles, circles, and finally

can suddenly turn to the place where the fires of truth are. What if they do not find the guards in their places and if they see that the sacred fires are not flaming with a full light? Many people whom God has given gifts which are not common to all should busy themselves with an affirmation of what is eternal, and not with a refutation of what is momentary. A man born with greater powers should educate himself deeply before battling with the world. If he reacts sharply to everything that is contemporary he will lose the state of mental tranquility without which our education is impossible. From everything it is clear that fashion will not long be maintained and that finally it will be dealt a strong blow, as before much that the world considered God and not subject to destruction has been dealt mortal blows. Thus, it seems to me that, in the sensible person, contemporary journal literature should produce indifference rather than any sincere disappointment. . . .

## N. M. Yazykov. November 4, 1843. (New Style). Dusseldorf.

. . . . I will tell you about one other spiritual discovery which is more and more confirmed the more you live in the world, though at first it was simply a presupposition, or, more accurately, prescience. It is that there is an endless multitude of powers in the soul of a poet. If a simple person struggles with unheard-of misfortunes and overcomes them, the poet must certainly overcome greater and stronger ones. Deeply studying the essence of those weapons with which simple people have overcome misfortunes we see with trembling that God has inserted a whole arsenal of such weapons in the soul of the poet. But the poet doesn't know of the greater part of them and doesn't try to discover them. No one knows powers which are scattered about—no one sees them or can ever say for sure what quantity of them there is. You find out about them only when they are gathered together. And only prayer can gather one's powers.

As a consequence of this I shift from this point directly to your illness. It seems to me that little by little it's necessary to toss all the liniments and ointments out the window. They have stimulated your body enough, it is even time to give it needed rest; and you should give work to your spirit instead. One must look on an illness as on a battle. It seems to me one should battle it in the same manner in which sainted hermits speak of battle against the devil. It is impossible, they say, to battle the devil with equal powers; one must go out to such a battle with greater powers, otherwise there will be an eternal

battle. You won't conquer him yourself, but when you have lifted yourself to God with prayer you will immediately turn him to retreat. The same must be applied to an illness. . . .


### S. T. Aksakov, M. P. Pogodin, S. P. Shevyrev. January 1844. Nice.

I wish you a Happy New Year, my friends, and with all my heart I wish you spiritual peace, i.e., the best we should wish each other. I feel that often you are not calm in spirit. There is a kind of ubiquitous emotional melancholy of the nerves; later it should become still more intense. In such cases mutual fraternal help is necessary. I am sending you advice; don't scorn it. It has come straight from spiritual experience; it is well tried and accompanied by great concern for you. Devote one hour of your day to concern about yourself; live this hour in an inner life concentrated within yourself. A spiritual book can place you in this condition. I am sending you *The Imitation of Christ,* not because there is nothing higher or better than it, but because for the use to which I am assigning it for you I don't know another book which would be better than it. Read one chapter each day, no more; and if the chapter is too long, divide it into two halves. In the course of reading devote yourself to meditation about what you have read. Consider what you have read from all sides in order finally to achieve an understanding of precisely how it can be applied to you, to that specific circle in which you move, in those specific circumstances in which you find yourself. Keep away from the thought that much which is here relates to monastic or some other life. If it seems thus to you, it means that you are still far from the real meaning and see nothing but the letters. Strive to perceive how all this can be applied specifically to life amid the noise of society and all its agitations. For this spiritual exercise choose a free and untroubled hour which would serve as the beginning of your day. Best of all is immediately after tea or coffee so that your very appetite doesn't distract you. Do not change this hour and do not surrender it for anything else. Even if you don't immediately see use in this, even if the remaining part of your day does not become better and more peaceful, do not stop, but go on. Everything can be acquired and achieved if only we ceaselessly and with increasing strength send from our breast our constant aspiration for it. May God help you![1] Farewell.

# S. P. Shevyrev. February 2, 1844. (New Style). Nice.

. . . . You say only that you do not know how to withdraw into yourself, what powers to use to force and coerce yourself. To this I can say only that it is extremely, extremely difficult. As a person who has spent many years of his life in a battle with himself and who has gained this right through hardships I have a right to say this. As a re-ward for persistence I discovered the following truth: *we can with-draw into ourselves amid all obstacles and alarms.* I have learned this truth, but I myself have not found the means to abide in it con-stantly. I can bring myself to such a condition only at times and for unprotracted moments. But this too is a very important discovery; a step has been made, and we must strive eternally. In any case everything we happen to discover we must share fraternally among ourselves. It seems to me, judging from the letters, yours as well as others that all of you (i.e., Aksakov, Pogodin, and you) often undergo emotional worries and troubles. They can stem from various causes, but they can all be reduced to a common denominator. I am sending you one remedy which I have already tried, which will surely help you to withdraw into yourselves more often and at the same time to resist all emotional worries. With this letter I am enclosing a letter to you all. You read it right now (alone first) and immediately buy four miniature copies of *The Imitation of Christ* in the French shop—for you, Pogodin, S. T. Aksakov, and Yazykov. Don't give the books without the letter, or the letter without the books, because the pre-scription for using the remedy itself is included in the letter; and be-sides I want this to be as if in the form of a New Year's gift to you com-ing from my own hands. I haven't the money to send you the books from here; at the end of the letter you will see laconic little inscrip-tions—cut them out with scissors and paste one in each copy. This gift is accompanied by a strong, sincere desire to offer you brotherly help, and therefore God will surely direct it to your good.

You both did right in not giving my letter to Pogodin. His pres-ent agitation and emotional worrying worries me. Apparently, it comes from the multitude of cares amid which he does not know how to moderate himself. Aren't there any ways to drag Khomyakov[1] into literary activity and make him work, at least polemically, in *The Muscovite?* It is surprising that *The Muscovite* has not intro-duced a single new talent to a career, hasn't aroused any of the lazy ones to activity, and relies solely on those who would be active even without it. There is something in Pogodin which makes young people feel dejected. He simply doesn't know how to stimulate and encour-age, and that is essential for young people. Encouragement is quite

an important thing for a Russian man. One can scold and swear and
nevertheless the young people will love you if the swearing and scold-
ing is based to some extent on a knowledge of their nature. But to demand that every person be exactly like a Pogodin and no one else—
there is absolutely nothing to be done in that case, and even all of the
fine rules and good intentions will be thrown to the wind. He doesn't
know the different aptitudes of the participants either, i.e., that one
is created for daily work, another to give one article in a month or
two, a third even more rarely than that. Without any compassion he
is ready to set one who is created for bigger work at small work, and
in the event of a refusal he will reproach him with egoism, saying
that his friends don't realize how he is working himself to exhaustion
and not one wants to help him. In a word, he will find occasion to
create disappointments for himself. But at the same time it is nevertheless necessary to urge Moscow to help *The Muscovite* to some
extent. It is absolutely not moving a bit in a bookish literary way. It
would be more appropriate to call *The Muscovite* a provincial, because for the most part its articles are sent from the provinces, from
inside Russia.

As for the second edition of *Dead Souls,* it seems to me this
matter can be postponed. I do not foresee a large sale. Meanwhile,
money can be gotten from Yazykov, which I imagine you have already done, and later . . . the morning is wiser than the evening. Now
I worry less than ever before about what will happen with respect
to money. At the end of last year I received 1,000 francs from the
Empress. I lived until February on this thousand, thanks among
other things to my good friends whom I found in Nice, with whom I
almost always dined and thus managed a certain savings of money.
Most of all I was tormented by my state of illness, which came at an
extremely bad time and cast my spirit into an insensate and inactive state in spite of all my efforts to move it. Now I'm much better.
. . .

*S. M. Sollogub. April 12, 1844. (N. S.). Frankfurt.*

Christ is risen!

Countess, you probably didn't expect a letter from me, but the
conversation I had with you before my departure from Nice remained in my thoughts and produced an incomprehensible distur-
bance in them. You told me about two dreams you had in which you
prayed in a way unlike that you pray in when awake, and in which

your soul experienced bliss such as it has never experienced before. I told you everything I thought about that at the time. I am not in the slightest a mystic; I have even been considered rather a staid and cold person than a passionate one who gets carried away. I did not believe and I do not believe in dreams just as I disbelieve all kinds of premonitions and omens; but I know for sure that dreams which have acted not on the imagination or the intellect but directly on the soul are holy dreams and direct from God. Such dreams played an extremely important role in the lives of the saints, served them as great guides, often a turning point in a whole life; and in general the fate of their entire life was connected to them. The other day I heard such a deep, sincere story about a person close to me who has suffered sincere grief and the strongest bodily ailments for several years, that I immediately grabbed up my pen to tell you that your dreams are beautiful. They are signs of God's mercy. Bring your soul to a state where you can pray in reality as you prayed in the dream, and your soul will surely tell you better than any wise men what these dreams mean and what God wants of you by them. . . .

## S. T. Aksakov. May 16, 1844. (N. S.). Frankfurt.

I received your dear and frank letter.[1] Having read it I mentally embraced and kissed you and then laughed. It is perceptible in your letter that you fear I might jump onto your back and you are standing like Fyodor Nikolaevich Glinka[2] when someone approaches to embrace him. All this agitation and mental battle of yours is nothing more than the business of our mutual friend who is known to all, to be precise—the devil. But don't you lose sight of the fact that he is a blusterer and consists entirely of hot air. What caused you to imagine that you have to wake up or lead a different life? Your life, praise God, is as irreproachable, fine and noble, as God grant to all. You have done much good and many services (partly known to me) which are worth many kopeks cast around to beggars, and they will be evaluated justly; your life is not contrary to Christian life in any respect. One reproach should be made to you—for an excess of passionate enthusiasm for everything—as in friendly attachment and your relations with people, so also in everything fine and noble that emanates from you. And so look firmly ahead, and don't be disturbed if there are empty and inactive years in your life. We need repose. There are such years in the lives of all people, even if they are the saints themselves. And if you discover any nasty things in yourself, you ought not to be disturbed by this, but rather to thank

God that we do have them in us. If these nasty things were not in us, God knows how we would puff up, and our pride would make us do a multitude of nasty things incomparably more significant. Without them you would not have this fine humility which is the first beauty of the soul.

And so your agitation is simply the doing of the devil. You pound the beast on the snout and don't be disturbed by anything. He is just like a petty civil servant who gets himself in town as if for an investigation. He scatters dust in everyone's eyes, scolds and screeches. All it takes is to be a little timid, to step back—and right on the spot he starts braving it. But as soon as you attack him he sticks his tail between his legs. We ourselves make a giant out of him, but in fact he is *the devil knows what.* A proverb does not err, and the proverb says: "The devil bragged he would possess the whole world, but God didn't even give him power over a pig." His tactics are well known: having seen he can't incline one to some vile deed, he'll run away full tilt and then approach from another side, in another guise, to see if he can't make one dejected somehow; he whispers: "Look how many vile things there are in you—wake up!" when there is no reason to wake up because you aren't asleep, but, simply, you don't see him. In a word, it is his business to frighten, to deceive, to make one dejected. He knows very well that God doesn't like a person who gets frightened and dejected—in a word, who doesn't believe in His heavenly love and mercy—that is all there is to it. Without looking at him you should simply carry out the prescription to the letter, guiding yourself just by the fact one doesn't look a gift horse in the mouth. Perhaps then you would find there only a confirmation of what you believe and what is in you, and everything would be fixed more clearly and affirmatively in its place, establishing by this means strict order in your soul.

About myself I will tell you that in general my nature is not at all mystical. Misunderstandings have come about because it occurred to me too early to speak of that which was extremely clear to me but which I could not express in my stupid and vague speeches —which I strongly repent, even where I did it in print. But inside I have never changed in my main positions. From perhaps the time I was twelve years of age I have been going along the same road I am on today, without ever hesitating or vacillating in my main beliefs; I haven't changed back and forth from one position to another, and if I ever encountered anything doubtful on the road, I did not stop and wrack my brains, but giving it up as a bad job I said: "It will explain itself later." I went further along my road; and to be sure God helped me and afterwards everything explained itself. And now

I can say that in my essence I am still the same person, though perhaps I have been relieved of much that hindered me on my road and, therefore, through that, I have become somewhat more intelligent, I see many things more clearly, and I call them bluntly by their own names—that is, I bluntly call the devil the devil, and I don't give him any fine costume à la Byron and I know that he wears a frock-coat made of [. . . .] and that his pride ought to be [. . . .] upon—that's all there is to it!

Ask Yazykov whether he sent me the books and with whom specifically. I still haven't received any though he promised me the following: (1) *The Loving of Good*, (2) Chronicles, (3) Innokenty, (4) the works of the holy fathers. Doubtlessly, they can be sent conveniently now because in the spring many people move out of Moscow for abroad. And I'll ask you if you can't send the complete *Muscovite* for 1843, then at least send Shevyrev's critical articles; but tell Mikhail Semenovich that he's a *swindler*, and tell his dear children that *the apple doesn't fall far from the apple tree*. He himself volunteered to get me Senkovsky's criticisms and the innocent remarks published in *The Son of the Fatherland*.[3] There has been sufficient time, and there needn't have been occasion for a foul-up in the sending, because by writing it on thin paper it could easily have been sent at any time divided into two or three letters—as I do with my essays which are considerably larger, and which helped him for his benefit night. He put me in the unpleasant and embarrassing position of writing to Senkovsky and requesting him to send the essays, because in many things it is entirely impossible to rely on those who are intimates and it is better to write to a person whom you know least of all. Sometimes a person you don't know is ashamed to show himself to be an unreliable person the first time, but friends are never ashamed to put off a matter.

Please deliver the enclosed letter to Nadezhda Nikolaevna.[4] It contains an explanation of a rumor which has been spread about in Moscow. I would make no explanation about this subject to anyone because I am lazy about such things, but since she asked me a question bluntly and guilelessly, it seemed to me shameful not to give her an answer. But I oughtn't to waste words with you about this. You are a *man-nebaba*.[5] A *man-nebaba* believes a *man* himself more than a *rumor about a man*; but a *man-baba* believes a rumor about a man more than the man himself. However, don't get proud of the fact you are a *man-nebaba*. This is no accomplishment of yours; it is less valuable than something acquired—it is God's will that you be a *man-nebaba*. Don't belittle the *man-baba* either, because except for this trait the *man-baba* may be the most perfect

man and have many traits that the *man-nebaba* will not succeed in acquiring. Our friend Pogodin is a *man-baba*, not because he hasn't led the kind of life he should or hasn't had firmness of character, but because sometimes he suddenly smells of the *baba's* skirt. This can even be brought to his attention because from now on everything between us should be simple and frank. Mikhail Semenovich,[6] for example, but he's not at all a *man-baba* . . . he's not a *baba*, but he turned out to be a *man*—[. . . .] about the matter mentioned below. Konstantin Sergeevich,[7] for example . . . but these men shouldn't be talked about; they are completely *in the hand of the future*. At least it is a good thing in the Russian's nature that if, for example, a German is a *man-baba* he remains a *man-baba* for all ages. But sometimes a Russian man can suddenly change into a *man-nebaba*. He emerges from *baba*-hood when he says solemnly in front of everyone that he is nothing more than a *man-baba*, and only by this does he enter knighthood, cast off the *baba's* skirt in view of every one and dress himself in pants.


*A. V., E. V., and O. V. Gogol.*[1] *January-May, 1844.*

. . . . For the course of a whole year you must answer only the questions I am going to be asking you in my letters. You can talk to your girl friends about trifles and other things, they are none of my concern: serious times have begun and therefore write only about what is important. This will not be difficult, because I myself will put the ladder up for you and teach you how to do it. I will demand no more than an hour a day from you for such a task. You can sacrifice this time, it doesn't seem like much. First of all I must find out what the peasants are like. Everything is based on the morality of the peasants; a good man is always a good master. Therefore, first of all begin by examining the huts yourselves. Divide the village into three parts and each of you take one as her share. And begin in order, a hut per day is sufficient. Examine how everything goes among them. Question each of them first about the person himself, then about the neighbors who are around him and what kind of people they are. Question the husband about the wife; question the wife about the husband. Question them both about their children. Then question the neighbors about this same family. Only in this way will you learn what a person is, and without it you won't learn. You must do this for me, and if you are intelligent you will know how to do something for yourselves as well, i.e., for your own souls by having done much good, just in passing, in various places, i.e., by reproaching one person if

he is acting badly and encouraging another if he conducts himself and his household well. You can take a piece of white bread or pie for those of their children who behave themselves best. But for those who are worst of all, you can tell the priest to rebuke them with a corrective word. And tell them all that the time is drawing near when all will have to live by the truth and pray more. Toward evening of the same day, so as not to forget later, write me about all of this in a letter—and every day in this way. And when the letter has accumulated and gets long, dispatch it to me immediately. And each of you act in this manner.

Observe the following order in this note-taking:

Day, month, and date. Hut such-and-such. . . . Head of house so-and-so—his name, age, what his appearance is like, what he is like in conversation and talking. What are the good qualities in him, what are the bad qualities in him? What is he like in the field and at work, and over and above the usual jobs, what special craft has he that other people do not know? Then—(1) in your own view what kind of person did he seem to you in general, (2) what does the steward say about him, (3) what do his neighbors say about him?

What is his wife like, what are her qualities? And what are her occupations? And does she control her husband or her husband her? What does her husband say about her, what do the neighbors say about her, what does the steward say about her? Sometimes it's not a bad idea to question the priest too what he thinks about some of them (if the priest is sensible).

How many children do they have, what ages, what qualities, how are their mother and father satisfied with them, and, finally, what order is there in the family, the hut, and their household affairs?

You must without fail have all these questions before you when you write to me and even more when you are doing the questioning and finding out. Don't leave any of them out. And God keep you from lying anything on your own. This is a sacred matter and what for now seems a trifle in your own eyes is very important for me. You must write not so that it can be seen in general, i.e., in a general sense, that so-and-so is good and so-and-so is bad.—But so that I can see precisely how one is good and precisely how the other is bad. In one word—so that I can see how each differs from the other. So that I can see, so to speak, his personality, portrait, in precisely what attributes and peculiarities one good man is distinguished from another good man, and one bad man is distinguished from another bad man.

Append to this every good deed that you happen to do for any of them. Describe it in the letter too. When you complete this task I

will give you another concerning other factors. And I will make my arrangements and give advice only when, in this manner, I find out absolutely everything, i.e., all sides of these matters; and you will see that from here, from far away, I will manage better than you, although you are standing with your face and even nose to things.[2] And if God helps, perhaps I will succeed in correcting the whole thing. . . .

### M. I. Gogol. June 12, 1844. (N.S.). Frankfurt am Main.

. . . . I also have a request of you, mama: never praise me in the presence of anyone. Also, you have my portrait. Hide it in a back room, sew it up in a canvas and don't show it to anyone.[1] Say that you sent it to Moscow at my request, in a word—that you don't have it. Do not allow anyone to make a copy from it, not even my sisters. That is my desire. . . .

### N. M. Yazykov. July 14, 1844. (N.S.). Frankfurt.

. . . . You ask whether *Dead Souls* is being written. It is being written and it isn't being written. It is being written too slowly and not at all as I would like, and the obstacles to this often stem from sickness, and even more often from me myself. At every step and every line I sense such a demand to become more intelligent, and besides the subject and task itself are so tied to my own inner education, that I simply don't have the power to write ahead of myself, and I must wait for myself. I go forward—and the work goes too, I stop— and the work doesn't go either. Therefore I often have need of changes in all circumstances—moves, turning to different occupations (those which don't at all resemble every-day ones), and the reading of books by which a person is educated. But . . . I fear to expatiate, lest I pile up some confusion. . . .

### A. S. Danilevsky. August 15, 1844. (N.S.). Ostend.

. . . . I am in Ostend for baths in the sea; the doctors sent me here because of violent nervous attacks which became unbearable, which troubled and tormented me to the point of exhaustion. After

the few baths I have already taken I cannot yet say anything positive; it seems as if I am a little better. Success is usually felt only after finishing.

I cannot say anything positive to your question of precisely when I am going to Russia. God alone knows this. If it pleases Him to give me health and the powers to consummate and complete my work, I will go as quickly as possible, because Russia and everything Russian has become dearer to me than ever before; but I cannot go with empty hands, my native land would not be my native land, and the joyful meeting with all my friends not a joyful meeting, but meanwhile write me a little more often and don't forget me. . . .

## N. M. Yazykov. October 26, 1844. (N.S.). Frankfurt.

. . . . For all its brevity, your report about the state of current literature is as accurate as, unfortunately, it is unconsoling; but in the first place it was always like that, and in the second, who is to blame? It has long been known to all that Petersburg writers are [. . . .] and Moscow ones are [. . . .]. As it seems to me your opinion of the new journal which is to be published in Moscow is rather well-founded, even though the journal itself doesn't exist yet. I also think that it will be something like Notes of the Fatherland. Not long ago I finally got to read one of your epistles, namely the epistle to Vyazemsky printed in The Contemporary.[1] In it I noted a special sobriety in the style and a rather manly disposition, but the same thing is still repeated in it, i.e., that it is timely and necessary to get down to the real task, but the real task itself still doesn't exist. However that may be, your soul has already tasted a different life; different things have happened within it. If you haven't drunk of it, at least you have already touched your lips to the higher spiritual spring—to which many, many, and all too many should have touched long ago. Why do you still display only your external state in your poetry, and not the internal—isn't poetry worthy of reflecting it, or are there too few subjects there? But the head will start to spin if we begin making a list of what still hasn't been touched by anyone.

Be careful that we ourselves are not subject to the reproaches with which we love to reproach current literature. Who knows, perhaps on us lies the sin that such a quantity of [. . . .] and [. . . .] has been bred in its midst. Incidentally, what a fellow Pogodin is, and what a trick he has played on me again![2] I boiled with indignation at Betzky for placing my portrait, and how could such a thing happen

—suddenly Betzky himself appears from Kharkov to Frankfurt to receive a personal bawling out from me. I learn from him that way last year it was Pogodin's pleasure to attach my portrait to *The Muscovite,* on his own authority, without any reservations, exactly as if it were his own—when I had already had extremely serious melees with him because of similar incidents. And meanwhile he stayed quiet as if nothing had happened (and none of my friends informed me of this!). I'm not mad now only because I have become disaccustomed to that, but I will tell you frankly that it would have been impossible to think up a worse insult to me. If Bulgarin, Senkovsky, and Polevoi combined had written the most malicious criticism of me, if Pogodin himself had joined up with them and written together with them everything conducive to my humiliation it would have been nothing in comparison with this. I have my own reasons for this, extremely legitimate ones of which I informed these gentlemen many times, which, however, I did not wish to explain to them, having legitimate reasons for that too. I don't think there has been such a degree of absence of sensitivity, of any decorum, and such a degree of lack of delicacy in any one man since the beginning of time. If in your youth you have written some trash which you didn't even think of printing, he no sooner sees it somewhere than he snaps it into his journal without a beginning, without an ending, for no reason at all, without asking, without permission. Like a pig that won't let a decent person [. . . .], as soon as it sees that he has squatted behind some fence, it jabs its snout under his very [. . . .] in order to snatch the first [. . . .]. You fling a stone at its oinker as hard as you can—that's nothing to it. It sneezes a bit and again jabs its oinker under your [. . . .].

The lovely rumors which are going around about my writing a multitude of works seem related to the same ones that went around last year about my readings from the second volume, wherein there is a witty comparison of Petersburg to Moscow—about which no thought ever entered my mind. I would sincerely wish that the current rumors were even half correct; I haven't even dreamed of *The Notes of a General in Rome,* though I find that the idea is not a bad one.[3] I suspect that in Moscow there is some tailor or other who sews for all Moscow using his own measurements—there are plenty of fools who order from him. I will have to spend the winter in Frankfurt, though it's not at all to my liking I'll try. What's to be done, we can't do everything as we would like, one must know how to be patient. . . .

## P. A. Pletnev. December 1-14, 1844. (N.S.). Frankfurt.

I received your letter. Thank you for your sincerity, reproaches, and opinions about me.[1] I'm not going to justify myself; I already said that in advance—besides, it's impossible. First, because if I justified myself in one thing, from other sides I would see so much rubbish in myself in many other respects that I would become ashamed just at the thought of it. Second, because for that I would have to raise my entire inner spiritual history which one couldn't write in a thick volume, let alone in letters. Third, because for some time the desire to appear better in the eyes of people and even in the eyes of a friend has been extinguished. A friend is prejudiced too. Just the feeling of friendship itself softens our soul and makes it sympathetic. Having noticed a few good qualities in our friend and especially an inclination and love toward ourselves, we involuntarily bend to his side. God knows, perhaps having learned something of my inner history you would have been imbued with sympathy, and I wouldn't even have received the letter from you that I have now received. And I need such letters as yours. But I heard a sorrowful voice in the expressions in your letter, the voice of seemingly chagrined and deceived feeling; and therefore to comfort you somewhat I will make just general remarks on a few points in your letter. My friend, the human heart is a deep inscrutable chasm. We make mistakes here every minute. I can still be less in error in conclusions about you than you about me. Your soul is more open; your character long ago took on its finished shape and has remained the same for always. Perhaps only the rubbish of the customs of society and habits which are acquired can hide both you and your soul somewhat, but that is for nearsighted people who judge a man from a few external features. In the eyes of an expert on the human soul you are always the same. He knows that the same soul which seems cold and slumbering to others will rouse itself to one sincere appeal. But how can one judge about a secretive person in whom everything is inside, whose character hasn't even taken shape, but who is still educating himself in his soul, and whose every move produces only misunderstanding? How can one make conclusions about such a person basing oneself on a few traits which have inadvertently stuck themselves out? Won't this mean the same as to conclude about a book by a few sentences torn out of it—not in order either, but from different passages? Of course, even sentences taken separately can give some idea about the book, but can one learn what the book itself is? God knows, sometimes they have a different sense in the book, sometimes even the opposite of what it first seemed. Your reproaches for

love of fame may be just, but I don't think I have it to such an extent, or that I loved offerings of thyme as much as you suppose. As proof I can cite only the fact that at the time when the author's fame moved me much more than now I was dazed only the first days after the publication of my book, but then after a little time I already felt almost disgust for my own creation, and its shortcomings revealed themselves before me in all their nakedness. I don't even think that it was due to lack of knowledge of the human soul that you formed such an opinion about me, but due to some of my external acts, unpleasant manners, and, finally, inappropriate and pompous passages scattered in my works—which, as a result of my incapacity to depict my thoughts more completely, took on even more of an appearance of self-assurance. All your remarks about my literary merits are correct and show an expert who knows how to judge this accurately. But alas! I did not find anything in them that I didn't know myself. And if I had printed the criticism which I myself wrote on *Dead Souls*[2] soon after its publication, you would see that I expressed myself more severely and more accurately than you. For each of your reproaches I must make a reproach to you too, because it is not worthy of your own elevated soul. My friend, aren't you ashamed to tell me I have traded you for someone else?[3] I will tell you only the pure truth in answer to this, even though I know that you won't accept it as the truth; people don't believe my words, how am I to dare to be frank, even if I had the power to be frank. And so, know that here is the pure truth for you; I will tell it whether you believe it or not. It will be a sin only for the one of us who has lied. Not only will I not trade you for anyone else, but I will not trade any person for any other person. And he who has once entered into my soul will remain there forever, no matter how he acts toward me afterward, even if he rejects me completely. I will not drive him from my soul. Praise God, the more time passes, the stronger this tie becomes, and it is no longer even in my power to drive it away even if I wanted to. But if these words of mine do not assure you of anything and you shake your head dubiously, for your comfort I will cite proof which you yourself can confirm. Everyone in Moscow, except perhaps Yazykov (who knows me a little more only because he ran into me during bitter and difficult minutes in life when, as is well known, more is learned about a person), everyone has the same opinion of me that you do; they also reproach me for secretiveness and distrustfulness, even more than you they are sure that I set no value on them and that I prefer you to them. Both times[4] I pushed everyone away from me, I avoided any explanations, and I feared even questions about myself, feeling myself that I didn't have the power to say anything. Every attempt to say anything was unsuccessful, and every time I repented even opening

my mouth, feeling that with my unclear and stupid words I had only brought on a new misunderstanding about myself. My friend, when a person avoids everyone, pushes everyone away from himself, seeks seclusion and voluntarily devotes himself to a wandering, or as you call it, gypsy life, then one must leave him alone for a time and not bother him. The set time will pass and he will appear before you himself; when a person hears the inner call within himself, he must leave everything, tear himself away for a while—even from what it is hard and painful for him to tear himself away. You were rather perspicacious, saying that the main blame for all my faults is my ignorance and lack of education. You felt this, but you were wrong in pointing out how I could spare myself this—a matter which demands extremely great study of the nature of the man to whom the instructions are given. You challenge an ignoramus to fight with ignorance; you demand that I show others the way and the straight road already, and, expressing it in your words, that I point out the delusion of the self-styled judges—but, my friend, everyone can tell me: "Physician, heal thyself first." I know too well that I must accomplish this. At the same time I know that one needs purity of soul and a better organization of oneself and an almost heavenly beauty of morals. Without this one can defend neither art itself nor all that is sacred for which it serves as a pedestal. The goal of which you speak stands before me invariably. It must be in the mind of everyone; but the aspirations toward it are different, and each person has his own road to this same goal. And if a person has already arrived at the point where he himself can see his shortcomings and vices and see his nature, he alone can know what road it is more possible for him to go on. One person requires unbroken contact with society, another person requires a gypsy life—for the very same reasons. And how can one tell him, "You are doing it wrong." When an animal gets sick it seeks a grass for itself and finds it, and this kind of medicine is better than any that the most intelligent doctors will prescribe for him. My friend, I am right in moving away for a time from where I couldn't live. You see my one premature contact with society—and what a mess was made.[5] Tight circumstances made me publish prematurely a few works which I didn't have time to look at even with the eyes I had then, let alone the eyes I have now; and in what sharp relief I displayed for all both my ignorance and my slovenliness, and with my own words I besmirched that which I wanted to elevate. And whole clouds of misunderstandings were generated in my prosaic affairs, in relations with my friends who were connected to all this. My friend, one who is still educating himself should not look into society even for a short time. . . . Children aren't allowed in the living room, they are kept in the nursery. My life amid society

will be useless until I have learned that without which I cannot enter society and even suffer that which other people do not suffer. Believe it, there will be no peace for me; on the contrary, either I will be offended or I will offend someone—or don't you know all the touchy situations that a writer is faced with in society—how many great characters have even perished prematurely because of it. For the same reason I cannot act well in my relations with friends now either. I don't yet have the strength to be a friend, even if I should want. In order to be a friend of someone, one must first make oneself worthy of friendship. But until then it is better to alienate people from yourself than to attract them. Look how accurately it is stated in the *Imiation de Jesus Christ:*

> Nous croyons quelquefois nous rendre agréables aux
> autres par une liaison que nous formons avec eux, et
> c'est alors que nous commençons à leur déplaire par
> le dérèglement de moeurs qu'ils découvrent en nous.

I will also say a couple of words about my distrustfulness. Everyone accuses me of distrustfulness, but is this really distrustfulness? Distrustfulness stems from ignorance of people and the human heart. A man fears people because he doesn't know them. But are signs of absolute ignorance of man and the heart really noticeable in me? But my works? For all their imperfection, they show that there is some knowledge of human nature in the author. This is not simply a good retentive eye; you know yourself that in all Russia I have rubbed elbows with only a few people, and that I was almost always inaccurate when I touched exact descriptions of locales or mores. Is this really distrustfulness? Well, what if I in my turn start reproaching others with distrustfulness in the same way; why were some qualities, words, and unclear and dubious acts counted on the bad side rather than on the good one—do you mean to say this is trustfulness? Having acknowledged me an odd eccentric fellow, why did they demand the same actions from me as from others? Before drawing a general conclusion about me from two or three acts, why didn't the one judging have doubts and say within himself: "I see the following symptoms within this man. In other people these symptoms mean the following—but this man is not like others; his life itself is different, the man is secretive besides." God knows, sometimes clever doctors have been mistaken, basing themslves on the same symptoms—and they took one disease for another. Why then without even admitting a doubt in themselves did they firmly conclude it to be such-and-such a baseness, such-and-such a quality, such-and-such an attribute. Of course I'll be wrong if I start making accusations. The matter wouldn't be exactly like this if I were right. My friend, well, what if we were to suppose that a sufferer were

found who has been befallen by such a strange thing that everything he does and says is taken in a distorted sense, that almost to a man everyone has doubted him and that a whole whirlwind of misunderstandings has started spinning before him and, let's suppose, he sees everything that is happening. If someone else fell into my position, someone with a more tender soul which had not yet been strengthened and was unable to bear grief, he too would see everything that was happening in the hearts of his friends and those close to him, his whole soul would wear itself out with suffering and pain, and at the time he would feel that he couldn't utter a word by way of justification of himself—like one who is in a lethargy. . . .

God knows what goes on in the depths of a man. Sometimes his position can be so strange that he resembles someone held by a lethargic sleep who sees and hears that everyone, even the doctors themselves, have pronounced him dead and are preparing to bury him in the earth alive.[6] But when, seeing and hearing all this, he doesn't have the strength to move one of his limbs. Isn't it because we conclude too early that we have discovered everything about a man that we don't know him? And therefore arm yourself with patience with regard to me. Cuss me—any such word will be pleasant for me, even if it is much harsher than the ones which are in your letter. But don't devote yourself to vain reflection and don't be angry with me in your soul. You see that there is much here which is still obscure and unclear; better give it time—that alone can resolve and clarify it. . . .

Now let's talk about a prosaic matter regarding my works. I thought your letter would solve everything for me, but this wasn't the case; I remained in the same darkness. My friend, you say that Prokopovich wants me to explain to him in a special friendly letter what I need to know from him. But examine my position yourself. I have already written two letters to him, but not one answer. I demanded a report—what's clearer than that? I demanded the numbers, to be informed how many copies are on hand, how many have been sold, how many sent out, how much money I have; I requested even the smallest details.[7] I needed that, without it my hands were tied and I couldn't act clearly and sensibly myself—and my circumstances demand immediate, quick arrangements. Could all this have been taken for distrustfulness? My patience exhausted by the silence, I wrote a harsh letter in which I reproached him for lack of sympathy for the position of another. I am not justifying my act at all, I was guilty; but, my friend, man is weak and circumstances are strong; I was squeezed tightly by them. On one hand my mother writes me that they want to auction off the estate if she doesn't pay the debts and interest very soon, on the other I do not get money

from anywhere myself; finally, I'm sick in body and spirit. In this letter, no matter how cruel it was, it at least mentioned that I was in tight circumstances. Help me first—then cuss me out. If I offended him so much that I can't even be forgiven, nevertheless in that case he should at least have written me in the following way: "You have offended me so much that I am breaking off all relations with you from this day forth. I do not wish to take care of your affairs; I will turn them all over to so-and-so; direct your inquiry to so-and-so." In a word, so that I would know what to undertake. How could he pay me with a year and a half's silence in place of all this? From the journals I see that almost all of the copies in Petersburg have been sold out. (In Moscow not one of a thousand has been sold.) And meanwhile at this time I am suffering, I am in need, and I can't understand anything from this strange story.

You say Prokopovich is more right than I. I believe it; he has been insulted by me, that's true, I'm not arguing about that. But you say he loves me. Friend, love is an extremely sacred thing; it's terrible to utter this word in vain. Everyone in the world understands love in his own way, and we are all far from its true meaning. Love knows how to endure even insult; love is magnanimous, and it makes the one who has insulted it ashamed. At least agree that as a consequence of acts so inexplicable to me I too could be dubious about much. But I swear it, I know how to believe the soul of a man more than all his acts; though everyone reproaches me for distrustfulness I know too well that there are so many different irrelevant things on earth—rumors, gossip, etc.—which so enshroud men in an impenetrable fog that they do not recognize each other a distance of two steps away, and that an honorable man can act in such a way that his deed will seem a riddle to a man standing apart, and not even far away. And so here is my word of honor for you—that in this matter I harbored mistrust only with regard to his punctuality, and not to anything else. From your present letter I have become even surer that this has gotten knotted up in so many irrelevant aspects that there will be no end to the explanations until I decide to cease all this at once and suddenly and by this means not untie, but cut through, the knot. There is one way to do this, and therefore let us turn this affair at one stroke from something mixed-up and stupid into something noble, intelligent, and sacred. I am to blame for everything; apart from all else I am to blame just for having produced all this entanglement, stirring everyone up, putting in unpleasant relations people who perhaps wouldn't clash among themselves if it weren't for me. The guilty one must be punished. I punish myself by forfeiting all of the money owed to me for my works.[8] My soul desires this

forfeiture because it is just and legitimate, and without it I would be pained. Every ruble and kopek of this money was bought by the dissatisfactions of and insults to my friends, and there is not a person whom I didn't insult; this money would be very heavy on my conscience. And therefore, in Moscow as well as Petersburg, I am giving this money away to poor but worthy students. They should get this money not for nothing, but for work. You must assign this work to them; from your own choice you will find what is necessary for all of us to translate or write. Whether these translations be useful for all, whether they are to be printed separately or in *The Contemporary*, the means and how much should be given to whom—all this no one is able to do better than you; and therefore even if I didn't ask you in the name of friendship you couldn't refuse. All the money to the last kopek for the copies sold in Petersburg, with the deduction, of course, of the interest (which after the deduction should be close to two hundred thousand) should go to you instead of me. Prokopovich will act nobly, I know this and I am more sure of him. His soul was born to be beautiful and therefore he will accept this sacred deed, casting aside even the thought of personal dissatisfactions. He will be more prompt, give an accounting of everything to the last kopek, and give all the money to you. Prokopovich will zealously carry out everything that he has to in connection with this matter. If after this he still harbors malice against me, it will simply be a sin on his soul; and if he really loves me, he will take this request as a sacred thing. This entire matter must remain a secret forever—for everyone except you two. Tell every one that the money for the copies is being sent to me.

Neither you nor he should say anything about it to anyone, no matter how close they are to you—neither during my lifetime nor after my death. I shouldn't know anything either—how, to whom, or for what the money is given. You can say that it comes from a rich man, you can even tell the Tsar about a person who wishes to remain unknown. Accounting for this is due God alone. The same will be done in Moscow with the thousand copies there. Only two there, Aksakov and Shevyrev (to whom it has been entrusted) have been let in on this matter. But you should never speak of this matter to them, nor they to you. This request must be fulfilled rigorously. No suggestions or objections about it. I expect one word. *Yes,* and nothing more. The will of a friend must be sacred. There is my answer. I must do it like this and no other way, and my conscience serves as proof of this. All of a sudden I feel light, and it seems a terrible burden has suddenly fallen from my soul. And so this matter has been decided, filed in the archives, and never a word about it. And you,

my friend, don't be indignant about the troubles which are ahead of you here. You will receive many inner pleasures by arousing young people to work and occupation. You will discover many talents among them. If you discover them, be the same thing for them that you were for me when I entered this career. Encourage, urge, and reproach, but do not be vexed if you notice something resembling ingratitude in them. Often this is just a capricious impulse of youthful pride; show him your love and impress him with new favors and he will be yours forever.

I thank you sincerely and with all my soul for your readiness to help me with your own funds. I'll ask you bluntly and without any excuses. But even before receiving your letter I had arranged things with Zhukovsky concerning that for the present.[9] I worry less about money now than ever before. The most difficult time of life's road has already passed, and now it's even ridiculous to me that I worried about that when I should have troubled about it less than anyone else on earth, and God made this obvious to me every time. When I thought about money I never had it, but when I didn't think, it always came to me. But farewell! I embrace you firmly! Love me simply, on faith and on my word of honor alone—and not because I might be worthy of love or because my deeds merit love—and believe me you will profit by it later.

Your Gogol


## S. T. Askakov. December 22, 1844. (N.S.). Frankfurt.

. . . . As I have heard *The Muscovite* has gone over to Ivan Vasilevich Kireevsky.[1] This will probably awaken a zeal for work in many. Konstantin Sergeevich can prepare a multitude of fine philological essays.[2] They will be interesting for everyone. I can say this in advance, because I myself listened with great pleasure when he explained the derivation of many words to me. But they must be written very simply and in the same order that they emerge in during conversation, without any thought about how to give them wholeness and completeness. Both these things will flow out by themselves much more satisfactorily than if he thinks about them. He must also take care the essay be as short as possible. The Russian mind doesn't like to have a thing explained to it for too long. The shorter and more compact his essay, the more interesting it will be. He shouldn't take large philological questions at first, i.e., those in which there are branchings into many others, but splinter them into separate ques-

tions which contain indivisible wholeness in themselves—and work on each separately, taking it as the subject of an essay; in a word, as Pushkin did—he cut paper into slips, wrote on each one the title of whatever he wanted to remember later. On one he wrote *The Russian Hut*,[3] on another *Derzhavin*,[4] on a third the name of some other noteworthy subject, and so forth. He stuffed all these slips in a heap into a vase which stood on his working table, and later when he happened to have free time he picked one out at random; at the name written on it he suddenly remembered everything which was connected to that name in his memory and he immediately made notes about it, everything he knew on the same slip of paper. The essays which were printed afterward in the posthumous edition of his works and which are so interesting precisely because his every thought remained alive, as it came from his head, were made up in this way. . . .

## A. O. Smirnova. December 28, 1844. (New Style). Frankfurt.

First of all I will tell you about the character of my relations with my literary friends and chums—among whom Pletnev also belongs. First of all, my acquaintances and relations began with writers because I myself was a writer. I always knew how to respect their merits and, from each of them, to make use of that which each of them was able to give me. I always had the intelligence for this. Since there was always many-sidedness in my intellect and I always had a willingness to make use of others and educate myself, it is not surprising that each of them became my friend and close to me—each as a person who had in him something which his other comrade did not have. As if on purpose all of them (which can happen only among us in Russia) are gifted with extraordinary and at the same time extremely original capabilities which are all unlike each other, varied intellects, varied characters (from this it is obvious why they battle among themselves so often and do not agree in their opinions). And so, knowing how to value them, I knew how to make use of something or other from each of them, but I always put off thanking them to a later time, i.e., to the time when I myself become more intelligent and am in a position to teach them what they lack. But I never foisted my friendship on any of them; I never asked any of them—or what is still more inaccurate—demand that anyone live with me as my soulmate, share my opinions with me, etc. In a word, I didn't make any promises to anyone, I didn't oblige anyone in any way regarding me. I didn't entrust to any of them either proposals or plans regarding me

myself or anything that relates to my personal fate—considering this unnecessary for many reasons, first because I myself could not tell them in a clear way what had been in me from my very infancy, second because even then, thank God, I had an adequate knowledge of people; and even then I could already feel how each man could be useful to me and therefore exactly what I should and what I shouldn't say to him, finally, third—even then I felt that we should love everyone more or less, according to their merits, but we should choose only God as a true and very close friend to whom we could entrust everything down to the slightest stirring of our heart. I should feel this more sharply and to a greater extent than others because, gifted by His own heavenly mercy with many sides to my character and abilities, I could never express everything about myself; and because even then I paid extremely dearly for every stupid attempt to be frank at the wrong time and out of place. And so already in the beginning I realized my position, and in relation to my literary friends I conducted myself as I should have conducted myself; I talked a little with them about my literary projects, but I did not talk to anyone about me myself, with regard to my inner mental state. I remained friends with all of them. And such was the state of affairs until my departure from Russia.[1] None of them knew me. From my literary conversations they were all sure that only literature interested me, and that absolutely nothing else on earth existed for me.

After I left Russia a great change took place in me. The *soul* occupied me completely, and I saw clearly that without the aspiration of my soul to its better perfection I didn't have the power to direct any of my ability or any aspect of my intellect towards the good and profit of my fellowmen, and without this mental education any work of mine would only be temporarily brilliant, but vain in its essence. How God led me to this idea, how my soul was educated unseen by anyone—God alone knows completely. You can't tell about this. Volumes would be needed for that, and these volumes wouldn't tell everything. And besides, why tell about what substances burned in me and burned out? If afterwards you smell the spreading redolence you'll guess yourself from what burning substances the redolence comes; but if you do not smell the redolence, then there is nothing to know about what burned in my soul. I will only tell you that God was heavenly-merciful to me, that His holy mercy helped me in my aspiration, and that now, whatever I am, though I see clearly the immeasurable chasm separating me from perfection, I also see that I am a far better person than I was before. But my literary friends could not learn everything that happened within me. . . .

It's no wonder: they all made my acquaintance when I was still the former person—knowing me rather slightly even then. On my arrival in Russia[2] they all met me with open arms. Each of them, busy with literature, some with a journal, others with something else, having become passionately attached to some one favorite *idea* and meeting opponents to their opinion in others, waited for me as for some kind of messiah that the Jews await, certain that I would share his thoughts and ideas, support and defend him against others, considering this the first condition and act of friendship, not even suspecting that (in an innocent way) these demands, apart from the absurdity, were even inhuman.[3] It was impossible for me to sacrifice the time and my work for the support of their favorite ideas, because, first, I did not completely share them, second, because I needed something to support my poor existence; and I could not sacrifice my essays for them by placing them in their journals; I had to print them separately as new and fresh ones in order to have an income.[4] All these trifles escaped view as much escapes the view of people who do not like to analyze the subtleties of the circumstances and situation of another person, but, rather, like to make hasty conclusions about a man; and therefore they make constant mistakes at every step. Those who have beautiful souls do bad things; those who have generous hearts act inhumanly without being aware of it themselves.

They took my coolness toward their literary interests for coolness toward them themselves. They didn't hesitate to make an egoist of me in their thoughts, one to whom the general good is nothing, to whom only his own literary fame is dear. In addition, each of them was so sure of the truth and justness of his ideas and positions that he considered anyone who didn't agree with him nothing other than an absolute apostate from the truth.

I leave it to you to judge for yourself what my position was among such people. But you will hardly guess what my inner sufferings were like—their beginning began at this point. (Pletnev was less the cause of them than any of the others, or, rather, he was completely innocent; but on the other hand he was the most ridiculous, and is just like a child to this day.) I will tell you only that something like jealousy began among my literary friends. Each of them started to suspect that I had traded him for someone else. And hearing from afar about my new acquaintances and about the fact that people unknown to them had started to praise me, they increased their demands still more, on the basis of the length of our acquaintance. I kept receiving very strange letters in which each one, setting himself forward and assuring me of the purity of his relations to me,

derogated and almost slandered others ignobly, assuring me that these people were flattering me only for their own advantage, that they didn't know me at all, that they loved me only for my works and not because they loved me myself (they are all still sure that I love all kinds of sky-high praises), and reproaching me at the same time with such things, accusing me with such base accusations as I would not make, I swear, to the worst person; and the acts ascribed to me I wouldn't ascribe not only to someone a little worse than I, but I wouldn't even ascribe them to anybody, because it would be an insane thing to ascribe them to anyone at all. In their thoughts they made a kind of toy out of me, a characterless person who doesn't know people at all, who changes his opinions and goes from one thing to another. And at the same time they attributed to me qualities which are obviously in contradiction with such a characterless person, like egoism, gloryloving, distrustfulness, secretiveness, and the like. In one word, they finally got completely confused and lost all sense. Each of them made up his own ideal in place of me, an image and character composed by himself, and he did battle with his own composition in complete certainty that he was battling with me. Now, of course, all this is ridiculous and having said, "Children, children!" I can turn to my work as before. But then it was impossible for me to do that. The misunderstandings reached the point of such offensive suspicions, such rough blows were dealt—and in addition on such sensitive and fine strings the existence of which could not even be suspected by those who dealt the blows, that my entire soul was exhausted from pain and suffering—and it was extremely difficult for me. This was all the more difficult that I didn't even have the possibility of justifying myself, no matter how I wanted to justify myself. It was impossible for me to justify myself because I would have had to make them understand too much, there was too much of my inner history I would have had to reveal to them. And at the thought of such work my very thought despaired, seeing endless pages before it. Besides, any justification of mine would have been an accusation of them, and they were not yet sufficiently mature in the soul and were not sufficiently Christian to hear out such accusations. One thing remained for me—to accuse myself for the time being in order somehow to quiet them until the right time; and having waited for the time when their souls would be softened, to reveal the real thing to them gradually, slowly, and little by little. There is a simple presentation of my relations with my literary friends—from which you can deduce my relations with Pletnev yourself. . . .

## S. S. Uvarov. End of April, 1845. Frankfurt.

I have received your letter. I thank you sincerely for your assistance and interest.[1] I say nothing of my gratitude to His Majesty; it is in my soul, I can express it only by a prayer for him. I will tell you only that I became sad after your letter. Sad, first, because nothing I have written so far merits great attention; though at its basis there lay a good thought, it was all expressed so immaturely, badly, trivially, and besides that to such an extent unlike it should have been expressed, that it is not in vain that the majority of people ascribe a bad sense rather than a good one to my works, and my countrymen glean gleanings from them for the harm of their souls rather than for the good. Second, I am sad because today I still stand before His Majesty with an unpaid debt—for his earlier help.[2] I swear I did not even consider asking His Majesty for anything now; in quiet I just kept on preparing the work which, really, would be more useful to my countrymen than my earlier scribblings, for which you too would perhaps say thanks to me—if it were completed in good conscience—for its subject would not be foreign to your own convictions. Until now I have been comforted by the thought that His Majesty, to whom the spiritual good of his subjects is truly dear, would with time perhaps say of me: "This man knew how to be thankful and knew how to express his gratitude to me." But now I am emburdened with a new beneficence; in comparison with what has already been done for me my work will seem poorer and more insignificant, my ruined health can even rob me of the possibility of doing it as I would wish and even as I could do it; and that is why I am sad. I am even sad that with your letter and your interest in me you have taken away from me the right to say what I wanted to say to you. I wanted to thank you for everything you have done for science, for our national history[3] (along with other people I had my share of good from these deeds), and—what is even more important—for awakening a firm Russian principle in the spirit of our enlightenment. Before I had the right to thank you for this as a son of the same land, as a brother of the same feeling in which we should all be brothers, and as one not obligated to you personally in any way. Now you have taken this right away from me, and what would have been a proper matter may now seem like a compliment. And so, in place of any expression of gratitude, accept rather this sincere statement of my spiritual condition; I cannot tell you anything else—I do not even add the polite ending which closes high-society letters, because I have forgotten them all, and I simply remain obliged and sincerely thankful to you.

N. Gogol

*V. A. Zhukovsky. July 14, 1845. Berlin.*

I was slow with a description of my lamentable travels, wanting to write you something comforting about myself. I left Frankfurt
in an absolutely indecisive state regarding my sickness. I was disturbed not by my sickness itself, but by the fact that I could not get
out of the doctors exactly what my sickness is. I perceived that I
had a nervous disorder, but what the source of it was remained a
problem for me; and the uninterrupted accumulation of ailments not
connected with the nerves, as well as nervous ones—the dehydra-
tion of my entire body and the coloration of a corpse which it has
taken on (the more time passes the worse it gets)—all this has confused the problem still more and has not given me the necessary
spirit to be brave enough for solitary treatment in seclusion—which,
given the spleen-filled mood that constantly pursues me, is dangerous. And therefore though I tried to take control of myself I was not
calm at any time during the journey. For my mental tranquility it
turned out to be necessary for me to confess and take Communion in
Weimar. Count Tolstoy also took Communion with me.[1] The kind
priest in Weimar advised me convincingly that while I was on the
road I should also consult with the renowned doctor in Halle, Kruck-
enberg. Seeing my intensifying attacks, emaciation, and the strange
sickly color of my skin, Count Tolstoy also urged me to do this. Kruck-
enberg paid particular attention to my back, attempting to find in it
the cause of my sickness, emaciation, weakening, etc. He undressed
me and felt me all over; he ran his fingers over and felt every vertebra in my back, tested my chest, pounding on every bone; and having
found both in good condition, made a conclusion like Kopp's, that
the whole trouble was in my nerves and that it was essential for me
to live at least three months by the open sea, bathing daily, and that
for this the island of Helgoland was most convenient for me—not far
from Hamburg—and that Gastein could get me too excited. This conclusion did not comfort me entirely and could not drive away the
doubts—first because I clearly felt something besides nerves within
myself, and second because I didn't have the strength to ignore such
a strong authority as Kopp who had recommended Gastein. I decided
to go to Berlin and present both possibilities for the judgment of
Schönlein, telling him of my entire critical position, and to venture
decisively to follow whichever opinion he agreed with, basing myself
solely on the majority of votes. But to my misfortune I didn't catch
Schönlein in Berlin; he had left for Hamburg, and I remained
entirely devoted to indecision. And I will let anyone who knows
what indecision is at such an important moment judge what that

position was. Meanwhile, passing time increased the difficulty of my position still more. In Berlin I was advised at least to go to Dresden to Dr. Karus. I went to Dresden. When I related the whole thing to him, Karus questioned me about the whole manner of my life and about all the excesses to which I had given myself in life which could produce such a strong nervous disorder in me. Not finding them sufficient to produce a complete disorder of the nerves, and finding my life rather temperate for that, he said that the causes must be other ones, and that he would come to my house to examine and feel me all over. Having undressed me completely he also felt me all over. He pounded against all the places and bones in my chest, found my chest healthy, felt my stomach and then again began to pound on the ribs of my right side. Here he stopped and found that the sound became hollow quite a bit higher than the location of the liver—which in his opinion is a clear sign that the liver has grown too large, leaving less and less room for the lungs, that the trouble was entirely in the liver, that the emaciation, green color of the skin, digestive disorder, nervous disorder, and poor circulation of the blood were all caused by it, that first of all it was necessary to treat the liver and that I should first of all go to Karlsbad without wasting any time. And so, there is my situation for you. I am going to Karlsbad because I must decide on something, because this was the last opinion, pronounced with the consideration of all the opinions of the other doctors, because Karlsbad is less secluded than the others and perhaps less dangerous with regard to spleen. But whether what I am doing is sensible I really don't know. . . .

*A. O. Smirnova. July 25, 1845. Karlsbad.*

. . . . You touched on *Dead Souls* and ask me not to get angry at the truth, saying that you are full of compassion for what you formerly laughed at.[1] My friend, I do not love my former works which have been printed up until now, especially *Dead Souls*. But you will be wrong if you are going to condemn the author for them because you take the ridiculing of the provinces for a caricature—just as you were wrong to praise him before. The subject of *Dead Souls* is not at all the provinces, and not a few ugly landowners, and not that which people ascribe to it. For the meantime it is still a secret which all at once, to the surprise of everyone (for not a soul among the readers has guessed), was to have been revealed in the following volumes— if it had pleased God to lengthen my life and bless my future work.

Again I repeat to you that it is a secret, and for now the key to it is only in the soul of the author. Much, even much of what was apparently directed to me myself was taken in a completely wrong sense. I did really have some pride, but not for my *present,* not for the attributes I possessed; the pride for the *future* stirred in my breast—for what stood ahead of me, the happy discovery by which, as a consequence of God's grace, to illumine my soul. In the discovery that one can be far *better* than man is, that there are means, and that for love. . . . But I have started talking at the wrong time about what does not yet exist. Believe me, I know very well that I am too much rubbish. And I have always more or less felt that in my *present* state I am rubbish, and that everything that has been done by me is rubbish, except what it pleased God to inspire me to do—and I did that in a way far from the way I should have.—But my hand grows tired. My friend, let us strengthen ourselves in spirit! . . .

## S. P. Shevyrev. November 20, 1845. (New Style). Rome.

I received your letter of October 4 in Rome where I am now God again saved me when I already thought my end was approach ing. Now I am incomparably better, although the weakness and ex haustion of my strength has not yet passed. Your letter was pleasant for me, but at the same time sad. Kireevsky is also ill.[1] You say, "Can it be there is no prayer which could save you?" and you an- swer, "There is—but you invoke it badly." Only God can know how a person prays. But if it has been decreed by His sacred will for some one of us to suffer, let that be His sacred will! And if it please His sacred will that my life, or the life of anyone else who should have done much good for Russia, be removed from the face of the earth, then surely that is better than if it were lengthened; and it is not for our small minds to judge about a great mind. I was also disturbed by your news about Konstantine Aksakov.[2] The beard, homespun coat, etc. . . . He's simply playing the fool; however this foolishness inevitably had to happen. He is a man sick with a superabundance of physical and moral strengths; both kinds have accumulated in him without having exits through which to erupt. But in a physical and in a moral respect he has remained a *virgin.* Just as in the physical respect a man who does not marry by the time he has reached thirty becomes ill, so it is in the moral respect. It would even have been better for him if in his youth, following the example of the young people, he had visited the whores once or twice a month. But ab- staining from all the diversions of life and the flesh directed all his

powers towards the spirit. He had inevitably to become a fanatic; I thought so from the very beginning. I thank you for the present news of him. I'll write to him; sometimes he heard from me the bitter truths that he didn't want to hear from others. Perhaps God will instruct me how to give him advice and him how to extract what is useful for him from my advice. . . .

## N. M. Yazykov. January 8, 1846. Rome.

. . . . I am glad that Ivan Aksakov has talent[1] and that Shevy-rev is preparing his lectures[2] for print—I await them impatiently. I wrote Ivan's father to send me his verses; you remind him too, or better send them yourself; I don't think it will be too much to ask you to have them all copied in small writing on a piece of letter paper. The news of the translation of *Dead Souls* into German was unpleas-ant to me.[3] Apart from the fact that in general I don't want Euro-peans to know anything about me before the right time, it is im-proper for that work to appear in translation under any circum-stances before its completion; and I wouldn't want foreigners to fall into the same stupid error into which a large part of my fellow coun-trymen did—taking *Dead Souls* for a portrait of Russia. If you hap-pen to get hold of this translation write how it is and what comes out in German. I think simply neither fish nor flesh nor good red herring. Also, if you happen to read any review in German journals, or simply a comment about me, write me that too. I have already read a little in French about the tales—in *Revue des Deux Mondes* and in *Des Débats*.[4] So far it's all right. It will sink in Lethe along with news-paper advertisements about new pills and about newly invented pomade for dyeing the hair, and there will be no more talk about it. But in Germany the literary commentaries which are disseminated have a longer life, and therefore I would like to keep track of every-thing that is said about me there. I don't know what to tell you of the news of Rome; to me at least it is not interesting. The most im-portant of events was the arrival of our Tsar. I admired him only from a distance and prayed for his soul. May God help him to arrange everything in our Russia for the best. . . .

## N. M. Yazykov. May 5, 1846. Rome.

. . . . Thank you for the excerpts from the introduction to the German translation of *Dead Souls*. The German judges things rather

sensibly.[1] It is the best view which a foreigner could have on these things. In spite of that it is extremely unpleasant that *Dead Souls* has been translated. However, what happened did not happen without the will of God. God only grant the strength to finish and publish the second volume. Then they will discover that we Russians have much that they never even guessed about, and that we ourselves do not want to recognize—if only it will please God to give me the strength amid infirmities and illnesses to fulfill the task honorably and devoutly.

The other day I read with interest and satisfaction the eulogy on Karamzin by Pogodin.[2] It is his best article. In it there is none of his rashness and various clumsy mannerisms. Everything is rather well proportioned. The passages and excerpts are arranged in good order so that Karamzin's whole character comes out before the reader. Karamzin is a truly extraordinary phenomenon. He was the first to show that the calling of the writer is worth the sacrifice of everything, that in Russia a writer can be completely independent, and he can say everything if he is full of love of the Good, love which is the most important thing in his entire organism and in all his actions. The censorship does not exist for him, and there is nothing about which he cannot speak. What a lesson and precept for us all! And after this how ridiculous are some of our fellow literary people who shout that in Russia one cannot speak the truth or that truth causes offense. Such a person does not know how to speak the truth himself; he expresses himself so loutishly and insolently that it is not so much the truth which gives offense as the words in which he expresses his truth, words which mark the internal slovenliness of his immature soul. And then he is amazed that people don't accept his truth. No, first have the harmonious and beautiful soul which Karamzin had, such pure aspiration and such love of men—and then boldly speak the truth. Everyone in the realm from the Tsar to his last subject will hear out the truth from you. But enough. I am hurrying to pack.

*A. M. Vielgorsky. May 14, 1846. Geneva.*

I just started *Poor Folk*,[1] I read about three pages, and glanced into the middle in order to see the particular stamp and manner of speech of the new writer. . . . Talent can be seen in the author of *Poor Folk*, the choice of subjects speaks in favor of his spiritual qualities, but it can also be seen that he is still young. There is

still a great deal of prolixity and little concentration within himself; everything would turn out much more lively and powerful if it were more compressed. However, I say this not yet having read it all the way through. I have so few contemporary Russian things to read now, that I read a little at a time—as if it were a sweet dessert.

## P. A. Pletnev. July 30, 1846. Schwalbach.

At last my request! You must fulfill it as the truest friend. Put all of your affairs aside and occupy yourself with the printing of this book with the title: *Selected Passages from Correspondence with Friends.*[1] It is necessary—too necessary—for everyone; that is what I can tell you at present; the book itself will explain everything else to you; when it is nearly all printed everything will become clear, and the misunderstandings which have troubled you till now will disappear by themselves. The beginning is enclosed. The continuation will soon be sent. I am still awaiting the return of a few letters; but there will be no postponement for these, because there are enough even with just those that have been returned to me. The printing should be done quickly; it is essential that no one except you and the censor should know about it. Choose Nikitenko as the censor; he is more favorably inclined toward me than others. I will write him a few words. Get his word also not to tell anyone about the fact that my book is coming out. It is necessary to finish printing it in a month so that it can come out by the middle of September. . . . Print two sets of 1,200 and prepare paper for a second edition which, in my reckoning, will soon follow; this book will sell better than my earlier works because it is my sole sensible book so far. After the notebook which is enclosed here, you will be receiving others without delay. I am putting my trust in God to support me in this work. . . .

## P. A. Pletnev. October 20, 1846. (New Style). Frankfurt.

Two days ago I sent you the fifth and final notebook. Because of exhaustion and the recurrence of many painful infirmities I haven't had strength to write about the final arrangements. I am writing now. For the sake of God, employ all efforts and means to have the book printed as soon as possible. This is necessary, necessary both for me and for others; in a word, it is necessary for the general good. I am told this by my heart and by God's extraordinary

mercy which gave me the strength to toil when I didn't dare to think about it, didn't dare even to expect the mental freshness required for that; and suddenly for that period of time everything was given to me; suddenly the most painful infirmities ceased, suddenly all the hindrances to my working disappeared, and all this continued until the last line of my work was completed. This is simply a miracle and the mercy of God, and it will be a grave sin for me if I start complaining about the return of the painful attacks of my illness. My friend, I acted firmly in the name of God when I was compiling my book; I took up my pen in praise of His holy name, and that is why all obstacles and everything which stops a weak man moved aside. When printing my book you act in the name of God too, as if you were doing this deed for the glorification of His name, forgetting all your personal relations to whomever might be concerned, keeping in mind only the general good—and then all barriers will move aside for you too. . . .

On publication of the book prepare copies and take them to every person in the Tsar's family, not excluding the children, to all the grand dukes, to the children of the heir, to the children of Maria Nikolaevna, to Mikhail Pavlovich's whole family.[1] Don't take gifts from anyone, and try to get out of that; say that the presentation of this book is an expression of that feeling which even I am unable to explain to myself, which has of late become still stronger than it was formerly, as a result of which everything which concerns their family has become close to my soul, even everything which surrounds them, and that just by the presentation of this book to them I give pleasure to myself, pleasure which is absolutely complete and sufficient, that as a result of both my ill health and my internal mental state, I am no longer interested in any of that which can still move and interest a man who lives in society. But if any one of them offers on his own accord money for assistance to those many whom I will meet going on a pilgrimage to the holy places, take this money boldly. My friend, there are many people who need help about whom we don't know or suspect, but whose tale of sufferings would make every heart, even the most callous, become dejected from sorrow. Many artists, many many talents should have at least some beggarly assistance so that they don't perish from hunger—in the literal sense. There are many who have already comprehended the higher secret of art and its higher calling, and for them the holy places and land of the Gospels are just as necessary as was manna for the Jewish people in the desert. . . .

*I. I. Sosnitsky.¹ November 2, 1846. (New Style). Nice.*

Turn your attention to the last scene of *The Inspector General.*
Consider it, ponder it again. From the concluding play, *The Denouement of The Inspector General*² you will comprehend why I am
fussing so about this last scene and why it is so important to me that
it have full effect. I am sure that you will look at *The Inspector General* with new eyes after this conclusion which for many reasons it
was impossible for me to publish then—and only now is it possible to
do so. Use all your efforts to see that *The Inspector General* is staged
well in all respects, that the actors do their job well. By this you will
be doing not only a good deed, but a truly Christian one. (The sale of
*The Inspector General* in its new form with the *Denouement* is earmarked to help the poor, and by your acting and production you can
increase the volume of sales.) Don't be too lazy to play the role of
Khlestakov before the actors preparatorily—a role which absolutely
no one except you can perform. By this you can give them the idea
once and for all. Theoretically, none of them can understand that this
character must without fail be played as a society man *comme il
faut*, not in the least with a desire to play a liar and blowhard, but on
the contrary, with the sincere desire to play the role of someone of a
rank higher than one's own—but so that it comes out of its own accord, in sum of everything, as a petty liar, a shabby underling, a
petty coward, and a blowhard in all respects. Only by your acting
can you impress all this upon them; no matter how convincingly
you tell them you will do nothing with words and instructions. You
know yourself that second-rate actors can imitate a character, but
they cannot create a character; in making forced efforts to produce
the latter, they will fall even below their own abilities. That is why
the example you give will lead them onto the right road more than
their own reasoning. As for the acting in the last play, that is in the
play, *The Denouement of the Inspector General,* read my lines about
that in my letter to Shchepkin.³ . . . . At the end of the play when you
make your curtain-call and have bowed to the public, ask them if they
wouldn't like to buy *The Inspector General* which is being sold together with *The Denouement* at the exit of the theater for a silver
ruble—the money to go to the poor. Whoever desires to give more
should present the money to you yourself and buy it personally from
your hands; and deliver all of this money to Pletnev who is entrusted
with the collection of the money and from whom it will go to those
who are responsible for dividing it among the poor. . . . See that the
sale in the theater booths is entrusted to reliable vendors, and don't
use some actor for this. I say this because one of these gentlemen

whom I took it into my head to trust, appropriated the money for himself and went on a spree with it, putting the blame on the vendors who didn't bring it to him; and when finally I took it into my head to question the vendors, the affair was revealed. Keep this in mind. . . .

### A. O. Smirnova. November 24, 1846. (New Style). Naples.

. . . . At present delays of various sorts concerning the printing of my book and my affairs in Petersburg in general are stopping the arrangement of all the circumstances conducive to the journey.[1] It must be the will of God for me to postpone my departure for a while. Various unforeseen delays have also occurred for many of the people who also wanted to go this year. It must be it is not God's will for me to set off on the road. As I look into myself I see that I am still far from being ready for this journey. There is still much, much I have not done and without which I will not have the power to pray as I ought to. My journey is not simple worship. My journey is for the solicitation of God's blessing for my great deeds in life, for those matters and great deeds for which He has given me abilities which I should not have displayed before the right time, but should have developed in myself first. A schoolboy who even though he has studied better than the others is nevertheless timid when thinking about the examination and his forthcoming graduation; how can a schoolboy who feels that he has studied carelessly not be timid? But let God's will be in all things! I still know nothing about whether I am going or not going this winter. . . .

### P. A. Pletnev. December 8, 1846. (New Style). Naples.

It is necessary to stop both the printing and performance of *The Inspector General.* Judging by the news that I have and by several obstacles, and, finally, taking into account several of Shevyrev's observations (set forth by him in a letter which I just received), I see that *The Inspector General with the Denouement* will have much more success if it is given a year from the present time.[1] Toward that time I myself will have time to examine this business a bit better, to correct the play and adapt it more to the concepts of the viewers. But in the form it is in now *The Denouement of The Inspector General* could produce an opposite effect, and with the bad acting of our actors it could come out simply as a ridiculous scene. There-

fore if, fortunately, the manuscript has not been given to the censors, keep it hidden with yourself. However, if it has been given to them, take it back immediately as if for some hurried change, keep it yourself, and make every effort possible to prevent it from being given general publicity. Incidentally, I learned from Shevyrev the news about which you didn't tell me anything—to wit that *The Contemporary* is no longer in your hands, but has been transferred to the hands of Nikitenko, Belinsky, and Turgenev.[2] And last week (knowing nothing about this) I sent you an essay about *The Contemporary* which you probably already have in your hands and have read. Now I don't dare make any remarks to you; they might be both erroneous and inapposite. I will tell you only that it seems to me that now, specifically at the present time, specifically with the coming year, 1847, your participation in literature is much more necessary than ever before. In all the time up to now it seemed absolutely fruitless to me. So it seems to me that it would be useful even if you were to start publishing *Northern Flowers*[3] in place of *The Contemporary*. . . . As for my essay, do with it as you think best. . . .

## A. O. Rosset. December 10, 1846. (New Style). Naples.

In my previous letter to you, Arkady Osipovich, I placed on you the troubles connected with the publication of *The Inspector General*; in the present one I take them from your shoulders. For many reasons, part of which you will probably fathom yourself, it is necessary to postpone *The Inspector General with the Denouement* for one more year. More important than all the other things the public must have time to read into my letters somewhat better and get accustomed to those words which still sound strange to their ears. I request you to tell me your opinion frankly when you read my book and to inform me what others are saying about it too. But still better, ask everyone you meet to write me a note from himself and candidly relate his impression as well as the thoughts of others about the book and about the degree of its necessity for society, without hiding its shortcomings in the least. . . .

## P. Pletnev. January 15, 1847. (New Style). Naples.

. . . . I read your letter again, again I weighed everything, again I imagined the entire content of the book in my thoughts, and

I absolutely cannot see a reason why *it is better* not to print those letters[1] which, it seems to me, will make some civil servants examine themselves a little more severely—especially those who have beautiful souls and good intentions and sin through lack of knowledge. If only two or three people in all of Russia look more clearly at many things after my book, then it is already extremely good. Also I still see no reason why *it is impossible even to think of presenting the book for the sovereign's examination* (as you expressed yourself), adding that I forgot how much business more important than ours he has. Nevertheless, his business is not about anything except his subjects; I am also his subject; I also have a right to present a petition to him personally, like everyone else in those cases when the judges placed over us do not take responsibility and authority on themselves. You also forgot that I am not publishing this book for my own pleasure at all—and not for the pleasure of others either; I am printing it with the assurance that by doing this I am fulfilling my duty and serving my service. Therefore, no matter what the book might be it is worth the attention of the sovereign—all the more so because there are things in it which relate directly to the government and the management of its affairs. Having considered all this, I decided to write a letter to the sovereign and dispatched it to Count Vielgorsky for delivery. . . .

### *S. T. Aksakov. January 20, 1847. (New Style). Naples.*

I received your letter, my good friend Sergei Timofeevich. I thank you for it. Everything in it which should be, has been taken into consideration. I ought to limit myself to this; but since great worry about me is visible in your letter, I consider it necessary to say a few words to you. Again I repeat to you once more that you are wrong in suspecting any new trend in my ideas. From my early youth I have had one road along which I go. I was secretive only because I was not stupid—it's as simple as that. The reason for your present deductions and conclusions about me (made by others as well as by you) was that I, putting hope in my powers and on my (seemingly) ripened maturity, dared start speaking of that which I should have been silent about for a little while longer—until my words achieved such clarity that they would be understandable even to a child. Here is the entire story of my mysticism for you. I should have worked quietly for more time yet, burned that which ought to have been burned, not said a word to anyone about my internal self, and not

responded to anything, especially not have given any answer to my friends concerning my works. The reason for the appearance of the essays which have so disturbed your spirit was partly injudicious urgings from their side, partly my inability to see what stage of my own education I had reached. On the other hand all this happened not without the will of God. The appearance of my book containing correspondence with many extremely remarkable people in Russia (whom, perhaps, I would never have met if I lived in Russia myself and remained in Moscow) will be necessary to many (in spite of all the incomprehensible passages) in many truly essential respects. But it will be even more necessary for me myself. My book will be attacked from all corners, from all sides and in all possible respects. At present these attacks are extremely necessary to me; they will show me *my own self* more closely and at the same time they will show me *you,* i.e., *my readers.* Without having seen more clearly what I myself am at the present moment and what my readers are, I would be absolutely incapable of doing my work effectively. But you will not be able to understand this for a while; better, simply take it on faith—you will profit by this. But do not hide any of your feelings from me! Immediately on reading the book, while nothing has grown cold, pour everything out on paper as it is, naked. Don't be at all disturbed if you express yourself in harsh words; that means absolutely nothing—why I even love them very much. The franker and more honest you are with me, the more you will profit. . . .

*M. I. Gogol. January 25, 1847. (New Style). Naples.*

. . . . For many reasons my will, made during my illness, had to be published in my book.[1] In addition to the fact that it was essential as an explanation of the very appearance of such a book, it is necessary in order to remind many about death; the living rarely think about it. It was not in vain that during my illness God let me feel how terrified one becomes before death so that I could pass on this sensation to others also. If you were truly instructed in Christianity as one ought to be, you would all know that consciousness of death is the first thing that a person ought to carry in his thoughts constantly. In the Holy Scriptures it is said that he who remembers his end at every moment will never sin. He who remembers about death and imagines it vividly before his eyes will not desire death, because he sees himself how many good things it is necessary to do to earn a good end and stand before the judgment of the Lord without

fear. Until the time when a person becomes accustomed to the thought of death and makes it seem as if it were awaiting him the next day, he will never begin living as one ought to; and he will postpone everything from day to day to a future time. The constant thought of death educates the soul in an amazing way; it lends strength for life and good deeds in life. Insensibly it strengthens our firmness, invigorates the spirit and makes us insensible to all that which exasperates weak, and faint-hearted people. . . .

## *A. P. Tolstoy. February 6, 1847. (New Style). Naples.*

. . . . A terrible muddle has resulted in the arrangement for my book in Petersburg. Something like an uprising of devils to prevent its publication has taken place. Some kind of mysterious parties of Europeans and Asians have joined together to confuse and befuddle the censorship. Instead of a thick book a little brochure came out —one which you have probably already received, because I wrote to send two copies to you. None of the essays and letters to various civil servants and people in government service which I considered the most essential have been passed.[1] However, all this has not put me out of countenance, in spite of my illness (for I have gotten sick again and feel out of sorts). All the essays not passed are going to the Tsar for examination, and within a month or two in place of the hunk of book eaten and gnawed around by the censorship which you received, you will receive the second edition in the form of a complete and respectable book. My heart tells me that everything will turn out all right. A month ago the sovereign was so generous to me too; learning of my journey which I am planning, he questioned Mikhail Yurevich Vielgorsky about me with interest and ordered the secretary to write to all of the embassies, missions, and authorities of those lands in the East that I am going to transverse to show me special patronage. And no matter what my book is like in its present form, nevertheless give me your open and frank opinion and tell me your impression of it. . . .

My illness consists of insomnia which has already continued for almost two months, a weakening of my body, eruptions on my legs; but by the mercy of God my soul is in calm equilibrium in spite of all this, even my distraught nerves. Even the death of Yazykov did not produce agitated feelings of sadness, but rather something indefinite and almost radiant. As if for me he hadn't died. Farewell! . . .

## A. O. Rosset. February 11, 1847. (New Style). Naples.

. . . . Pletnev committed a great imprudence by publishing this one fragment instead of the whole book. He should have waited patiently for permission from above to pass all those letters which were supposed to serve as support of the thoughts expressed in this fragment. Almost everything which explains how to apply what is said to actual deeds was not passed—all the letters to people in government jobs, to civil servants in Russia in which I explain the possibility of doing truly Christian deeds in any position in our secular offices. A trifle! I did *not* compile this book to anger the Belinskys, Kraevskys, and Senkovskys; I was looking into the inside of Russia, not at literary society. Now the book consists of generalities, and instead of those people and subjects which should have stepped out before the readers, I alone have stepped out on the stage, exactly as if I were publishing my book in order to display myself. . . .

In addition to the journals being sent to me, I will ask for Kukolnik's *Illustration*[1] of last year, bound in one book. I don't want this year's. In the book there are stories by Dal[2] which I need very much. I respect this writer because one can always collect some positive information from him about various escapades in Russia. There are other stories from Russian daily life, too. Please don't forget that you should send me only those books wherein something of Russia can be smelled, even if it is rather stinky. . . . I don't need the books which are written for good people, but those which are produced by the current school of literary people who are trying to describe and civilize Russia. Any Petersburg and provincial scenes, mysteries, etc. Last year a book called *Petersburg Heights*[3] was published; send me both parts of it. But enough. I am tired. . . .

## S. P. Shevyrev. February 11, 1847. (New Style). Naples.

. . . . I will begin by saying that your comparison of me to Princess Volkonskaya with regard to religious exaltation, self-gratification, and turning God's will to one's self personally—as well as your finding signs of Catholicism in me—seemed incorrect to me. As for Princess Volkonskaya,[1] I have not seen her for a long time; I have not peered into her soul—and besides, this is the kind of thing that only God can know the real truth about; as for *Catholicism* I will tell you that I came to Christ by the *Protestant* path rather than the *Catholic*. The reason that I met Christ was an analysis of the soul of man such as others do not make. I was amazed first at the human

wisdom in Him and knowledge of the soul unknown till then—and only then did I worship His divinity. There is no exaltation in me, but rather mathematical calculation. I simply add the figures themselves. Nothing that I think is based on theories either, because I don't read anything except my own internal book and various kinds of statistical documents about Russia. . . .

## S. T. Aksakov. March 6, 1847. (New Style). Naples.

Thank you, my good and noble friend, for your reproaches; though I sneezed from them, I sneezed in health. Also thank good D. N. Sverbeev[1] and tell him that I always value the observations of an intelligent man when they are articulated frankly. . . . Also thank his dear wife for her short letter. Tell them that many of their words have been taken into consideration and made me examine myself more severely an extra time. We are so strangely constituted that we don't see anything in ourselves until others lead us onto it. I will note only that they did not take into consideration one circumstance which would point a certain thing out to them in a different aspect, to be specific: a man who seeks with such greed to hear everything about himself, catches up all judgments and is able to value the observations of intelligent people even when they are harsh and severe—such a man cannot be blinding himself fully and absolutely. And, my friend, I will make a small reproach to you. Don't get angry; the agreement was to accept reproaches from each other mutually without getting angry. Haven't you relied on your intellect and the infallibility of its deductions too much? Making *observations* is another thing, every intelligent person and even, simply, every person has a right to do that. But draw a *conclusion* about a whole man from these observations—this is already a certain kind of self-opinionation. This means to assert that one's intellect has risen to a height from which it can survey a subject *from all sides*. Well, what if I relate the following story to you? A cook volunteered to treat to a good and even extraordinary dinner some people who (although they had eaten rather tasty dinners) had not been in a kitchen themselves. The cook himself volunteered; no one ordered the dinner from him. Only he did say in advance that his dinner would be prepared in a new way, and therefore it would demand more time. What should those who were promised this treat have done? They should have kept silent and waited patiently. No, they started shouting, "Bring on the dinner!" The cook says, "That is physically im-

possible, because my dinner is prepared in a completely different way than other dinners; for this it is necessary to raise a clamor and fuss in the kitchen such as you cannot even imagine." The answer to him: "You lie, brother!" The cook sees that there's nothing to be done; he finally decided to conduct the guests themselves into the kitchen, trying, in so far as possible, to arrange the saucepans and all the kitchen gear in such a way that one could draw at least some kind of conclusion about the dinner. The guests saw a multitude of such strange and unusual saucepans and, finally, implements which it was impossible even to imagine could be required for the preparation of a dinner, that their heads started to whirl about. Well, what if there is a little particle of truth in this story? My friend! You see that for the meantime this business is still obscure. . . .

*V. A. Zhukovsky. March 6, 1847. (New Style). Naples.*

. . . . The publication of my book burst forth exactly like a slap in the face—a slap in the face of the public, a slap in the face of my friends, and, finally, a stouter slap in my face. After it I came to my senses exactly as if after some dream, feeling like a guilty schoolboy who did more mischief than he intended. I turned out to be such a Khlestakov[1] in my book that I don't have the courage to peep into it. But nevertheless from this day hence the book will always lie on my table, like a true mirror into which I must peep in order to see all my slovenliness and to sin less in the future. For all that my book is useful. Every copy of it disappeared in one week[2] (although 2,400 were printed). All of the former questions in literature have suddenly been replaced by others, and all the topics of conversations among the intelligent people of our societies have been replaced by other topics. I expect that after my book several intelligent and pertinent works will appear, because there is something in my book which urges a man to intellectual activity. Although it is not itself a fundamental work of our literature, it can engender many fundamental works. But I confess it was more joyful for me to hear the news of your beneficial plan to write letters about my letters. I think that their publication can be the most proper and *necessary* event in Russia, because after my book everything is somehow strained; the opponents as well as the defenders are more or less in an uneasy state, and many are simply nonplussed as to where to turn, being unable to make many apparently contradictory things harmonize— because of the sharpness with which they were expressed. The ap-

pearance of your letters can have a beneficial and conciliatory effect now. But how ashamed I am of myself, how I am ashamed before you, good soul! Ashamed that I was conceited, as if my school education had already ended and I could stand on a level with you. Really, there is something Khlestakovian in me. . . .

### A. O. Smirnova. April 20, 1847. (New Style). Naples.

. . . . Address the answer to this letter to Frankfurt in care of Zhukovsky. I am departing from here the first part of May. I am spending the summer at the waters, July and August in Ostend for bathing in the sea, and from there to Italy for the autumn in order to leave from there to Jerusalem. And at the sepulcher of the Lord I will be fortified in spirit and body—and could it be otherwise? God is merciful. Wasn't it He Himself who instilled in me the aspiration to work and serve Him? Who else besides Him can instill this aspiration in us? Or shouldn't I do anything to glorify His name, when every creature glorifies Him and when even those who don't have the power of speech perceive His power. I am blamed for starting to speak about God, accused of having no right to this since I am infected with egotism and pride unheard of until now. What is to be done if I feel like speaking of God even if I am possessed by these vices? What is to be done if there comes a time when involuntarily one feels like speaking of God? How can one be silent when even the stones are ready to cry out about God? No, the wits will not upset me by saying I am unworthy, that it is not my business, that I have no right; to the last man every one of us has this right, we should all teach each other and instruct each other as Christ and the Apostles command. . . .

### S. P. Shevyrev. April 27, 1847. (New Style). Naples.

. . . . A word about my renunciation of art.[1] I cannot understand how this absurd thought about my renunciation of my talent and art settled in your head when from my own book one could, it seems, see (if only a few) what sufferings I had to endure because of my love of art, desiring to coerce and force myself to write and create when I did not have the strength, when from my foreword to the second edition of *Dead Souls* one can see how I am occupied with the same thought and how I thirst to collect the information

which I need for my work. What can be done if the soul has become
the subject of my art; am I guilty of this? What can be done if I have
been forced by many special circumstances of my life to view art
more severely? Who is guilty here? He is guilty without whose will
not one event takes place.

The publication of my book, in spite of all its monstrousness,
is a step which is extremely important for me. My book has the quality of a test stone; believe me, one can test the man of today with it. . . .
Believe me, a Russian man cannot be forced to start talking until
you make him angry. He will just keep on lying on his side and de-
manding that the author treat him to something which "reconciles
one to life" (as is said). A bagatelle! As if you could *invent* something
which reconciles one to life. Believe me, no matter what kind of work
of creative literature you put out, it will have no influence now if it
does not contain just those questions around which present-day
society turns, and if the people whom we need now in the present
time are not presented in it. If this is not done, it will be killed off by
the first novel that appears from Dumas'[2] factory. . . .

## N. Ya. Prokopovich. June 20, 1847. (New Style). Frankfurt.

. . . . The other day I read Belinsky's criticism in the second
number of *The Contemporary*. It seems he thought the entire book[1]
was written against him personally and read in it a formal attack on
all who share his ideas. That is false; in my book, as you see, there
is an attack on everyone and everything that goes to extremes. He
probably took personally the goat[2] which was directed to the journalists in general. This irritation made me very sorrowful—not because of the cruelty of the words (which I supposedly cannot bear);
you know that I can hear out the harshest words. But because, no
matter what else, during the course of ten years this man talked
about me sympathetically.[3] In spite of excesses and enthusiasms
this man nevertheless pointed out correctly many features of my
works which others who considered themselves on a higher level of
understanding than him did not notice. And I would be paying the
man with ingratitude, when I know how to render justice even to
those who search out and exhibit only my shortcomings! On the contrary, in that case I simply deceived myself; I considered Belinsky
above that, less capable of such a nearsighted view and trivial conclusions. I don't know why it is so painful to bear the reproach of ingratitude, but for me this reproach was the most painful of all the

reproaches, because in reality my soul is grateful, and I love to show gratitude because I feel a personal pleasure in this. Please have a talk with Belinsky and write me what mood he is in now with regard to me. If bile is seething in him, let him pour it out against me in *The Contemporary* in whatever expressions he thinks best, but let him not harbor it against me in his heart. If on the other hand his displeasure has waned, give him the little letter (which you can read too) enclosed with this.

From everything I see that I will have to make a few explanations about my book, because not only Belinsky but even those people who could know me much better as regards my own person are drawing such strange conclusions that one is simply astounded. Apparently, there is incomparably more obscurity and vagueness in me than I see myself. One more request. Please find out what other Gogol, supposedly my relative, has appeared.[4] So far as I can remember I didn't have a single relative Gogol except my sisters who, firstly, are female and, secondly, don't venture into literature. My father had two cousins who were priests, but they were simply Yanovskys without the addition of Gogol, which stayed only with my father. If the Gogol who has appeared is one of the sons of the priest Yanovsky (of whom to this time, however, I have seen none with my own eyes), then he might really be my second cousin, but I don't understand why he should kidnap the name Gogol! I don't say this because I stand up so for the family name Gogol, but because, really, some dirty tricks could result from this—imbroglios with the booksellers, frauds and forgeries in the book business. Therefore, in order to avoid any printed publicity, I request you to inform the booksellers personally to be careful; and if anyone by the name of Gogol approaches them and starts proposing something or acting in my name, for them to remember that properly speaking I have no relative by the name Gogol and have never laid eyes on him. . . .


*V. G. Belinsky. About June 20, 1847. (New Style). Frankfurt.*

I read your article about me in the second number of *The Contemporary* with sorrow. I was not sorrowful because of the abasement in which you wanted to display me before all, but because the voice of a man who is angered at me can be heard in it. And I did not want to anger even a man who does not love me, all the less you whom I always thought of as a man who loved me. I didn't in the least have in mind distressing you in any passage of my book. I still cannot

understand how it happened that to the last man everyone in Russia has become angry at me. The Easterners,[1] the Westerners, and the neutrals—all were distressed. It is true, I had in mind a little fillip to each of them, considering this necessary—having experienced the necessity of this on my own skin (we all need a little more humility)—but I didn't think that my fillip would come out so crudely-clumsy and so offensive. I thought they would forgive it magnanimously and that the embryo of general reconciliation, and not discord, was in my book. You looked at my book with the eyes of an angry man and therefore took almost everything the wrong way. Ignore all those passages which are still a riddle for many, if not for all, and turn your attention to the passages which are comprehensible to every sensible and reasonable man, and you will see that in much you are mistaken.

It was not for nothing that I implored everyone to read my book several times, foreseeing all these misunderstandings in advance. Believe it—it is not easy to judge a book in which the personal spiritual history of a man is involved, a man who is not like others and, in addition, a secretive man who has long lived within himself and suffered from the inability to express himself. Also it was not easy to decide on the heroic deed of holding myself up to general shame and ridicule by displaying a part of my inner cell, the real sense of which will not soon be felt. Such a deed alone should have made a thinking person fall pensive and without hurrying with a presentation of his own opinion of it, read it in various spiritual frames of mind—when this frame of mind is calmer and more inclined to its own confession, because only at such moments is the soul capable of understanding the soul—and my book is a matter of the soul. Then you wouldn't have made the false conclusions with which your article is filled. For example, how can one draw the conclusion that the critics who have spoken of my merits were inaccurate from my saying that there is much that is accurate in the critics who have spoken of my shortcomings? There can be such logic only in the head of an angered man who continues to look only for that which can anger him, who does not calmly survey the subject from all sides. Well, what if for a long time I was keeping in mind and considering how to start talking about those critics who spoke about my merits and who, apropos of my works, spread many fine thoughts about art. And if I wanted to define impartially the merit of each and those delicate shadings of aesthetic sensibility with which each of them was more or less gifted in his own way? And if I was just waiting for the time when I would be able to talk about that or, more accurately, when it

would be *proper* to talk about that—so that it would not be said afterwards that I was guided by some selfish goal and not by a feeling of impartiality and accuracy? Write the harshest critiques, apply all the words that you know to abase a man, to promote the ridicule of me in the eyes of your readers without sparing the most sensitive strings of, perhaps, a very tender heart—my soul will endure all this, although not without pain and the throes of sorrow. But it is painful for me, very painful (I say this to you truthfully), even when an evil person harbors personal malice against me—not just a good man, and I always considered you a good man. There is an honest statement of my feelings.

N. G.

*A. P. Tolstoy. August 2, 1847. (New Style). Ostend.*

. . . . I am appending the answers to Grubi's[1] questions to this letter. I don't know how to thank him. It seems to me I have gotten a little better. But I still cannot bathe except on the warmest day and when there is absolutely no wind. The wind acts extraordinarily strongly on my skin and I feel a great weakness. A slight wind throws me first into a sweat, then chills. . . .

Answers to Grubi's questions:

1. The reason for the propitious condition of my health may be partly the agitation following the trip. The first day I walked around the city a lot, especially after dinner, which I have not done formerly.
2. Sleep is fairly sound.
3. After dinner there are small belches, about three hours after eating there is a heaviness in my stomach.
4. I don't have a big appetite even after bathing.
5. Rumbling near the heart occurs mostly before dinner in the evening and the next day before breakfast.
6. I also feel crumbs in my mouth much later—after eating.
7. A bitterish taste in the mouth.

After a good dose (double) of Zeidliz tablets my bowels loosened and since then I have . . . . . . , but almost everyday.

I feel pain (especially in the mornings lying in bed) in my upper back, between my two shoulder-blades, a little lower than the first vertebra—as if *inside*.

## V. G. Belinsky. July-August, 1847. (New Style). Ostend.

How shall I begin my answer to your letter?[1] I will begin it with your very own words: "Come to your senses, you are standing on the edge of an abyss!" How far you have wandered from the true road, what an inside-out view of things you have! In what a crude, ignorant sense you have taken my book! How you have interpreted it! Oh, may the holy powers bring peace into your suffering, tormented soul. What reason was there for you to change from the peaceful road you had once chosen! What could be finer than showing the readers the beauties in the works of our writers, elevating their souls and powers to an understanding of everything beautiful, enjoying the excitement of the interest aroused in them, and having a fine effect on their souls in this way? This road would have led you to a reconciliation with life; this road would have made you bless everything in nature. As for political events, society would come to peace of its own accord if there were conciliation in the spirit of those who have influence upon society. But now your lips breathe bile and hate. What reason was there for you with your fervent soul to get into the political whirlpool, into these murky events of contemporaneity—amid which even a firm, prudent, many-sided personality loses itself? How can you not be lost—you with your one-sided intellect which is as flammable as gunpowder and which is flaring up even before you have managed to find out what the truth is? You will burn up like a candle, and you will burn others. Oh, how my heart aches for you at this moment! What if I am guilty, what if my works serve to delude you? But no, no matter how I examine all my former works, I see that they could not mislead you. No matter how one looks at them, there are none of the lies of some contemporary works in them.

What a strange delusion you are in! Your lucid intellect has been befogged. Such a wrong view you have taken of the meaning of my works. My answer is in them. When I wrote them I held in reverence everything which man should hold in reverence. In my work there is no dislike and mockery of authority, not of the basic laws of our country, but of perversion, of deviations, of incorrect interpretations, of bad application of them, of the scabs which have accumulated, of a life inappropriate to it. I have never mocked that which forms the basis of the Russian character and its great powers. There was mockery only of triviality unnatural to its character. My error was in the fact that I revealed little of the Russian man; I did not take the cover off him, bare him to those great fountainheads which are preserved in his soul. But that is not an easy matter. Even

though I have observed Russian man more than you, although a certain gift of clairvoyance could help me, I did not blind myself; my
eyes were clear. I saw that I was still not mature enough to contend
with the most powerful characters, with events which were above
those which had appeared in my works formerly. Everything could
seem exaggerated and forced. This happened in my book which you
attacked so violently. You glanced at it with inflamed eyes, and you
saw everything in it the wrong way. You did not see it for what it was.
I am not going to defend my book. How can I answer any of your
charges when they all miss the point? I myself attacked and attack
it. It was published in quick haste uncharacteristic of my prudent
and cautious personality. But the move was an honorable one. I did
not want to flatter or blandish anyone with it. With it I only wanted to
stop a few hotheads ready to go spinning and get lost in this whirlpool
and disorder in which everything in the world had suddenly found
itself. I fell into extremes, but I say to you that I didn't even notice
it. Even formerly when the temptations of the world still interested
me somewhat I had no selfish aims, and still less now when it is time
to think about death. I had no selfish motive. I did not want to beg
for anything with it. This is not in my nature. There is charm in
poverty. You could have at least recalled that I do not have even a
corner to call my own, and I am trying only to lighten my small
traveling case so that it will be easier to part with the world. You
might have exercised some restraint in branding me with those offensive suspicions which I would not have spirit enough to stain the
worst possible villain with. You should have remembered that. You
use your anger to excuse yourself. But how is it that you decide to
talk about such important matters in a mood of anger and that you
do not see that your angered mind blinds you and excludes tranquility.

How can I defend myself against your attacks when the attacks
are irrelevant? My words to the emperor reminding him of the
sacredness of his calling and his high duties seemed lies to you. You
call them flattery. No, each of us should remember that his calling is
sacred—all the more the emperor. Let him remember what a stern
answer will be demanded from him. But if the calling of each of us
is sacred, then all the more the calling of the one who has received
the difficult and terrible lot of caring for millions. Why remind one
of the sacredness of a calling? Yes, we must even remind each
other about the sacredness of our duties and calling. If one doesn't
do this, man will sink into the muck of material concerns. You say,
incidentally, that I sang a song of praise to our government. Nowhere did I sing. I said only that the government consists of us our-

selves. We attain higher ranks and constitute the government. If then the government is a huge band of thieves, or do you think that none of the Russians know that? Let us examine things more closely, why is this so? Isn't this complexity and monstrous accumulation of laws a result of the fact that we all pull in different directions? One person looks to England, another to Prussia, a third to France. One sets off on one set of principles, another on others. One jabs one project at the Tsar, a second a different one, and a third still another. However many people there are—there are as many various ideas and projects; however many cities—as many various ideas and projects. How could thieves, all possible kinds of roguery, and injustices fail to appear in the midst of such dissension, when everyone sees that obstacles have developed everywhere; everyone thinks only about himself, and about how to provide himself with a cozier little apartment. You say that Russia's salvation lies in European civilization. But what an infinite and unqualified pronouncement that is. You could at least define what one should understand by the term (which everyone repeats senselessly) "European civilization." Here is the Phalangist, and the Red, and what have you; and they are all ready to gobble each other up, and all have such destructive, such ruinous principles, that even in Europe every thinking person is already trembling and asking involuntarily "where is our civilization." And European civilization has become a phantom which so far no one has really seen; and if they attempted to grasp it in their hands it dissolved. And "progress"—it too existed until they started thinking about it; but when they started to grasp it, it too dissolved.

Why did it seem to you that I also sang a song of praise to our vile, as you put it, clergy? Was it my saying that the preacher of the Eastern Church must preach by means of his life and deeds? And why are you possessed by such a spirit of hate? I have known very many bad priests, and I can tell you a multitude of amusing anecdotes about them—perhaps more than you can. But on the other hand I have also met those whose great deeds and holy lives amazed me; and I saw that they are a creation of our Eastern Church and not of the Western one. Therefore, I did not in the least render up a song of praise to the clergy who have disgraced our church, but to the clergy who have evaluated our church.

How strange this all is! How strange my position is—that I have to defend myself against attacks which are all directed neither against me nor against my book! You say that you read my book seemingly a hundred times, while your own words prove that you haven't read it once. Anger has befogged your eyes and has not permitted you to see anything in its true sense. Glints of truth wander

here and there amid a huge heap of sophisms and thoughtless youthful enthusiasms. But what rank ignorance glitters on every page! You separate the church from Christ and Christianity, the same Church, those same pastors who with their martyr-deaths sealed the truth of every word of Christ, who perished by the thousands under the knives and swords of murderers while praying for them, and who finally exhausted the very executioners so that the victors fell to the feet of the vanquished, and the entire world professed this word. And it is these same pastors, these martyr-bishops, who bore the sanctity of the church on their shoulders whom you wish to separate from Christ, calling them false interpreters of Christ. Who—who in your opinion can better and more exactly interpret Christ now? Do you mean to tell me it is the present-day communists and socialists who explain that Christ ordered us to take away property, to rob those who have made a fortune? Come to your senses! You name Voltaire as having done a service to Christianity, and you say that every schoolboy knows it. But when I was still in the gymnasium, even then I was not in ecstasy over Voltaire. Even then I had enough sense to see in Voltaire only a clever wit, far from a deep man. Developed and mature minds could not go into ecstasy over Voltaire; adolescents who hadn't finished their studies were ecstatic over him. Voltaire, in spite of all the brilliant flourishes, remained the same old kind of Frenchman. One may say about him what Pushkin[2] says in general about the Frenchman:

> A Frenchman—is a child,
> Thus he will jokingly
> Destroy a throne,
> And give a law;
> And he's quick as a glance,
> And empty as nonsense,
> And he'll amaze
> And make one laugh.

Never does Christ say to anyone that one must acquire things, but on the contrary—and persistently—commands us to give them away: if someone is stealing your clothes, give up your last shirt; if someone asks to go one mile with you, let him go two.

It is impossible to judge about such matters with the lightweight education of a journalist. One must study the history of the church for this. One must read over again, and with careful reflection, the entire history of humanity in its original sources, and not in light of present-day brochures written by God knows whom. These superficial encyclopedic bits of information do not concentrate one's intelligence; they scatter it in various directions.

What am I to answer you to the biting remark that the Russian peasant is supposedly not inclined to religion, and that when he talks about God, he scratches himself below his back with the other hand, a remark which you utter with such self-confidence—as if you had spent your entire life in the society of the Russian peasant. What is there to say to this when the thousands of churches and monasteries which cover the Russian land speak so eloquently. They are built not with the gifts of the rich, but with the donations of the poor, those very people who you say talk about God with disrespect, and who share their last kopek with the poor and God, who bear bitter privation about which each of us knows, in order to have the opportunity of giving earnest alms to God. No, Vissarion Grigorevich, it is impossible for one who has lived his whole life in Petersburg to judge about the Russian people, one who has busied himself with the light magazine articles and novels of those French novelists who are so prejudiced that they don't want to see that truth comes out of the Gospels and who do not notice what an ugly and trashy way they use to depict life. Now, allow me to say that I have more right than you to start talking about the Russian people. All my works, at least according to unanimous conviction, show a knowledge of the Russian character; they reveal a man who has been observant with the people and, therefore, already has a gift of understanding their life—about which much has been said—which you yourself confirmed in your critical articles. And what will you offer as proof of your knowledge of human nature and the Russian people; what have you produced where this knowledge can be seen? This subject is a large one, and I could write books about it. You yourself should be ashamed of the coarse interpretation that you placed on my advice to the landowner. No matter how this advice was chopped up by the censors, still there is no protest against literacy in it—but perhaps only a protest against the corruption of the Russian people by reading and writing instead of it being given to us to direct man toward the higher world.[3] Your comments about the landowner generally smell of Fonvizin's times. Since then very, very much has changed in Russia; and now much that is new has appeared. What is more advantageous for the peasants—the rule of one landowner who is pretty well-educated now, who has been schooled in the university and who somehow evidently must be aware of many things—or being under the government of a bunch of civil servants who are less educated, who are selfish and worry only about how to make a fortune? And there are many subjects about which each of us should think ahead of time, before discussing emancipation with the zeal of an unrestrained knight and youth—so that the emancipation would not be worse than slavery.

Somehow we Russians generally tend to be concerned more about the change of names and titles. Aren't you ashamed to see our diminutive names[4] (which we occasionally give to our comrades too) as a debasement of humanity and sign of barbarism? That's the kind of childish conclusion to which an incorrect view of the main subject leads. . . .

I was also amazed by the brave presumption with which you say: "I know our society and its spirit" and you vouch for it. But how can you vouch for this chameleon which is changing every minute? With what facts can you confirm that you know the society? Where are your means to do this? Is there any place in your writings where you have shown that you are a deep sage of the soul of man? Have you passed through the experience of life? Living almost without contact with people and society, leading the quiet life of a journal contributor constantly occupied with feuilletons, how can you have an understanding of this vast monster which with its unexpected moves ensnares us in that trap into which all young writers fall, writers who discourse on the entire world and all humanity when we have enough troubles around ourselves. First of all one must take care of these things, then society will move along all right by itself. But if we ignore the duties to people who are close to us and chase after society, then we will lose both the former and the latter in exactly the same way. Lately, I have met a great many fine people who are utterly confused. Some think that the world can be corrected by reorganizations and reforms, by turning in one or another direction; others think that by means of some special, rather mediocre kind of literature (which you call *belles-lettres*), it is possible to have an effect on the education of society. But neither disorders nor hotheads can lead the well-being of society to a better condition. No constitutions can correct discontent within. . . . Society forms and molds itself—of its own accord; society is made up of individuals. It is necessary for each individual to fulfill his duty. Man must remember that he is not at all a material brute, but an elevated citizen of an elevated heavenly community. Until he begins to live at least a little bit the life of a citizen of heaven, the earthy community will not come into order.

You say that Russia has prayed long and in vain. No, Russia has not prayed in vain. When it prayed, it was saved. It prayed in 1612 and was saved from the Poles; it prayed in 1812 and was saved from the French.—Or do you call it prayer when one out of a hundred prays, and all the rest go on a spree like mad from morning till night at all kinds of shows and spectacles, mortgaging the last of their

property to enjoy all the comforts with which this dunderheaded European civilization has endowed us?

No, let us leave such doubtful propositions aside and look at ourselves honestly. Let us attempt not to bury our talent in the ground. Let us exercise our trade according to our conscience. Then all will be well, and the condition of society will be corrected of its own accord. The sovereign means a great deal in this. He has been given a duty which is important and much higher than all others. In our country all people follow the example of the sovereign. All he has to do is rule well without distorting anything, and everything will go along by itself. Who knows, perhaps he will get the idea of living his free time modestly, in seclusion, far from the corrupting court, from this entire mess. And of its own accord everything will turn out to be simple. They will want to abandon this insane life. The landowners will disperse to their estates and start getting to work. The civil servants will see that it isn't necessary to live richly and will stop stealing. And the ambitious man, seeing that the important jobs are rewarded neither with money nor rich salaries, will leave the civil service. Leave this world of those who have become insolent, which is half-dead, for which neither you nor I were born. Allow me to remind you of your former works and writings. Allow me also to remind you of your former path. The man of literature exists for something else. He ought to serve art, which introduces a higher reconciliatory truth into the soul of the world—not hostility; love for man—not bitterness and hate. Again take up the calling from which you have wandered with the thoughtlessness of a youth. Begin your study from the beginning again. Take up those poets and sages who educate your soul. You yourself confessed that the chores of a journalist wither the soul and that you are finally aware of emptiness in yourself. It could not be otherwise. Remember that you studied haphazardly, that you did not even finish the university. Compensate for this by reading the great works and not present-day brochures written by inflamed minds which lead one astray from the true view...

You took my words about literacy in a narrow, literal sense. These words were spoken to a landowner whose serfs are tillers of the soil. Why it was even amusing to me when you understood my words to mean I was attacking literacy. Just as if that were the question now when this question was already decided by our fathers long ago. Our fathers and grandfathers, even the illiterate ones, decided that literacy was necessary. That is not the point. The idea which runs through my entire book is this: how can we enlighten the literate first (rather than the illiterate), how first of all to enlighten

those who have close contact with the common people (rather than the common people themselves), all these minor civil servants and officials who are all literate and who are nevertheless guilty of many abuses. Believe this—it is more necessary to publish for these gentlemen the books which you think are useful for the common people. The common people are less spoiled than all this literate population. But for these gentlemen it is necessary to publish books which could reveal to them the secret of how to treat the common people and subordinates who are entrusted to them—not in the general sense with which a precept is repeated: don't steal, observe the truth, or remember that your subordinates are people just like you, etc., but books which could reveal to him specifically how not to steal and precisely how to observe the truth.

I couldn't answer your letter right away. My soul has been exhausted; everything in me has been shaken; I can say that even before I received your letter there were no sensitive strings left which had not been dealt blows. I read your letter almost without feeling, but nonetheless I did not have the strength to answer it. And what is there for me to answer. God knows, perhaps there is some truth in your words. I will tell you only that I have received about fifty different letters about my book; not one of them resembles another, there are not two people whose opinions about one and the same subject are in agreement; what one refutes another asserts is correct. And besides that, there are equally noble and intelligent people on every side. So far I have seen only one thing as an indisputable truth —the fact that I do not know Russia at all, that much has changed since I was there, and that now I have to learn almost everything that is there anew. And from all this I have drawn the conclusion for myself that I should not publish anything—not only not *living images*,[5] but not even two lines of any writing whatever—until such time as I go to Russia and see a great deal with my own eyes and feel it with my own hands. I see that those who have reproached me with ignorance of many things and not taking into consideration many aspects have revealed to me their own ignorance of much, their own failure to consider many aspects. Not all the cries have been heard, not all the sufferings have been weighed. It even seems to me that some of us don't understand the *present* time when the spirit of *building what is more complete,* is so clearly manifested, than ever before: however that may be, everything is coming out into the open now, everything asks that it too be taken into consideration; the old and the new are going out to battle, and no sooner do they flow over and fall into excess on one side than in rebuff to that they pour over on the other side too. The coming age is the age of reasonable aware-

ness; it weighs everything without passion, taking all sides into con-sideration—without which it is impossible to discover the reasonable middle road of things. It orders us to scan things with the many-sided glance of an old man, not to show the zealous nimbleness of a knight of past times; we are children in the presence of this age. Believe me, both you and I are guilty before it in equal degrees. Both you and I have gone over into excess. At least I admit this, but do you admit it? Exactly as I lost sight of *contemporary* affairs and a multitude of things which should have been considered, exactly in the same man-ner you too lost sight; as I *concentrated* within myself too much, you *scattered your energies* too widely outside yourself. As I need to learn much that you know and I do not know, so you too need to learn at least part of what I know and which you wrongfully disdain.

But for the meantime take care of your health above all. For-get contemporary questions for a while. Afterwards you will return to them with more freshness, therefore with more usefulness to your-self as well as to them.

With all my heart I wish you spiritual tranquility, the first blessing without which it is impossible to work and act reasonably in any field of endeavor.

N. Gogol

## *P. V. Annenkov. September 7, 1847. (New Style). Ostend.*

. . . . In your letter you mention that Herzen[1] is in Paris. I have heard many good things about him. People of *all parties* speak of him as a most noble man. At the present time this is the best repu-tation. When I am in Moscow I will make his acquaintance without fail, but in the meantime inform me what he is doing, what interests him most, what the subject of his observations is. Inform me whether Belinsky is married or not; someone told me that he got married. Also draw a portrait of young Turgenev[2] so that I get a conception of him as a man; I know him a little as a writer: so far as I can judge by what I have read he has *remarkable* talent and promises great activity in the future . . . .

## *M. A. Konstantinovsky.[1] September 24, 1847. (New Style). Ostend.*

May God reward you for your kind lines! Much in them came at just the right moment for my soul; I agreed with much even be-

fore your letter came. For example, about not justifying oneself before the world. In fact, God is going to judge us, not the world. I don't
know whether I will cast off the title of a literary man, because I
don't know whether that is God's will; but in any case my reason
tells me not to publish anything for a long time, until I have matured
more myself *internally* and *spiritually*. But for now I am making
a trip to Jerusalem; I will pray at the sepulcher of our Lord insofar
as I have strength to pray. Pray for me, kind soul, that I might have
the strength to pray warmly and strongly. Ask God to tell my heart
everything that I need—in the same place where the footsteps of His
only begotten Son passed. From the day of this my worship I would
like to carry the image of Christ everywhere in my heart, keeping it
before my mind's eye constantly. I confess to you that I am still confident that one can carry Christ's law with himself anywhere, even
inside the walls of a jail; and it is possible to fulfill His command-
ments in every calling and social class. One can also fulfill it in the
calling of a writer. If a writer has been given talent, then no doubt
it is not in vain and not for the purpose of turning it into evil. If a
painter has a predilection for painting, surely God and no one else is
the cause of this predilection. The painter was free to draw seductive
scenes of debauched amusements and human abasement instead of depicting elevated subjects with his brush, why can't a writer also, in an
interesting story, depict living models of people better than other
writers depicted—present them in a lifelike way just as the painter
does? Examples are more forceful than discussions; but for this the
writer has first to make himself good and to some extent please God
with his life. I would not even think about being a writer if there were
not such a universal inclination for reading all kinds of novels and
stories now, for the most part seductive and immoral ones which are
read simply because they are written captivatingly and not without
talent. And I, having talent, being capable of depicting people and
nature in a lifelike way (on the assurance of those who read my initial stories), can it be that I am not obliged to depict with equal cap-
tivation good, believing people who live in God's law. That is the
reason (I will say it frankly) for my writing—and not money and not
fame. But . . . now I am putting off everything until the right time and
telling you that I will not publish anything for a long time, and I will
try with all my powers to discover God's will, how I should act in this
matter. If I knew that in some other career I could act better than in
this one for the salvation of my soul and accomplishment of everything that I should accomplish, I would shift to that career. If I
knew that I could get away from the world in a monastery, I would
go to a monastery. But the same world surrounds us in a monastery

too; the same temptations are around us, it is necessary to struggle and fight with our enemy just as much. In a word, there is not a career or place in the world in which we can get away from the world, and that is why for the time being I have planned the following for myself: now, right from the day of the receipt of your letter, I plan to double my daily prayers, to devote more time to reading books of spiritual content; I will again reread Chrysostom, Efrem Siryanin, and everything that you advise to me, and then—whatever God wills. After reading of this kind and alloting my time in this manner, it would be impossible for my heart not to be in better harmony and not to tell me more clearly what my road is. And I ask you, since you have already begun your prayers for me and already know something of my soul (oh, how I would like to open my entire soul to you, to be with you in Rzhev, to confess, and receive the sacrament of the body and blood of Christ offered by your hand!), I ask you to pray for me meanwhile, especially during my journey to Jerusalem. I will leave for there around Easter. . . .

## V. A. Zhukovsky. January 10, 1848/December 29, 1847. Naples.

I am guilty before you, my soul! Every day I intend to write —and an incomprehensible *reluctance* holds me back. Naples, Vesuvius, and the sea are before me again! The days run by busily; time flies so that one doesn't know where to get an extra hour. I am studying like a schoolboy all that which I neglected to learn in school. But what should I tell about this! I would like to talk a little about that which I can talk of only with you: about our dear *art*, for which I live and for which I am now studying like a schoolboy. Since my journey to Jerusalem stands before me now, I want to confess to you, if not to you then to whom else? To be sure, literature has occupied almost my entire life, and my main sins are here. Here it has been almost twenty years already since the time when I, a youth who was barely entering into the world, came to you for the first time, to one who had already completed half the road in this career. That was in Shepelev Palace. That room is no longer there. But I can see it all now, to the smallest furnishing and knickknack. You gave me your hand, and you were so full of desire to aid a future associate! How benevolently loving your look was! What brought us, unequal in age, together? Art. We felt a kinship much stronger than ordinary kinship. Why? Because we both felt that art is a sacred thing.

It is not my business to decide to what degree I am a poet; I only know that before understanding the meaning and purpose of art I felt with all the sensitivity of my soul that it should be sacred. And almost from the time of this first meeting of ours it already became what is *first* and *central* in my life, and everything else *secondary*. It seemed to me that I should no longer tie myself to earth with any other bonds—neither with family life nor with a citizen's life of civil service, and that the career of letters is also service. I did not yet realize (but could I realize it then) what the subject for my pen should be, but already creative strength was stirring and the actual circumstances of my life stumbled onto subjects. Everything happened as if independently of my own free will. For example, I never thought that I would have to be a satirical writer and make my readers laugh. It is true when I was still in school I felt an inclination to gaiety from time to time, and I bored my comrades with inappropriate jokes. But these were temporary attacks; in general I was of a more melancholy character, and disposed to meditation. Subsequently illness and the spleen were combined with this. And the same illness and spleen were the reason for the gaiety which appeared in my first works: in order to amuse myself I invented heroes, without further aim or plan, and put them in amusing situations—there is the origin of my tales! The passion to observe man which I nourished from childhood lent a certain naturalness to them; people even started calling them true portraits from nature. One more circumstance: in the beginning my laughter was goodhearted; I never thought of ridiculing anything for some purpose, and when I heard that people were offended and that whole levels and classes of society were even angry at me, I was surprised to such an extent that I finally fell thoughtful. "If the power of laughter is so great that it is feared, then it should not be wasted purposelessly." I decided to gather everything bad that I knew of and to ridicule it all at once—that is the origin of *The Inspector General.* That was the first of my works conceived with the goal of producing a good influence on society, which, however, did not succeed: people started seeing in the comedy a desire to ridicule the established order of things and governmental forms, while I had the intention of ridiculing only the willful departure of a few people from the formal and established order. The performance of *The Inspector General* produced a painful impression on me. I was angry both with the spectators, who didn't understand me, and with myself for being to blame that they didn't understand me. I wanted to run away from everything. My soul demanded solitude and a very severe consideration of my work. For a long time I had been occupied by the thought of a *large work* in which all that is good and bad in Russian man would

be presented and the *character* of our Russian nature would be revealed before us more visibly. I saw and embraced many parts separately, but I simply could not clarify and define the plan of the whole firmly enough that I could take it up and begin to write. At every step I felt that I was lacking in many things, that I did not know how to put together and unravel events, and that I had to study the structure of the large works of the great masters. I took them up, beginning with our dear Homer. Already it seemed to me that I was beginning to understand something, and even to acquire some of their devices and flourishes—but the ability to create still did not return. My head ached from the strain. With great efforts I somehow managed to publish the first part of *Dead Souls,* as if to see in it how far I still was from that to which I aspired. After this a nonbeneficial condition was again upon me. My pen got gnawed to pieces, my nerves and powers got irritated—and nothing came out. I thought that already the ability to write had simply been taken away from me. And suddenly illnesses and painful mental conditions, tearing me away from everything at one stroke and even from the very thought of art, turned me to that which I had a desire for even before I became a writer: to inner observation of man and of the *human soul.* Oh, how much more deeply this knowledge opens up before you when you begin the task with your own soul! On this path you involuntarily meet *more closely* with the One who (alone among all who have so far existed on earth) showed in Himself a complete knowledge of the human soul, and even if His divinity has been denied by the world, it has absolutely no power to deny the latter quality except if it becomes not just *blind,* but simply *stupid.* By this sharp turn, which did not happen of my own will, I was led to peer more deeply into the soul in general and discover that its more elevated degrees and forms do exist. From that time the ability to create began to awaken; living images begin to emerge clearly from the darkness; I feel that the work will move ahead, that even the language will be correct and sonorous, and that the style will become more solid. And perhaps a future district teacher of literature will read a page of my future prose to his pupils immediately after yours, saying: "Both writers wrote correctly, even though they do not resemble each other." The issuing of the book *Correspondence with Friends* which (because of the joy that my pen had gotten in a writing mood) I so hurried, not thinking that before being of any use I might confuse many people with it, was of use to me myself. In this book I saw where and in what respect I had crossed over into that excess into which nearly every person who is going forward falls during the period of our present transitional state of society. In spite of the prejudice in the criticisms

of the book and their differing ideas, in sum one could hear a common voice pointing out to me my place and the boundaries over which I, as a writer, should not trespass. In fact, it is not my business to teach by means of a sermon. Even without that art is teaching. My business is to speak by means of *living images,* not by means of cogitations. I must exhibit the face of *life,* not write tracts about life. The truth is obvious. But the question is: could I become a worthy producer of art without this long detour? Could I exhibit life in its depth so that it would become a teaching? How could I depict people if I didn't first find out what *the human soul* is? If a writer is gifted with the creative power of creating his own images, let him first educate himself as a man and citizen of his land—and only then take up the pen! Otherwise everything will be irrelevant. What is the use of attacking a shameful and depraved man, of putting him on exhibition for all, if the ideal of the fine man who is his opposite is not clear in your own self. How can you exhibit human shortcomings and demerits if you haven't asked yourself the question—"Just what is merit in a man?" And if you haven't given yourself a somewhat satisfactory answer. How can one ridicule exceptions if you still haven't learned clearly the rules out of which one puts exceptions on exhibit. This would mean destroying the old house before having an opportunity to build a new one in its place. But art is not destruction. The seeds of creation, not destruction, hide in art. This has always been perceived, even in those times when everything was ignorance. Cities were built under the sounds of Orpheus' lyre. In spite of society's concept of art which has still not been purified, everyone nevertheless says: "Art is reconciliation with life." That is true. A true creation of art has something in it which is becalming and conciliating. During the reading the soul is filled with a well-formed harmony, and after the reading it is satisfied: nothing is wanted, nothing is desired, in the heart no emotion of indignation towards one's brother raises up, but rather the balm of all-forgiving love for one's brother flows through it. And in general one does not strive toward *censure* of the actions of another, but toward *contemplation* of oneself. If, however, the creation of the poet does not have this quality in it, it is just one noble, ardent burst, the fruit of a temporary condition in the author. It will remain as a notable manifestation, but it will not be called a creation of art. It serves him right! Art is reconciliation with life!

Art is the establishment of harmony and order in the soul, not confusion and disarrangement. Art should depict the people of our land for us in such a way that each of us would feel that these are *living people,* created and taken from the same body that we have been

taken from. Art should show us all our heroic *national* qualities and attributes, not excluding even those which, not having space to develop freely, haven't been noticed by everyone and evaluated so accurately that every person would feel them in himself and burn with the desire to develop and cherish in himself that which he has abandoned and forgotten. Art should show us all our bad national qualities and attributes in such a way that each of us will search out traces of them in ourself and think first how to cast from our own self everything which obscures the nobility of our nature. Only then and acting in this way will art fulfill its designated purpose and bring order and harmony into society! . . .

If you find this letter not without merit, save it. In the second edition of *Correspondence* it could be given the title *Art is Reconciliation with Life*[1] and put at the front of the book in place of my *Testament* which is to be thrown out.

I keep wanting to ask and I keep forgetting: do you have the Latin supralineal translation of the *Odyssey* which was printed together with the original not long ago in Paris? An extremely beautiful edition. All of Homer in one volume, in a large octavo. . . .

*M. A. Konstantinovsky. January 12, 1848. (New Style). Naples.*

. . . . To be sure with my precipitant book[1] (which you read) I showed some gigantic designs on something like universal teaching. But this book is a product of my transitional spiritual state, a temporary state barely freed from disease. Saddened by several unpleasant events happening in our country and by the un-Christian tendency of contemporary literature, I precipitantly rushed ahead with this injudicious book and without realizing it I strayed where it is unseemly for me to be. And the devil, who was right on the spot, puffed up to monstrous overstatement even that which was not intended to teach—which always happens to those who rely a bit on their own powers and on their *significance* in God's eyes. The point is that this book is not my kind of book. But what had long and more continually absorbed me was to depict in a large work what good and evil there is in our Russian land, after which Russian readers would know their land better, because among us many people, even civil servants and officials, fall into great errors on account of lack of knowledge of the Russian man's basic qualities and the national spirit of our land. I have always had the facility for noting all the characteristics of each man, from small ones to big ones, and, afterwards, for depicting

him before the eyes so that, on the assurance of my readers, the man I had depicted remained in the head like a nail, and his image seemed so lifelike that it was difficult to forget it. I think that if I, with my ability to depict characters in a lifelike manner, find out a little better about many things in Russia and what goes on inside her, I will lead the reader to greater knowledge of the Russian man. And if, by the grace of God, I myself become more imbued with the knowledge of man's duty on earth and knowledge of truth, then because of this imperceptibly in my work too, good Russian characters and qualities of people will acquire attractiveness and bad ones such unattractiveness that the reader won't love them even in himself, if he discovers them. That is what I thought, and therefore I studied everything that relates to Russia, studied the souls of people, and the soul of man in general, beginning with my own. I still didn't know myself how I would manage this and how I would succeed, but I already believed that this would be possible for me when I became better myself. That is what I believe my writing to be. And so, is this teaching? I only wanted to present to the writer the most remarkable Russian subjects in such an aspect that he himself would see and decide what he needs to take and would, so to speak, teach himself. I didn't even want to introduce moralizing; it seemed to me (if I myself became better) that the reader himself would conclude all this, imperceptibly, apart from me. There is the confession of my writing career for you. . . . Only now am I amazed at my pride, amazed that God did not strike me and wipe me from the face of the earth. Oh my friend and confessor sent to me by God Himself! I am burning with shame, and I don't know where to hide from the numberless multitude of weaknesses and vices I didn't suspect in myself before. And there is my confession for you—no longer just with regard to my writing. I could fill pages for you in witness of my cowardice, superstition, and fear. It even seems to me that I have absolutely no faith; I acknowledge Christ to be the God-man only because my intellect so orders me, not faith. I was amazed by His infinite wisdom, and with a certain terror I felt it was impossible for an earthly person to have room for it in himself; I was amazed at His deep knowledge of the human soul, feeling that only its Creator Himself could know the soul of man like this. That is all; but I have no faith. I want to believe. And in spite of all this I now dare to go and worship the Holy Sepulchre. . . .

*V. A. Zhukovsky.* *February 28/16, 1848. Jerusalem.*

I am writing you a few short lines, priceless friend. And I, like many others, have been vouchsafed to see the place and land where

the deed of our redemption took place. I arrived here safely, without any difficulties, hardly noticing that I had crossed from Europe into Asia, almost without any hardships, and even without exhaustion. I have already managed to pronounce your name at the grave of the Lord. Oh, God help us, both you and I, to collect all our strength for the production of creations cherished in the depths of our souls for the good of our land, and may He illumine us with the light of the reason of His Holy Gospel. I won't remain here long, hurrying to return to Russia with my old schoolmate Bazili, with whom I arrived here also, and who, being our General Consul in Syria, manages affairs in Jerusalem. So don't worry on my account. If God is not against the desire, we will see each other in Moscow and start living close to each other. If you want to write a few lines about yourself (for which I thirst) before July, inscribe on the packet: To Poltava; if after July—to Moscow in care of Shevyrev at the University. . . .

## V. A. Zhukovsky. June 15, 1848. Poltava.

I received the nice little letter which you sent from Frankfurt to Poltava. And I read the big one printed in *The Muscovite*[1] in Odessa the day after I set foot on the Russian shore. It is very, very much to the point; it pleased many people and refreshed me. Never yet has the duty of the writer been discussed so correctly and so beautifully. Perhaps never before has it been as necessary to discuss this as at the present time. . . . What is it to us whether our words have an influence, whether we are heeded? The point is that we ourselves remained true to the Beautiful to the end of our days, that we were able to love it so as not to be disturbed by anything happening around us and so as to sing it an unceasing song, even at the moment when the earth would be collapsing and everything earthly would be destroyed. To die with singing on the lips—isn't that the irresistible duty of a poet, as a soldier's is to die with his weapon in his hands. . . .

## A. M. Vielgorskaya. October 29, 1848. Moscow.

How are you? How is your health, my most kind Anna Mikhailovna? As for me, I'm just getting over my insomnia which has continued even here in Moscow, and only now is it beginning to let up. Moscow is isolated, peaceful, and propitious for work. I'm still not laboring as I would like; I feel a slight weakness, I still don't have the beneficial disposition of spirit which is necessary for crea-

tion. But my soul senses something, and my heart is filled with the tremulous anticipation of that desired time. Write me a few short lines about your occupations and the state of your spirit. I'm curious to know how your Russian lectures began. For now I am still not sending you the list of books which ought to make up Russian reading in relation to history. There is much I must comprehend and examine beforehand so as to be able to give you one thing after another in order, so that the soup doesn't turn up after the sauce and the dessert before the main course. Write how my adjunct-professor[1] is managing things and in what order he is serving you the dishes. I'm very confident that he will tell you much that is good and necessary, and at the same time confident that there will remain a place for me to insert my speech and add something which he will forget to say. This is not because I am more well read and learned than he, but because every man who is talented at all has his own original sensitivity which belongs specifically to him, in consequence of which he sees a whole side which is not noticed by another. That is why I would very much like for my lectures to you to begin with the second volume of *Dead Souls*. After that my soul could more easily and freely talk about many things. There are many sides of Russian life which to this time still have not been revealed by a single writer. I would like for people of all parties and opinions, after reading my book, to say: "He really knows Russian man. Without hiding a single shortcoming of ours, he felt our merit more deeply than anyone." I would also like to start talking about what my soul has loved to ponder since the days of childhood, that about which vague sounds and hints were scattered already in my very first works. Not everyone noticed them. . . . But that aside. Don't forget to read the history of the Russian Church along with Russian history; without it much in our history is obscure. The entire work of Filaret Rizhsky has now come out—five books.[2] They can be bound in one volume. I think Matvey Yurievich[3] has this book, in which case embrace him firmly for me. About your health, here are instructions for you again: for God's sake don't sit in the same place for more than an hour and a half; don't bend over the table—your chest is weak, you ought to know that. Try by all means to go to bed no later than 11:00. Don't dance at all, especially wild dances; they agitate your blood, but they do not provide the correct movement which the body requires. And besides, dances do not become you at all—your figure is not that graceful and light. You are not pretty. Do you know that for sure? You are pretty only when some noble feeling appears in your face; it's clear the features of your face are arranged so as to express spiritual nobility; as soon as you lose this expression you become homely.

Give up all social calls, even the small ones. You see that society has gotten you nothing; in it you searched for a soul capable of responding to yours, you thought to find a man with whom you wanted to go through life hand in hand, and you found trivia and vulgarity. Give it up altogether. There are nasty things in society which stick to us like burrs no matter how careful we are; something of it has already stuck to you—specifically what I won't say at present. God also save you from any feeble attempts at so-called social amiability. Preserve the simplicity of a child—that is best of all. . . . Don't pass up talks with people from whom you can learn a great deal; don't be disturbed if they have a coarse exterior. Just be attentive to them; know how to question them, and they will start talking with you. Remember that you must become really Russian—in soul and not in name. Apropos: don't forget that you promised me every time that you meet Dal to make him tell you about the life of the serfs in various districts of Russia. It is especially among the serfs that one perceives the originality of our Russian mind. When you happen to see Pletnev don't forget to question him about all the Russian literary people with whom he has had relations. These people were more Russian than people of other classes, and therefore you will certainly learn much which will explain Russian man to you more satisfactorily. . . .

## A. S. Danilevsky. February 25, 1849. Moscow.

. . . . Concerning Volume II of *Dead Souls* I can only say that it is still a long time to print. Besides the fact that the author himself hasn't prepared it for print, it is not the right time to print anything, for I don't think that peoples' minds themselves are in condition to know how to read a calm artistic creation. I see this from the *Odyssey*. If Homer was met indifferently, what is there for me to expect?[1] Besides that ailments give me little opportunity to work. Somehow I have become sick this winter. The severe northern climate is beginning to plague me. . . .

## S. T. Aksakov. March 19, 1849. Moscow.

Dear friend Sergei Timofeevich, two friends are to turn up at your place for dinner today: Peter Mikhailovich Yazykov and I, both sinners and meat-eaters. I make reference to this circumstance for the reason that you will be able to order a hunk of beef added for one extra mug.

All yours N. Gogol

## *A. M. Vielgorskaya.[1] March 30, 1849. Moscow.*

. . . . It is easier to become Russian in language and knowledge of Russia than Russian *in soul*. The words *populism* and *nationalism* are fashionable now, but so far these are just shouts which spin heads and blind the eyes. What does it mean to become Russian in fact? What is the attractiveness of our Russian race which we are now constantly striving to develop, casting aside all that is alien to it, unbefitting and uncharacteristic. What is this? The high merit of the Russian race consists in the fact that more than others it is capable of taking into itself the elevated word of the Gospels which leads to the perfection of man. The seeds of the heavenly sower were scattered everywhere with equal generosity. But some fell close to the public road and were all devoured by birds which swooped down; others fell on stone, germinated, but dried up; a third kind fell among the thorns—they germinated but were quickly smothered by harmful weeds; only the fourth kind which fell on good earth brought forth fruit. This good earth is the receptive Russian nature. Christ's seeds, well-cherished in the heart, gave all that is best in the Russian character. Therefore, in order to become Russian it is necessary to turn to the source, to have recourse to the means without which a Russian will not become Russian in the higher meaning of this word. Perhaps only the Russian is destined to feel the meaning of life more closely. The truth of these words can be witnessed only by one who has penetrated deeply into our history and who comprehends it completely—having thrown off in advance all sapient cogitations, suppositions, ideas, self-assurance, pride, and conviction—as if he had already achieved an understanding of what it is all about, when he had hardly approached it. Yes. A marvelous thing can be noticed in the history of our people. We had debauchery, disorders, rebellions, the dark consequences of ignorance, just as we had dissensions and all kinds of disagreements—perhaps to even a greater extent than anywhere else. They stand out sharply on all the pages of our chronicles. But to make up for that, at the same time the light shines in the chosen ones more brightly than anywhere else. Also perceptible everywhere in the chronicles are the traces of a secret inner life, the detailed story of which they did not transmit to us. One can perceive the possibility of founding a country on the purest Christian laws. Lately, in the dust and rubbish of antiquity people have continually been discovering documents and manuscripts like Sylvester's *Domostroy*[2] where the entire ancient life of Russia is revealed in the most detailed detail—as the ancient world was in the ruins of Pompei. It shows not the political structure of Russia, but

everyday personal family customs and life, illuminated by the light in which it should be illuminated. In the instructions and outlines about how to run one's house, how to act with people, and how to keep order in one's earthly and heavenly household one is struck, apart from the liveliness of such customs in olden times, by the deep experience with life and the completeness with which all duties are considered, how the head of the household should preserve the image of God's goodness in his treatment of everyone. How his wife and the mistress of the house should act with her husband, with the children, with the household affairs, how to educate the children, how to educate the servants, how to manage everything in the house, to sew, clothe, clean, fill the storerooms with supplies, to be able to look after everything—and all this with extraordinary detail, with the terms for the things that were in use then, with the names of the dishes which were prepared and eaten then. You fairly see before your eyes cordial old-times with their satisfaction, hospitality, joyous, intelligent treatment of guests—with an amazing absence of the boring etiquette considered essential by the present age. In a word, we see the journey of Martha and Mary together or, better, we see Martha not grumbling at Mary, but agreeing that she has chosen a good part, not inventing anything better than to remain at Mary's command—i.e., to worry only about the smallest things in the earthly household in order through this to have an opportunity of busying herself with the heavenly household together with Mary.

Lately manuscripts of this type are constantly being discovered. More than anything else these books acquaint one with what is best in the Russian man. . . .

## S. M. Sollogub. May 24, 1849. Moscow.

. . . . I came to Moscow to sit down at *Dead Souls*, the end of which is connected with everything I have and even with the means of my existence. At first the work was going well, I spent part of the winter in fine shape, then my mind again grew torpid; the beneficial mood and the elevated spiritual mellowing during which work is completed with inspiration did not last. And suddenly everything within me grew bitter, my heart grew callous. I fell into vexation, spleen, and almost into malice. There were no people close to my heart whom I did not then insult and offend in an attack of a kind of cold insensitivity of the heart. I acted as only a man in a state of insanity can act—and imagining at the same time that I was acting in-

telligently. But God is merciful. He punished me with a strong nervous disorder which began with the arrival of spring with an illness
which is the most terrifying of all illnesses for me, after which, however, a beneficial mood almost always set in if I bore it submissively
and became humble. Suddenly my melted soul began to ache from
the terrible cruelty of my heart. With terror I saw that nothing but
egoism lay in it, that in spite of the ability to value elevated feelings
I had absolutely none of them in myself; I was becoming worse, my
character was being spoiled, and my every act was an offense to
someone. Now I was terrified for myself as never before. . . . You ask
me what I am going to do with myself—and where I will move. I don't
know myself. Before me there is nothing but a shoreless sea. I feel
only that I have to go somewhere, because the road would be useful
for my nerves—where I don't know. . . .

## V. A. Zhukovsky. Fall 1849. Moscow.

A million kisses and nothing more! The news of the completed
and printed *Odyssey* left me speechless. Chichikov, the beast, has
barely got to the halfway point of his wanderings. Maybe that's because a Russian hero has to be incomparably more shifty with the
Russian people than a Greek one with the Greeks, and maybe it's
because the author of *Dead Souls* has to be much better in the soul
than the beast Chichikov. I will write a letter, and it will be a long one.

## K. I. Markov.[1] December 3, 1849. Moscow.

I am very grateful for your letter. I did not answer the earlier
one because I didn't know your address. As for Volume II of *Dead
Souls*, I did not have in mind precisely a *hero of virtues*.[2] On the
contrary, almost all the characters can be called heroes of shortcomings. The point is simply that the characters are *more significant* than the earlier ones and that the intention of the author here
was to enter more deeply into the meaning of the life we have vulgarized, to do this by revealing more clearly the Russian man not
from some *one side*. We will discuss the other points of your letter
personally; it seems we are neighbors.

## A. O. Smirnova. December 6, 1849. Moscow.

I had just dispatched a letter to you when two hours later yours came. Apparently, there are many scurvy things around you. But how should it be? If they didn't exist we couldn't attain the kingdom of heaven. Man would soon forget that he is here to bear a cross. As for gossip, don't forget that the devil spreads it about, not people, in order to confuse and bring us down from the elevated calm which is essential to us for living the higher life, surely it is the one which man should live. As soon as this long-tailed beasty notices that a man has become cautious and insusceptible to big temptations, he immediately hides his snout and begins to sally forth with *trifles,* knowing very well that even the intrepid lion must finally start to roar when impotent gnats attack him from all sides in a swarm. The lion roars because he is an animal, but if, like a man, he could consider that no one dies from gnats, fleas, and so forth, that with the inception of cold spells all this would vanish, that perhaps these bites were even necessary for letting excess blood, then perhaps he would have the magnanimity to bear all this patiently. I have become absolutely convinced that gossip is woven by the devil, not by man. From idleness and often stupidly a man blurts out a word with no sense, one which he didn't want to say. The word is off on its travels; another person will idly utter another about it, and little by little a tale weaves itself without anyone's knowledge. It is insane even to search for its real author because he cannot be searched out. Don't blame any of your domestics either; you will be unjust. Remember that everything in the world is deception; nothing seems to us what it is in actual fact. In order not to make mistakes about people, it is necessary to see them as Christ orders us to see them. May God help you in this!
. . . .


## V. A. Zhukovsky. December 14, 1849. Moscow.

. . . . The year and a half of my stay in Russia has swept past like a quick instant, and there hasn't been one event that would refresh me, after which, as after a tub of cold water, I would feel that I was acting soberly and really acting. The trip to Jerusalem seems to me the only sober act. My working is lazy. Trying not to let a minute of time get by, I don't leave the table, I don't move the paper away, I don't let the pen out of my hand—but the lines are sculpted sluggishly, and time flies irretrievably. Is forty-two really old-age for

me, or is it that my *Dead Souls* should not come out at this confused
time when society, not yet having managed to become sober, is still
a child, and people have still not reached a condition to read a book
as they should, i.e. properly—and not holding it upside down? Everyone here, both the youth and the oldster, has his ideas so entangled
that he cannot give account to himself. Some in utter ignorance are
finishing chewing up chaws that have already been spit out by the
Europeans. Others are regurgitating their own spew. Rare ones, very,
very rare ones perceive and value what really makes up our *strength*.
One can say that only the Church is still a healthy body among us. The
publication of the *Odyssey* was not for the present time. It was
greeted by people who are already on the way out, who were joyful
for themselves—that they could still feel the immortal beauties of
Homer—and for their grandchildren—that they would have radiant
reading which does not benight the mind. I know people who have
read the *Odyssey* several times in a row with full gratitude and deep
thankfulness to the translator. But, alas, there are few of these! No
time yet has been so poor in readers of good books as the one which
has begun. Shevyrev is writing a review; he will probably say many
good things in it, but no reviews have the power to make the present
generation, which is deceived by political unrest, sit down to read
that which is radiant and becalms the soul. Sometimes it seems to
me that Volume II of *Dead Souls* could serve Russian readers as a
kind of step towards reading Homer. Sometimes I get a desire to read
you something from it, and it seems that this reading would refresh
and urge me on—but . . . When will that be? When will we see each
other? There's all I have strength to say. . . .


*P. A. Pletnev. January 21, 1850. Moscow.*

    I can't understand what's happening to me. I don't know
whether it's from old age, which works torpidly and lazily in us, or
from the enervated state of illness, or from the climate which produces it, but I simply do not manage to do anything. Time flies as I
have never yet recalled. I get up early, I take up the pen in the morning; I don't admit anyone into my room, I put all other matters aside,
even letters to people close to me,—and nevertheless so few lines
come out of me! It seems I have been sitting at work no more than
an hour, I look at the clock—it's already time for dinner. There is not
even any time to walk and stroll about. There's my whole story for
you. The end of the task is still far off, i.e., I have in mind the end of

*Dead Souls.* Almost all of the chapters have been thought out and even sketched, but, precisely, no more than sketched; only two or three have actually been written. I don't even know whether one can create a real artistic work rapidly. Perhaps only God knows this, He who controls everything; both reason and the word are with Him. Though man has words at the ready, he has to search for reason. . . .

## A. M. Vielgorskaya. Spring 1850. Moscow.

It seemed to me essential to write you at least a part of my confession.[1] Undertaking to write it I prayed God only to say just the real truth in it. I wrote, I corrected, I crossed out—I began to write anew, and again I saw that it was necessary to tear up what had been written. Is my confession really necessary to you? Perhaps you will glance coldly at what lies next to my very heart, or else from some other viewpoint; and then everything can appear in a different light, and what was written to clarify the matter can only obscure it. An absolutely sincere confession should belong to God. From this confession I will tell you only one thing: I have suffered much since I parted with you in Petersburg. My entire soul was anguished, and my condition was painful, so painful that I do not know how to tell you. It was even more painful because there was no one for me to explain it to, there was no one from whom to request advice or sympathy. I could not confide it to my closest friend[2] because relations to your family were mixed up in this; and everything that relates to your home is sacred to me. It will be a sin for you if you are going to continue to be angry with me because I surrounded you with dark clouds of misunderstandings. There was something odd about this, and I still cannot explain to you how it happened. I think everything happened because we still did not know each other well enough, and we looked upon much that is *very important* lightly, at least more lightly than we ought to have. You would have got to know me better if we had happened to live somewhere together somewhat longer—not idly, but at work.[3] In fact, why don't you go live on your estate near Moscow? You haven't seen your serfs for more than twenty years already. As if that were a trifle: they feed us (but call us the ones who feed them), and we don't even have time to glance at them in twenty years! I would come to your place too. We could all undertake to manage the estate together and worry about them—and not about ourselves. Really, it would be good for the health and merrier than the usual senseless life at summer villas. And if in addition each of

us prayed more firmly to God for Him to help us do our duty, after a while we would all certainly get into the relations to each other in which we ought to be. Then it would become clear and apparent to both you and me *what* I ought to be in relation to you. And I *must* be something in relation to you; it is not in vain that God brings people together in such a strange way. Perhaps in relation to you I should be nothing more than a faithful dog obliged to protect the property of his master in some corner. But don't be angry; you see that although our relations have been made resentful for a time by some fleeting resentment, nevertheless, they are not such as you should regard me as an alien person from whom you must hide even what your offended heart would like to utter at a moment of distress. May God protect you. Farewell. Embrace all of your family firmly.

All yours to the grave,

N. Gogol.

*Official Letter to A. Perovsky or others.[1] July 10-18, 1850. Vasilevka.*

. . . . However, the subject of my work is not of little import. In the remaining parts of *Dead Souls,* on which I am working now, Russian man no longer steps forward with the trivial features of his character, not with banalities and oddities, but with all the depth of his nature and the rich variety of the inner powers contained within him. If only God will produce everything as my soul desires perhaps I will serve a service to my land, one no smaller than that which all noble and honorable people in other callings serve it. Much which has been forgotten, ignored, and cast aside by us ought to be depicted brightly in living, speaking examples capable of acting strongly; man in general and the Russian in particular ought to be reminded about much that is essential and central. Therefore it seems to me that I have a certain right to take care of myself and be concerned about my self-preservation. . . . Of course, I could have funds if I decided to publish my work in an unprepared and incomplete form— but I will never decide on that. There is, praise God, a conscience which would not allow me that even in the event that I found myself at the last extremity. Every man ought to fulfill his calling on earth honorably and conscientiously. Feeling (in proportion as the years are added) that for every word said *here* I will give an answer *there,* I have to submit my works to incomparably more consideration and circumspection than does a young writer who is not experienced in

life. It was possible for me to write, meditate, and publish faster before when the task only touched on what deserved ridicule in the Russian man, only what is banal, insignificant, and constitutes a temporary disease and excrescences on the body—not the body itself; but now when the task is getting to the point of displaying in the open all that is healthy and strong in our nature, and displaying it so that even those who do not acknowledge this will see and admit it, and those who have neglected the development of the great powers given to the Russian will be ashamed—one cannot rush with such a task. Such work is not consummated quickly. For this one must mature in both intellect and soul and be at a distance from everything which disturbs the elevated disposition of the spirit, many secret prayers, powerful inner tears are needed . . . in a word much is needed which I cannot explain and which it is not proper for me to explain.

It seems to me that if for three years I were provided with the opportunity of making three summer trips to the inside of Russia and three winter sojourns outside of her in the salubrious climate of the south which has always worked refreshingly on my powers and creative ability—such a boon would not be in vain. In addition to the large work to which I have made reference, then I could finish a book which is essential and necessary among us, one the thought of which has interested me for a long time and for which (if only God grants me the strength to fulfill it as I wish) many fathers of families will thank me.[2] We need a living, not a dead depiction of Russia, her basic, speaking geography outlined in a powerful, living style which would put the Russian face to face with Russia—already during the first part of his life when he is put under control of foreign tutors, but when all his capabilities are fresher than at any time thereafter, and his imagination is keen and retains forever whatever strikes him.

Such a book (it has always seemed to me) could be compiled only by a writer who knows how to catch accurately and depict powerfully and graphically the features and characteristics of the people, and how to set up and depict every *locale* with all its colors in such a life-like manner that it would always remain in the eyes, who, finally, would have the ability to concentrate the work into one interfused whole so that the entire land from border to border with all the peculiarities of its locales, the characteristics of the mountain ranges and lowlands would be chiseled into the memory as if alive—even into that of an immature boy, and it would be obvious to him even in childhood what specifically is characteristic and proper for each corner of Russia, and later when he arrived at a mature age he would not get it into his head (trusting foreign industrialists who are concerned about their own temporary profit) to institute factories and manu-

factures which are not characteristic of it. And so that in exactly this way as a child he would see in their true form the qualities and characteristics of the Russian people with all the variety of attributes by which its branches and tribes are distinguished, so that as a child he would be able to see exactly what each of these tribes is capable of as a result of the arms and powers which have been given to it and later, when at a mature age, God made him a statesman, would turn his attention to the attributes of each of them, would respect the customs, engendered by the laws of the locale itself, and would not demand universal fulfillment of what is good in one corner and bad in another.

This book has long been the subject of my meditations. It is maturing along with my present work, and perhaps it will be ready at the same time. For its success I rely not so much on my powers as on love of Russia which, praise God, is constantly increasing within me, on the succor of all the people who truly know it, to whom its future fate and the education of their own children are dear—but most of all on God's mercy and help without which nothing is completed and the undertaking of the cleverest person perishes at the outset.

*A. P. Tolstoy. August 20, 1850. Vasilevka.*

. . . . If Odessa's climate were even a little like that of Naples, of course I wouldn't even think about a departure for abroad. But salubrious air and warmth which is not from a stove are essential to my mind and body, especially when I am working. And I must work hard this whole winter to prepare Volume II for print, bringing it to an end once and for all. For the time being, praise God, the task is not going badly. Before my departure from Moscow when I read to a few people who, like you, were familiar with the first two chapters, it turned out that the latest ones are stronger than the first and that the further it goes, the more deeply *life* is revealed.[1] It must be that in spite of the fact that I am getting old and my body is falling into decay, my mental powers, praise God, are still fresh. But for all that I simply cannot be confident of the work. If God doesn't help, nothing will come of it. Never have I felt so clearly as now that for every line I should cry out: Lord, have mercy and help me! . . .

## *V. N. Leshkov.[1] Summer 1851. Moscow.*

Having learned that in the censorship there are new prohibitions as a result of which not only all the new works, but also the old ones which were printed earlier are again being submitted to severe reexamination, I am having recourse to you with a request to save my previously published works from destruction, changes, corrections, or omissions and to provide an opportunity for their publication in the form in which they have been published until now. My manner of thinking is well known to both the Emperor and the Crown Prince. The ridicule in my works is not ridicule of the government—but of people who are miscreants, who use the trust of the government for evil—not of established rules, but of misuses of them. In the mind of a censor who is not farsighted all this often gets confused and makes him look with fear at an innocent sentence which is a bit harsh as one which is harmful and unworthy of Russian [. . . .], makes him look suspiciously [. . . .]. I am also requesting this of you because for their own profit the booksellers are already beginning to spread the rumor that my works will be forbidden by the censorship; and for the few copies which are left now they ask (and people pay) a price which is six times too big. Of course, the destruction of two or three harsh sentences and expressions doesn't [. . . .] anything for me with [. . . .]; this wouldn't bother those who know my works by heart; their omission will be filled in mentally. . . .

## *Father Makarius.[1] September 25, 1851. Optina Monastery.*

One more word Father Makarius, friend of my heart and soul. Driving up to the cloister after the first decision which I made in my soul, it was peaceful in my heart and quietness. After the second it was somehow uneasy and disturbed, and my soul was disquieted. When you were saying good-bye to me why did you say: "For the last time." Perhaps all this is happening because my nerves are upset; in this case I greatly fear that the road will completely shake me. It somewhat terrifies me to turn up sick in the middle of a long journey. Especially when I will be consumed by the thought that I have left Moscow where people wouldn't leave me alone with the spleen.

All yours.

Tell me, doesn't your heart tell you I would be better off not to leave Moscow?

## *V. A. Zhukovsky. February 2, 1852. Moscow.*

Thank you very much for the book and kind letter. Don't re-proach me for not being able and not managing to write you any-thing except: "God help you!" I ought not even to write that I remem-ber you often in my sinful prayers. I ought to pray for you much more ardently, as for a person to whom I owe a great, great deal.

You have my sincere condolences for your blindness, although I know that God is merciful and arranges everything for the good of our soul.[1] But meantime I am sending you a medical recipe which works extraordinarily successfully in curing blindness. One must in-hale (either mixed with an equal part of tobacco or simply by itself) the dried leaf of the well-known Jerusalem artichoke, a root plant which is eaten by us. People relate the following incident of this dis-covery: the servant girl of an old blind woman who took snuff, be-cause of a shortage of it began to mix the snuff for her in the snuffbox with the leaf of this plant ground into a powder. The mistress who began to notice an unusual discharge of mucus through the nose and even the sniffles—the maid was interrogated and admitted everything. But feeling that she saw better the old woman continued until she was completely cured of blindness. It is said this treatment is confirmed everywhere by experiments, curing amaurosis, even the most chronic, of old people. What is there to say about myself? As before I am sitting at the same thing; I am busy with the same thing. Pray for me, for my work to be truly conscientious and for me to be even a little worthy of singing a hymn to heavenly beauty.

Be healthy and God help you, dear brother close to my soul!

## *M. A. Konstantinovsky. February 6, 1852. Moscow.*

I was already going to write you one letter yesterday in which I asked forgiveness for offending you.[1] But suddenly through some-one's prayers the mercy of God visited hardhearted me, and my heart wanted to thank you warmly, so warmly; but what can I say about that? Only I regretted not exchanging coats with you. Yours would have warmed me better.

Obliged to you with eternal gratitude both here and beyond the grave,

All yours Nikolai.

## M. I. Gogol. About February 10, 1852. Moscow.

Thank you, my priceless mama, for praying for me. It is always so sweet for me during the moments when you pray for me! Oh, how much a mother's prayer does! For God's sake take care of yourself for us. Protect your health, which is precious to us. Lately you have become susceptible to inflammation of the blood. Perhaps in the spring you need treatment with herbs, of course together with moderation in food and diet. In general all plethoric people, as you know yourself, ought to avoid all strong foods. For God's sake, consult with a good doctor. Pray for me and pray for yourself at the same time. Oh, how we need your prayers! How we need them for our internal peace! God grant you spend Lent spiritually and beneficially for you all. My health still needs something for it to be strengthened. I still cannot take up any work, as I ought to, nor ordinary affairs which have therefore come to a halt. Oh, may God make you understand everything; do not be disturbed by anything around you, not by any failures; just pray and all will be well.

All yours, your loving son

Nikolai.[1]

# Notes

*Introduction*

1. The full family name was Gogol-Yanovsky. In school Gogol was known as Yanovsky, not Gogol. Later he dropped the second part of the name claiming it was a nasty invention of the Poles.

2. In 1835 only 16 percent of the squires in Russia owned more than 100 serfs. [See S. Durylin, *Geroj našego vremeni M. Ju. Lermontova* (M. 1940), p. 77.] But the estate produced virtually no money income; Gogol had to rely on his literary earnings and loans from friends.

3. Any names with which the reader wishes to familiarize himself may be looked up in the notes to the letters. In the index the page reference given in italics is the one which gives the main explanation of each name.

4. For example, Gogol's highest grade was in German, but as he and his friends all wrote, he knew almost nothing about the language. In one of the plays performed at Nezhin he had a long speech which began "O mein Vater" and ended "nach Prag." Gogol labored for hours to memorize the lines. At the performance he strode onto the stage and began "O mein Vater," hesitated, stumbled, turned red—and finally waved his arm in disgust, crying out firmly, "Nach Prag." The audience, incidentally, did not notice the hiatus.

5. My translations of quotations from memoirs are made from V. Veresaev, *Gogol' v žizni* (M. 1933), a fine volume from which all English accounts of Gogol's life are cribbed.

6. "The fox knows many things, but the hedgehog knows one big thing," said the Greek poet Archilochus. Berlin suggests: "Taken figuratively, the words can be made to yield a sense in which they mark one of the deepest differences which divide writers and thinkers, and, it may be, human beings in general. For there exists a great chasm between those, on one side, who relate everything to a single central vision, one system less or more coherent or articulate, in terms of which they understand, think and feel—a single, universal, organizing principle in terms of which alone all that they are and say has significance—and, on the other side, those who pursue many ends, often unrelated and even contradictory, connected, if at all, only in some *de facto* way, for some psychological or physiological cause, related by no moral or aesthetic principle; these last lead lives, perform acts, and entertain ideas that are centrifugal rather than centripetal . . ." *The Hedgehog and the Fox* (Mentor Books, 1957), pp. 7-8.

7. Actually, Gogol did do a great deal of reading, and the surviving notes (made while reading and preparing lectures) show that he did know something about history. But these 250 pages of notes suggest he was very unsystematic.

8. Letters to Pogodin and Maximovich on January 22, 1834.

9. There was another storm-interrupted reading of *Dead Souls* in 1843, after which Gogol said, "God Himself didn't want me to read what is still not completed and hasn't received my inner approval . . . and in His wrath God threatened me."

10. Lev Pushkin, the poet's brother, records that when in 1851 he showed a group of guests a glove which had been removed from Lermontov's hand after his fatal duel, Gogol was the only one who displayed no interest in the relic.

11. The horrifying story of his last days proves this. One of their treatments was to surround his body with warm loaves of bread. The series of diagnoses made by various doctors makes sad and farcical reading.

12. The quotation is from one of the four letters on *Dead Souls* in *Selected Passages*.

Monday-morning quarterbacks of the literary world have maintained that Gogol was trying to accomplish an impossible task. This kind of thinking combines the advantages of hindsight with self-assurance one could suppose only in a divinity. The fact that Gogol did not achieve his aim does not necessarily mean it was *per se* a bad or impossible idea. —If Tolstoy had outlined sweeping plans for *War and Peace* in 1855 and twelve years later had left only one hundred pages of a rough draft we would all say it was an impossible task he had chosen and wonder at his delusions of grandeur.

13. Described in detail below in note 1, July 30, 1847.

14. See below, Gogol's reply of July-August, 1847.

15. With typical attention to detail Belinsky claimed to have read the book one hundred times.

16. They *were* inferiors.

17. This was Goncharov's first novel; his *Oblomov*, which owes a considerable debt to *Dead Souls,* was not published until 1859.

Nekrasov's memory was a little foggy: he recalled that Belinsky was also present at this meeting—when in fact Belinsky was dead at the time. And Nekrasov had political reasons for disliking Gogol.

18. As the reader is going through the letters which follow and considering Gogol's biography and character, he might keep in mind the classical characteristics of the schizophrenic personality. These are some signs listed by A. Brill (*Lectures on Psychoanalytic Psychiatry*) and Karl Menninger (*The Human Mind,* New York, 1937): extreme bashfulness, dislike of unfamiliar people, general inability to get along with people, dislike of rough games, reserve, serious-mindedness, and eccentricity, excitability, fondness for books and arts with a tendency to make artificial worlds because of the unacceptability of the outer world, many emotional conflicts, sexual idiocy, delusions of grandeur, regression to childish habits, existing for years as a vagrant or at the expense of others, flaunting of conservatism, tendencies to attack everything and stir up resentment, and religious convictions of divine inspiration. The term schizophrenia covers a very broad area. This is what Menninger says about "the artistic type" schizoid personality:

"The artist and the poet are similarly detached from 'normal' life—to their sorrow, often, and to our profit. They submit to us fragments of their inner world—bits of dreams and visions and songs that we—out here—don't hear except as they translate them. But this same esotericism, this same otherworldliness, may appear as religious fanaticism, artistic grotesqueries, pseudo-psychological bunk, spiritualism, mysticism, all sorts of fad faiths and cures." (p. 82)

19. Gogol's sex life is filled with booby-traps for biographers. There are legends that Gogol's problem was guilt-ridden autoeroticism; these are totally unsubstantiated and stem from the dismal days when nervous mothers and witch doctors believed the art of onanism culminated in madness. There are speculations he was a latent homosexual; these are based on a shaky interpretation of a letter to Danilevsky and some motifs in Gogol's works—and while fiction can be evidence for a writer's biography, it is notoriously unreliable evidence. It is true that if Gogol ever had any love affairs he did not tell anyone about them. The only concrete testimony about his love-life is a report from Dr. Tarasenkov that Gogol said he had occasionally whored, but that he felt little need for it or pleasure from it. The only firm conclusion that follows this confession is that Gogol was atypical.

20. On Konstantinovsky's character see below, note 1, Sept. 24, 1847. He had arrived at Count Tolstoy's for a visit around January 26, so biographers have often used him as an easy explanation. The story that at one of their last meetings Father Matvey demanded Gogol renounce Pushkin because he was a sinner and a pagan is from a highly questionable source. Although of course he could have been lying, Konstantinovsky said he believed artistic talent was a God-given gift, and he flatly denied having asked Gogol to renounce art. A letter which Gogol wrote to Konstantinovsky on February 6 indicates they had quarreled the day before, but it does not suggest that his soul had been shattered.

*April 23, 1825*

1. Gogol's father, Vasily Afanasevich Gogol-Yanovsky, died in the second part of March. At this time Gogol was a student in the gymnasium at Nezhin.

2. A Nikolsky, *The Founding of Russian Literature* (St. Petersburg, 1822). The incongruous postscript is paralleled years later; in a letter (March 16-28, 1837) on Pushkin's death there is a similarly peculiar shift from the tragic to the trivial.

*March 19, 1827*

1. Gerasim Ivanovich Vysotsky had graduated from the gymnasium at Nezhin in 1826.

2. F. E. Sevryugin—music teacher at the gymnasium.

3. Denis Ivanovich Fonvizin (1745-92) —Russian neoclassical writer of satirical verse and prose in various genres. *The Minor* (1782) is his best play.

Yakov Borisovich Knyazhnin (1742-91) —Russian poet and satirical playwright.

August Friedrich Ferdinand von Kotzebue (1761-1819) —a popular German dramatist (author of more than 200 plays) and sometime Russian spy.

Jean-Pierre Claris de Florian (1755-94) —French writer of romances and plays.

*April 6, 1827*
   1. Prokopovich is reported to have said that "Gogol soon lost patience trying to make sense out of Schiller" and that "it was just a momentary enthusiasm."

*October 3, 1827*
   1. A distant relative of Gogol.

*September 8, 1828*
   1. Vasilevka was Gogol's small family estate.

*January 3, 1829*
   1. In "The Overcoat" Akaky Akakievich pays eighty rubles for his new coat.

*April 30, 1829*
   1. One verst equals 3500 feet.
   2. Alexander Semenovich Danilevsky (1809-88)—one of Gogol's closest friends throughout his life, from Vasilevka and Nezhin to Petersburg and Paris.
   3. Gogol used some of the material his mother sent in the stories of *Evenings on a Farm near Dikanka* (1831-32) and *Mirgorod* (1835).
   4. Gogol's father wrote two comedies (in Ukrainian) for the domestic theater (made up of family members and serfs) of the Troshchinskys. Only the second, usually entitled *The Simpleton*, . . . has survived and been reprinted—several times.

*July 24, 1829*
   1. One of these failures was the poor reception of his *Hans Küchelgarten*, an idyllic poem of some 1,200 lines.
   1. One of these failures was the poor reception of his *Hans Küchelgarten*, an idyllic poem of some 1,200 lines.
   2. It is probable that the story about this Petersburg angel is false. In his first letter from Lübeck he gives a totally different excuse for the trip abroad—as if he had completely forgotten what he tells his mother here.
   3. The money was a payment on the Gogols' mortgaged estate.

*September 24, 1829*
   1. Gogol's mother put the angel he discusses in his letter of July 24 together with the rash mentioned in that of August 13 and concluded her Nikolai had contracted a venereal disease.

*February 2, 1830*
   1. A short poem, "Italy," had appeared in *Son of the Fatherland* in 1829, and a short story, "St. John's Eve," was published in *Notes of the Fatherland* in 1830. Nothing is known of any printed translations of Gogol.

*June 3, 1830*
   1. Although he had taken a civil service job, Gogol, of course, had not given up his literary activities.

*October 10, 1830*

1. *Notes on the Fatherland*—a political and literary journal discontinued in 1830. It began again in 1839 under A. A. Kraevsky and Vissarion Belinsky.

*August 21, 1831*

1. Peter Alexandrovich Pletnev (1792-1865)—close friend and literary agent of Pushkin, editor of *The Contemporary* after Pushkin's death. Critic, poet of small talent, professor of Russian literature, member of the Russian Academy.

2. Gogol's first collection of short stories, *Evenings on a Farm near Dikanka*, was being published. See Pushkin's reply to Gogol in a letter dated August 25, 1831.

3. Alexander Anfimovich Orlov (1790-1842) published his six novels about various Vyzhigins in 1831 and 1832. His novel *The Falcon Would Be a Falcon, But the Hen Ate Him, or The Runaway Wife*, was also printed in 1831.

4. Thaddeus Benediktovich Bulgarin (1789-1859)—talentless author of various works, including patriotic and didactic novels like *Ivan Vyzhigin* (1829) and *Peter Ivanovich Vyzhigin* (1831), literary enemy of Pushkin and Gogol, agent of the Tsar's secret police.

5. Mikhail A. Bestyuzhev-Ryumin (1800-1832)—publisher of the satirical *Northern Mercury*, literary opponent of Pushkin and his circle.

6. Alexander F. Voeykov (1779-1839)—writer, editor of *The Russian Invalid* (and the *Supplements* to it), literary enemy of Bulgarin and Senkovsky.

7. Nikolai I. Nadezhdin (1804-56)—historian, ethnographer, one of the critics who railed against romanticism in the late 1820's. Parts of his dissertation *De origine, nature et fatis Poëseos quae Romantica audit* were published in 1830.

8. Under the pseudonym Feofilakt Kosichkin, Pushkin was publishing a piece in which he parodied Orlov and attacked Bulgarin. See J. Thomas Shaw, "The Problem of the *Persona* in Journalism: Puškin's Feofilakt Kosičkin," *American Contributions to the Fifth International Congress of Slavists.* (The Hague, 1963), II, 301-27.

*September 10, 1831*

1. Vasily Andreevich Zhukovsky (1783-1852)—dulcet-tongued sentimental poet, influenced strongly by German romantics; talented translator of everything from *The Odyssey* to "Leonore" and "The Prisoner of Chillon"; friend and protector of Pushkin and Gogol; tutor of the Tsar's children. His aesthetic and religious beliefs had considerable influence on Gogol.

2. The first section of *Evenings.*

3. Alexandra Osiponvna Smirnova (née Rosset—or Rozetti) 1809-82. Beautiful lady-in-waiting of the Empress. A friend of Zhukovsky, Vyazemsky, and Lermontov. Like other poets, Pushkin (who introduced her to Gogol) had written poems to her. Her husband was a rich diplomat to whom she was indifferent (in her memoirs she wrote, "I sold myself for 6000 souls for my brothers"). She frequently acted as *"notre dame aux bons secours"* when her literary friends ran afoul of the censorship. After a rather rowdy youth, her moral development (in the forties) took the same direction as Gogol's. He became her very close spiritual friend.

4. The quotation is from *Eugene Onegin*, VI, XXXII.

5. "Folktales"—the two poetic imitations of Russian folktales to which Gogol refers are "The Tale of Tsar Berendey" and "The Sleeping Princess." Pushkin's was "The Tale of Tsar Saltan."

*November 2, 1831*

1. The real title of Pushkin's comic poem was "A Little House in Kolomna" (1830).

2. *Ruslan and Ludmila* was Pushkin's first long poem (1820).

3. "The Tale about the Priest and His Workman, Balda."

4. See note 5, September 10, 1831.

*March 30, 1832*

1. Nikolai Mikhailovich Yazykov (1805-46)—primarily an elegist—was one of the most important poets of the period. Later, Gogol considered Yazykov a kindred soul, but Yazykov's own letters are full of nasty remarks ridiculing Gogol. His "Earthquake" was Gogol's favorite poem.

2. "Ivan Fedorovich Shponka and His Auntie" (1832)—the penultimate story in *Evenings*.

3. Nestor Vasilevich Kukolnik (1809-68)—schoolmate of Gogol at Nezhin, author of many historical dramas, including *Torquato Tasso* (1832). Mr. Plato was Kukolnik's brother, Pelikan a doctor.

4. *Boris Godunov* (1826), Pushkin's Shakespeare-modeled play in blank verse, was the first example of a romantic tragedy in Russian drama.

*December 20, 1832*

1. Danilevsky had fallen in love.

2. The identity of the creatures who led Gogol to the abyss is a mystery.

3. What specific works by Pushkin Danilevsky had criticized we don't know—perhaps his southern poems.

4. Again, this refers to remarks in a letter (which has not survived) from Danilevsky.

5. A nickname for Nikolai Ya. Prokopovich (a school chum), who was marrying a young actress.

6. Yakov G. Bryansky—a well-known Petersburg actor.

7. Vasily Yakovlevich Prokopovich—the elder brother of Nikolai.

*February 1, 1833*

1. Mikhail Petrovich Pogodin (1800-1875), writer, critic, publicist, professor of Russian history at the University of Moscow, editor of *The Moscow Herald* (1827-30) and *The Muscovite* (1841-56), was a friend of the literary circle of Pushkin and Gogol and an ardent Slavophil.

2. A. F. Smirdin (1795-1857)—an important and highly successful publisher and bookseller.

*February 8, 1833*

1. Prince Vladimir Fedorovich Odoevsky (1804-69)—admirer of Hoffmann, author of short stories, music historian, friend of Pushkin and Gogol. *Motley Tales* was a collection published in 1833.

2. Nikolai Ivanovich Gnedich (1784-1833)—elegant lyric poet with a taste for classical literature. His accurate and sonorous translation of the *Iliad* is still used today.

*February 20, 1833*

1. *Vladimir of the Third Degree*, Gogol's first play, was never finished.

*October 2, 1833*

1. Two of Gogol's sisters. The word *vospitan'e* means both education and upbringing.

2. Probably a domestic.

3. In his biography (*Gogol*, London, 1957) Magarshack takes this to mean Gogol was debauched by house serfs at a tender pubertal age. An interesting fantasy.

*November 9, 1833*

1. Mikhail Alexandrovich Maximovich (1804-73), a collector and publisher of Russian and Ukrainian folk songs—an undertaking in which Gogol was extremely interested—was later a successful ethnographer and historian.

2. An almanac Maximovich planned to publish.

3. "The Story of How Ivan Ivanovich Quarreled with Ivan Nikiforovich." Gogol's excuse for not giving the story to Maximovich does not ring true.

4. There were no external events in Gogol's life at this time which could have made him suffer so terribly.

5. Gogol's megalomaniacal plans to write a multivolumed history ended in *Taras Bulba* only.

6. Zoryjan Dolega-Chodakowski (pseudonym of Adam Czarnocki (1784-1825), a Polish historian, had compiled a two-volume manuscript of Ukrainian folk songs. Maximovich put the manuscripts at Gogol's disposal for a short time, and Gogol inserted a number of supplements and variants.

7. For some of the songs Gogol collected and copied see *Pamjati Zhukovskogo* (St. Petersburg, 1908).

*January 11, 1834*

1. *The Library for Reading*—an extremely successful monthly journal "of literature, sciences, arts, industry, news and fashions" begun in 1834 by Smirdin and Osip Ivanovich Senkovsky (1800-1858). Senkovsky, professor of Arabic, Turkish, and Persian at the University of St. Petersburg, was a high-handed editor. Under the pen name Baron Brambeus he wrote a considerable amount of fiction which enjoyed popularity in certain circles.

2. Thaddeus Benediktovich Bulgarin—see note 4, July 21, 1831.

3. Gogol refers to Senkovsky's *The Fantastic Journeys of Baron Brambeus* (1833) and Bulgarin's own *Verisimilar False Tales* (*pravdopodobnye nebylicy*), or *Wanderings Through the World in the 29th Century* (1824).

4. *The Northern Bee*—a political and literary newspaper published by Bulgarin and Grech in the 1830's.

*May 13, 1834*

1. S. S. Uvarov (1786-1855)—president of the Academy of Sciences and director of the "Ministry of People's Enlightenment." With his patronage Gogol hoped to be appointed professor of history at Kiev University.

2. In a note to Gogol (May 13, 1834) Pushkin promises to see Uvarov and "apropos of the death of *The Telegraph* I'll start telling about yours too. From this point I will imperceptively and artfully shift to the immortality which awaits him. Perhaps we'll fix things up."

*End of December 1834*
   1. Gogol's story was published in late January 1835.

*About January 22, 1835*
   1. A recently published collection of stories (including "Nevsky Avenue," "The Portrait," "Notes of a Madman"), and essays (such as "On the Middle Ages," "A Few Words about Pushkin," "On Present-Day Architecture," "Thoughts about Geography," "On the Teaching of Universal History," "Sculpture, Painting, and Music," "On Little Russian Songs," and "The Last Day of Pompei").

*March 22, 1835*
   1. Gogol's second collection of tales (1835), made up of "Old-World Landowners," "Viy," "Taras Bulba," and "How Ivan Ivanovich Quarreled with Ivan Nikiforovich."

*March 23, 1835*
   1. Gogol did not know that the first issue of the long-awaited new journal had already appeared on March 15. His story "The Nose" was published in Pushkin's *Contemporary* in 1836.
   2. A paper published at the University of Moscow.

*April 12, 1835*
   1. Gogol's mother frequently ascribed to him the works of other authors—as well as, if we are to believe one memoirist, the invention of the steam engine and the train.

*October 7, 1835*
   1. His comedy *The Marriage* was not completed until 1842. Natalya Nikolaevna—Pushkin's wife.
   2. This is the first reference to *Dead Souls* in Gogol's letters.
   3. According to Gogol, Pushkin did suggest a plot, and the result was *The Inspector General*.

*January 18, 1836*
   1. *The Inspector General.*
   2. Gogol published no such collection. "The Nose" appeared in Pushkin's *Contemporary*.
   3. M. Pogodin, *A Dramatic History of Dmitri the Pretender*, Moscow, 1835. *An Outline of Russian History for Schools*, Moscow, 1835. *Lectures of Professor Pogodin on the Politics, Communication, and Trade of the Main Peoples of the Ancient World According to Heeren.* Part One, Moscow, 1835. Arnold Hermann Ludwig Heeren (1760-1842) was the foremost historian of the Göttingen school. His *Ideen über die Politik, den Verkehr und den Handel der vornehmsten Völker den alten Welt* was published in 1793-96.

*February 21, 1836*
   1. *The Contemporary* was one of the most prominent and influential literary journals of the ninteenth century. It was founded by Pushkin and first appeared in April 1836.
   2. Prince Peter Andreevich Vyazemsky (1792-1878) —graceless but witty poet and critic, staunch defender of romanticism, one of Pushkin's closest friends and cleverest correspondents.

*March 2, 1836*

   1. A scene from an unfinished play.
   2. A short story.
   3. "On the Tendency of Journal Literature." Gogol's abrasive essay deploring the level of journal literature and criticism in general (and attacking Senkovsky in particular) was published anonymously in the premier issue of Pushkin's *Contemporary*—along with "A Civil Servant's Morning" and "The Carriage."

*April 29, 1836*

   1. Mikhail Semenovich Shchepkin (1788-1863)—one of the first great Russian actors. Gogol met him in 1832. As his letters show, Gogol valued Shchepkin's talents highly and relied on him to keep *The Inspector General* from being played as a traditional farce.
   2. Tsar Nikolai I allowed the play to be printed after the censors had forbidden it.
   3. *The Marriage*, Gogol's most important play after *The Inspector General*, was not completed until 1840, not published until 1842.

*September 22/10, 1836*

   1. Here Gogol uses *Rus'*—an older more poetic name for Russia.

*October 12, 1836*

   1. Maria Petrovna Balabina (1820-1901). In 1831 Pletnev procured Gogol a position as tutor of the Balabin children, one of whom was Maria. Gogol remained a good friend of the family for years. His whimsical letters to Maria suggest that in his own peculiar way he felt particular affection for her.
   2. The meaning of this allusion (if that is what it is) remains unclear to the translators.

*November 28, 1836*

   1. In the first part of this letter Gogol objects to Pogodin's plans to begin a new journal and warns him that he should not expect short stories from him. It was not until 1841 that Pogodin finally started *The Muscovite*.
   2. His comedy *The Marriage* was not completed until 1840. In the interim Gogol gave several contradictory versions of what happened to the manuscript.

*January 25, 1837*

   1. More precisely, "idle lucky fellows" (*prazdnye schastlivcy*), a phrase from Pushkin's one-act tragedy *Mozart and Salieri*.
   2. Jules (Jules Janin) was Gogol's nickname for Pavel V. Annenkov (later an important biographer of Pushkin and a memoirist). In the early 1830's Gogol had given his friends such nicknames as Hugo, Dumas, and Balzac.
   Mlle George was the stage name of Marguerite Vemmer (1787-1867). In 1837 she was only fifty. There are several references to her in *War and Peace*.
   3. *The Huguenots* (1836), *Robert* (1831)—Meyerbeer operas.
   "Copper pots and plates"—Gogol's culinary metaphor for kettle drums and cymbals.
   4. "The Field Commander" (*Polkovodec*)—a verse fragment (fifty-

four lines) by Pushkin which was to be devoted to Michael Barclay de Tolly. *The Captain's Daughter*—Pushkin's short historical novel set during the Pugachev Rebellion. Both these works were published in *The Contemporary* in 1836.

## March 28/16, 1837

1. A Petersburg banker.

## March 30, 1837

1. On January 27, 1837, Pushkin was fatally shot by George d'Anthès in a duel.

2. In Gogol's *Author's Confession* (written in 1847, published posthumously) he claimed Pushkin had advised him to write a serious long work and had given him the plot for *Dead Souls*, saying he had intended to use it for a poem himself and that he would have given it to no one but Gogol.

3. These are civil service ranks.

4. It is not true that the Tsar honored Pushkin's talent; he was merely interested in (1) keeping Pushkin from penning anything seditious, (2) seducing Pushkin's elegantly empty-headed wife.

## April 18/6, 1837

1. These two stories were published first in *Mirgorod* (1835).

2. Zhukovsky persuaded Nikolai I to give Gogol 5,000 rubles.

## October 30, 1837

1. See note 2 April 18/6, 1837.

2. Gogol had worked briefly as a government clerk when he first arrived in St. Petersburg. He was a notably unsuccessful lecturer on world history at Petersburg University in 1834-35.

## February 2, 1838

1. Julietta Grisi (1811-69)—an Italian opera singer.

2. The antecedent of "they" is as impossible to find in Russian as in the translation.

3. Varvara N. Repnina and her brother Vasily (who was married to the eldest daughter of the Balabins) were wealthy friends of Gogol.

## April 23, 1838

1. Pushkin's unfinished story "Egyptian Nights" was published in *The Contemporary* in 1837, as was Lermontov's "Galub."

2. See note 2, September 3, 1837.

3. Adam Mickiewicz (1798-1855)—Poland's greatest poet. His epic, *Pan Tadeusz*, was published in 1834. Judging by the request—and some other evidence—Gogol could read Polish.

## End of April 1838

1. Giuseppi Gioachomo Belli (1791-1863)—an Italian poet known for his numerous sonnets.

2. Including works by Tassoni, Braccolini, Dottori, Parini, Casti, and other luminaries.

## May 13, 1838

1. Censored.
2. Ivan Andreevich Krylov (1769-1844)—Russia's most prodigiously lazy and prodigiously talented fabulist.
3. Nikolai Ivanovich Grech (1787-1869) —editor of *Son of the Fatherland* and coeditor (with Bulgarin) of *The Northern Bee*. Grech and Bulgarin were arch-conservatives; apparently for this reason they were going to boycott the dinner for Krylov—whose pungent satire knew no conservatism.

## May 16, 1838

1. Pavé—the young ward of a mutual friend, Z. A. Volkonskaya.

## August 14, 1838

1. Gogol refers to *Dead Souls*.
2. In order to send Gogol the money Pogodin, S. Aksakov, E. A. Baratynsky (a major poet), and N. Pavlov (a minor prose writer) each contributed 250 rubles; the remaining 1000 rubles were provided by a rich patron, I. E. Velikopolsky. Gogol did not know about this—and apparently he never repaid the loan.
3. *Dead Souls*.

## April 2, 1839

1. Stepan Petrovich Shevyrev (1806-64) was professor of literature at the University of Moscow (and thus Pogodin's colleague). Frequently attacked by radicals of his own and our age, he was nevertheless one of the best critics of the time. His essays on Pushkin and Gogol are well worth reading. He was among Gogol's regular correspondents.
2. Kraevsky—see note 1, October 10, 1830.

## May 30, 1839

1. The son of Count M. U. Vielgorsky, a dilettante composer who was close to the royal family. Iosif died on June 2, 1839. Gogol remained a friend of the family until, much later, he proposed to one of Iosif's sisters.

## June 5, 1839

1. The next Tsar, Alexander II.

## June 22, 1839

1. E. G. Chertkova—wife of A. D. Chertkov. Gogol had met her in Moscow; in Rome they both cared for the dying Vielgorsky.

## September 5, 1839

1. Exactly what Gogol said about "northern" vs. "southern" poetry is not known.

## September 10, 1839

1. Shevyrev had begun translating *The Divine Comedy*, a chore which he did not finish. Gogol over-compliments Shevyrev's poetic talents.
2. The play based on Ukrainian history which Gogol had begun.

## First Half of October, 1839

1. Gogol arrived in Moscow in October and attended a performance of *The Inspector General* at the Maly Theater. According to Sergei Aksakov,

Gogol virtually lay down in his box so that he could not be seen by the audience. But the play went well, and the spectators called the author to the stage at the conclusion of the third act. Gogol left his seat and Aksakov followed to show him to the stage, but he saw Gogol rushing toward the exit. Gogol refused to go with Aksakov and ran out the door. The public considered itself affronted, and Gogol wrote this letter to Zagoskin—but Pogodin and Aksakov kept it from being delivered and made public.

Aksakov said Gogol gave him the same excuse he had given in the letter —that he had just received bad news from home. This, it would seem, was pure fabrication. Shortly after this Gogol's mother reported that there had been no bad news at all.

*January 4, 1840*
   1. Through Zhukovsky, Gogol had suggested that Smirdin publish his complete works. After Smirdin's insultingly low offer Gogol received others.
   2. *The Marriage* was originally called *The Bridegrooms*. The "unfinished comedy" is probably *Vladimir of the Third Degree*.
   3. A publisher.
   4. Zhukovsky himself loaned the money to Gogol.

*January 25, 1840*
   1. One of Gogol's reasons for visiting Russia was to take his sisters from the institute where they had been studying and place them in the home of some protectress in Moscow.

*April 12, 1840*
   1. A rich landowner whom Gogol had met when he was still studying in Nezhin.
   2. Owner of an estate bordering on Gogol's Vasilevka and son of a well-known poet, Vasily Kapnist (1757-1823).

*June 10, 1840*
   1. Sergei Aksakov (1791-1859)—the late-blooming author of one of Russia's greatest classics, *A Family Chronicle* (1846-56), a work begun partly at Gogol's urging. As Mirsky says, Aksakov's house was a "stronghold of pure Russianism in Moscow society." His *Story of My Acquaintance with Gogol* is a vital source for Gogol's biography. Gogol was idolized by Aksakov's entire family.
   2. One of Aksakov's sons, an essayist and Slavophil.
   3. Gogol had a small passion for miniature editions. The miniature *Eugene Onegin* was published in 1837 (and recently republished with Vladimir Nabokov's translation of *Onegin*).
   4. A play (published in 1825 by Alexander Sergeevich Griboedov (1795-1829). It is generally regarded as the finest Russian comedy in verse.
   5. Ivan I. Dmitriev (1760-1837) was the author of a number of flabby fables.
   6. I. F. Saxarov's *Songs of the Russian People* were published in 1838 and 1839.

*June 25, 1840*
   1. A friend of P. A. Elagina (see next letter). With Elagina's help Gogol settled his younger sister Elizaveta in Raevskaya's house.

*July 7, 1840*

1. Chief of Police in Moscow.
2. Aksakov.
3. Maximovich's *Ukrainian Folk Songs* were published in 1827 and 1834.
4. Shchepkin.

*October 17, 1840*

1. In 1839 Pogodin began collecting ancient manuscripts dealing with Russian history. His collection became one of the most important archival sources.
2. Johann F. Overbeck (1789-1869) —a German artist.

*December 28, 1840 (Aksakov)*

1. In 1840 V. A. Panov had left Moscow with Gogol and lived with him, first in Vienna then in Italy.

*December 28, 1840 (Pogodin)*

1. This is the earliest known reference to Gogol's work (or plans for work) on further volumes of *Dead Souls*.

*January-April, 1841*

1. See note 4, January 4, 1840.

*March 5, 1841*

1. Shchepkin and Aksakov.

*March 13, 1841*

1. Pogodin had just started *The Muscovite*, a journal with Slavophil leanings.
2. *Dead Souls.*
3. Gogol did not keep his promise, but later he sent the fragment *Rome*, which appeared in the third issue of *The Muscovite* in 1842.

*September 27, 1841*

1. Mikhail A. Bakunin (1814-76)—the ebullient anarchist.
2. P. M. Yazykov—Nikolai Yazykov's older brother.

*First Part of October, 1841*

1. Alexander A. Ivanov (1806-58)—a Russian artist. He lived in Italy from 1830 until the year of his death. Gogol met him in 1838, and they became close friends. The painting referred to is his "Christ Appears to the People."
2. "The Triumph of Religion in the Arts" (1840).

*January 7, 1842*

1. *Dead Souls.*
2. In his correspondence Gogol is inconsistent about the genre of *Dead Souls*, sometimes calling it a novel, sometimes a "poem"; but on the fanciful skull and scroll-embellished title page he created for the first edition, the title itself is dwarfed by the genre-specification *POÈMA*—a Russian term usually applied only to rather long works in verse.

*February 10, 1842*

1. "*Al'pijskaja pesnja*" and "*Pesnja baltyskim vodam*," two short poems, appeared in *The Muscovite*.

*February 17, 1842*

1. In August 1840. (See his letter of October 17, 1840.) Some biographers consider Gogol's illness in Vienna a sharp turning point in his development, but I think the evidence is inconclusive.

2. Richter (1763-1825) —the German writer was popular in Russia, but Gogol had scant respect for him.

*March 4, 1842*

1. Alexander Vasilevich Nikitenko—a censor. In a letter to Pletnev (February 17, 1842) Gogol says: "Besides his views on the censor's duty, he understands the calling of the censor in the sense of the ancient Roman censors, i.e., watchers after purity of morals; and therefore many of my expressions will suffer greatly from him." Also see Gogol's letter of April 10, 1842.

*Between February 24 - March 4, 1842*

1. Gogol enclosed this letter with the following one to Pletnev, but Pletnev did not deliver it because Nikitenko passed *Dead Souls* on March 9.

*March 17, 1842*

1. For nearly a month Gogol's anguished efforts to locate the MS of *Dead Souls* were unsuccessful.

1. For nearly a month Gogol's anguished efforts to locate the MS of *Dead Souls* were unsuccessful.

2. The changes and additions were basic and extensive. Gogol's new moral stance and his attempt to defend the aesthetics of *Dead Souls* are clearly visible in the new version.

3. Soviet editors conjecture Gogol means "observations" made by Belinsky in 1835—this sounds like wishful thinking.

4. *The Contemporary.*

5. Perhaps an allusion to Baron Delvig's almanac *Northern Flowers* (1825-32) to which Pushkin was a regular contributor.

6. "The Portrait."

*April 9, 1842*

1. The "Tale of Captain Kopeikin" in Chapter Ten of *Dead Souls.* Gogol rewrote it, and the cautious censors authorized the eviscerated version.

*May 9, 1842*

1. Before leaving Russia in 1842 Gogol solemnly announced a forthcoming pilgrimage to the Holy Land. He did not make the trip until 1848.

*May 11, 1842*

1. Vissarion G. Belinsky (1811-48)—a very famous, very earnest critic who displays only moderate sensitivity in his wretchedly written essays.

*June 4, 1842*

1. Gogol's *Collected Works* (dated 1842) were published in late January 1843.

*August 18/6, 1842*

1. His projected trip to the Holy Land.

*October 30, 1842*

1. This dramatic piece is an important statement of Gogol's aesthetic beliefs at the time. It has particular relevance for *Dead Souls.*

2. Pletnev wrote his friend Ya. K. Grot: "Nikitenko came to me and showed me a letter from Gogol in Rome in which he showers praises on him because Nikitenko censors his works. I blushed for the abasement to which authors are led by the censorship at present; they are forced to debase themselves in front of people. . . . What if Nikitenko publishes this letter in his memoirs sometime? Delvig and Pushkin weren't like that." (See Gogol's letter of May 11, 1842, for his other view of Nikitenko.)

## November 28, 1842

1. On September 9 in St. Petersburg's Alexandrinsky Theater a certain N. I. Kulikov presented "Comic Scenes from the New Poem, Dead Souls."

2. A. M. Gedeonov, director of the Imperial Theaters in Petersburg, soon promised Pletnev to stop any further literary privateering.

## December 3, 1842

1. The Marriage, The Gamblers, and several dramatic fragments were published in Gogol's Collected Works. Shchepkin staged the first two together (over Gogol's objections) on February 5, 1843.

## February 28, 1843

1. Prokopovich handled the publication of Gogol's Collected Works.

2. See note 1, December 3, 1842.

3. He had rewritten Taras Bulba as well as "The Portrait."

4. Gogol's request angered Pogodin and Shevyrev. Only Aksakov helped Gogol—he sent 3000 rubles.

## March 2, 1843

1. The previous letter (February 28).

## May 28, 1843

1. Paul de Kock (1793-1871)—a prolific and popular French novelist and playwright whose name became a synonym for trash. (As a curiosity it may be noted that among his works is a novel called The Gogo Family in which there is a character named Nicolas Gogo.)

## June 10, 1843

1. Zhukovsky was translating the Odyssey.

2. "Mateo Falcone"—a verse version of Merimée's tale, and "Captain Bopp."

3. Perhaps Zhukovsky's "Tale of Ivan-Tsarevich and the Gray Wolf" (1845).

4. In addition to Belinsky, Shevyrev, and K. Aksakov, the inky brawls about Dead Souls were joined by Senkovsky (Library for Reading), K. P. Masalsky (Son of the Fatherland), Pletnev (The Contemporary), N. Grech (The Northern Bee), N. Polevoi (The Russian Messenger), and M. Sorokin (St. Petersburg News).

5. M. D. Mizko, "A Voice from the Provinces," Notes of the Fatherland, No. 4 (1843).

## September 1, 1843

1. Being a creature of politics rather than literature, Belinsky considered Paris exciting and complained that Gogol had a nastily one-sided view of it.

*September 20, 1843*
  1. Pogodin.

*January 1844*
  1. Aksakov waited three months, then replied: "My friend, I did not doubt the sincerity of your conviction or your desire of good for your friends; but I confess, I am dissatisfied with that conviction, and especially with the forms in which it manifests itself. I am even afraid of it. I am 53 years old. I was reading Thomas à Kempis before you were born. . . . And suddenly you set me, like a child, at reading Thomas à Kempis, without knowing anything of my convictions—and how besides?—At a specified time, after coffee, and dividing the reading into chapters, as if into lessons. . . . It's both amusing and maddening. . . . I fear mysticism like fire; and it seems to me it can somehow be seen in you. I can't bear moral recipes or anything that resembles belief in talismans. You are walking on the blade of a knife! I tremble lest the artist suffer."

*February 2, 1844*
  1. Alexei Stepanovich Khomyakov (1804-60)—a poet, Slavophil philosopher of history, and theologian.

*May 16, 1844*
  1. See note 1, January 1844, for a translation of part of Aksakov's letter.
  2. Glinka (1786-1880) was a poet whose themes were primarily religious.
  3. K. Masalsky's essay on *Dead Souls* was not so "innocent."
  4. N. N. Sheremeteva.
  5. *Baba* means "peasant woman"; any woman might be called a *baba* contemptuously. A *nebaba* (Gogol's neologism) would be a "nonwoman."
  6. M. S. Shchepkin.
  7. K. S. Aksakov.

*January - May, 1844*
  1. Anna, Elizaveta, and Olga Vasilevna—Gogol's sisters.
  2. The stimulus for this letter was the atrocious mismanagement of the family estate.

*June 12, 1844*
  1. Gogol's dread of having his portrait reproduced reached pathological proportions. In a letter to Shevyrev (December 14, 1844) he wrote: "And for the same reasons it also cannot be comprehensible to someone else why the publication of my portrait is so unpleasant for me. Some can ascribe it to excessive humility, others to caprice, others to the fact that nothing has any rhyme or reason with an eccentric, and the odd fellow must be seen in every act. I won't even hide the fact that the placing of my portrait in just that manner, i.e., lithographed from the portrait I gave to Pogodin, increased the unpleasantness still more. I am depicted there as I was in my own den several years ago. I gave this portrait to Pogodin as a friend, and in no way suspecting he would publish me. Judge for yourself whether it is useful to exhibit me before the world in a dressing gown, disheveled, with long rumpled hair and moustaches. Can it be you don't know yourself what importance people give to all this? But it is not grievous to me myself that I was exhibited like a debauchée. But, my friend, I knew I would be torn out of the journals.

Believe me, youth is stupid. Many of them have pure aspirations, but they always feel a need to create some idol for themselves."

*October 26, 1844*

1. "To Prince P. A. Vyazemsky," *The Contemporary*, XXXV, 96-98.

2. Pogodin had reprinted a portrait of Gogol. There is no rational explanation for Gogol's truculent reaction. Relations between Gogol and Pogodin were severely strained for years after this and Pogodin's demands that Gogol contribute to his Slavophil *Muscovite*. (See below, Gogol's letter of December 14 to Shevyrev.)

3. Yazykov had reported to Gogol the rumors that Part Two of *Dead Souls* was finished along with the (nonexistent) work about a general in Rome.

*December 1- 14, 1844*

1. Pletnev accused Gogol of being "a secretive creature—egotistical, haughty, distrustful—who sacrifices everything for the sake of fame," of having no faith in his former friends (i.e., Zhukovsky and Pletnev himself), of being taken in by Pogodin and Shevyrev—false friends, "schismatics who hate truth and enlightenment" and who flattered Gogol shamelessly only to attract him to their obscurantist Slavophil circle.

2. Unfortunately, no such critique has ever been discovered.

3. See note 1.

4. Evidently, Gogol is referring to his visits to Russia in 1839-40 and 1841-42.

5. It is not clear what "one contact" Gogol has in mind.

6. As he wrote in his "Testament" (in *Selected Passages*) Gogol was morbidly afraid that he would somehow be buried alive.

7. Owing to laziness and lack of business acumen rather than dishonesty, Prokopovich had mismanaged the printing and selling of Gogol's *Collected Works*. Aksakov and Shevyrev had attacked him for this, while Pletnev defended him. Misunderstandings arose, and Prokopovich thought Gogol was accusing him of dishonesty.

8. At this time Gogol had no money, his mother and sisters were in difficulty, and he owed substantial sums to his friends, but he overruled all of their objections and insisted this capricious "punishment" be carried out. Shevyrev distributed 5,000 rubles to needy students over a period of several years.

9. Besides making another personal "loan" Zhukovsky managed to get Gogol a yearly pension (for three years) of 1,000 rubles from Nikolai I. A few months later Alexandra Smirnova wrote in her diary: "I reminded the Sovereign about Gogol; he was well-disposed. 'He has much dramatic talent, but I do not forgive him overly coarse and base expressions and turns of speech.' —'Have you read his *Dead Souls*?' I asked.—'Do you mean that's his? I thought it was Sollogub's." (See also Gogol's letter to Uvarov in April 1845.)

*December 22, 1844*

1. I. V. Kireevsky (1806-56)—a Slavophil critic of some talent. By the end of 1845 he had quarreled with Pogodin and left the editorship of *The Muscovite*.

2. Konstantin Aksakov was writing a dissertation entitled "Lomonosov in the History of Russian Literature and the Russian Language." He also did some work towards the compilation of a Russian dictionary.

3. This is the title of one of the divisions in Pushkin's posthumously published essay on Alexander Radishchev's *Journey from Moscow to Peters-burg.*

4. Gavrilo Romanovich Derzhavin (1743-1816)—neoclassical author of a few fine odes and a number of very bad ones. Pushkin (who found more brass than gold in Derzhavin's verses) did not finish an essay on him.

*December 28, 1844*

1. Apparently, Gogol means his departure from Russia in 1836, though 1840 is also a possibility.

2. Gogol is referring either to 1839 or 1841.

3. Three "parties" were vying for Gogol's support: Zhukovsky and Pletnev (friends of Pushkin and Gogol's first protectors, both were partial to religionism and mysticism); Pogodin, Shevyrev, and the Aksakovs (the Moscow Slavophils) ; and the "furious" Vissarion Belinsky (for the Western-izers) . While Pogodin bedeviled Gogol with demands for contributions to *The Muscovite,* Belinsky persisted for his journal. On April 20, 1842, Belinsky had written Gogol:

> I am very sorry that *The Muscovite* took all you had ["all" was the fragment "Rome," C. P.], and that you have nothing for *Notes of the Fatherland.* I am sure this is a matter of fate and not of your own good will or your exclusive predilection in favor of *The Muscovite* and to the disadvantage of *Notes of the Fatherland.* For a long time fate has played a strange role in relation to everything that is decent in Russian literature: it deprives Batyushkov of his sanity, Griboedov, Pushkin, and Lermontov of their lives—and leaves Bulgarin, Grech, and other such good-for-nothings in Petersburg and Moscow in good health; it adorns the pages of *The Muscovite* with your works and deprives *Notes of the Fatherland* of them. . . .

4. See note 1, December 1-14, 1844.

*End of April, 1845*

1. Zhukovsky, Pletnev, and A. O. Smirnova had asked Nikolai I for a pension of 5,000 rubles for Gogol. Uvarov, often called the "Minister of De-Enlightenment," lowered the sum to 3,000 (over a three-year period). Of course Gogol didn't know this and was happy to get anything. Uvarov used this letter to spread the word that Gogol was changing the direction of his ideas (the government and many other blind people regarded Gogol as a revolutionary). A. V. Nikitenko, the censor, wrote in his diary: "Sad self-abasement on Gogol's part! . . . A pity, a pity!"

2. Gogol had received financial aid in earlier years as well.

3. In fact Uvarov had done little for history, science, or literature.

*July 14, 1845*

1. Alexander Petrovich Tolstoy—a rich, superreligious, and hypochon-drical friend of Gogol during the last several years of his life.

*July 25, 1845*

1. She had written: "I recall your *Dead Souls* often, but unfortunately I can no longer laugh at these shortcomings; now they arouse only pity in me." There are passages in her letters to him in late 1844 which show her attitude toward Gogol: "Pray for Russia, for all those who need your prayers, and for me, a sinful woman who loves you very, very much and with living gratitude.

You have made life easy for me; it had lain on my shoulders like a Tyrolese waggon. And should I confess my sins to you? I don't pray at all except on Sundays. . . . You know the heart well—look into mine more deeply and tell me whether some baseness is nesting there. . . ." "I am bored and sad. Bored because there is not a soul with whom I could think and feel aloud as with you; bored because I have become accustomed to having Nikolai Vasilevich with me and because there is no such person here, and one isn't likely to find another Nikolai Vasilevich in life. . . ."

*November 20, 1845*

1. Ivan Vasilevich Kireevsky.

2. Young Aksakov had grown a beard, donned a peasant coat, and decided to sacrifice everything for the Russian folk.

*January 8, 1846*

1. Ivan Aksakov was one of Sergei Aksakov's Slavophil sons. Shevyrev had informed Gogol that young Aksakov was writing poetry.

2. Lectures on Old Russian literature read at the University and later (1862) in Paris. See S. P. Shevyrev, *Lekcii o russkoj literature* (St. Petersburg, 1884).

3. *Dead Souls* was translated by Phillip Loebenstein and published in Leipzig in 1846.

4. In 1845 Ivan Turgenev and his beloved's husband, Louis Viardot, had published French translations of "Old-World Landowners," "Viy," "Notes of a Madman," "The Carriage," and *Taras Bulba*.

Among the reviews was one by Sainte-Beuve (with whom Gogol had once chatted on a steamer) in the *Revue des Deux Mondes*, XII (1845), and an anonymous one in *Journal des Débats* (No. 16, 1845).

*May 5, 1846*

1. See note 3, January 8, 1846.

2. A speech made by Pogodin at the unveiling (August 25, 1845) of a monument to the influential Russian writer and historian Nikolai Mikhailovich Karamzin (1766-1826).

*May 14, 1846*

1. Dostoevsky's first published work (1846), an epistolary novel which was both strongly influenced by and hostile to Gogol's works.

*July 30, 1846*

1. This was Gogol's last book. It was published in 1847. The volume is made up of thirty-two essays, some of which were originally letters written to Gogol's friends:

I.    Testament
II.   Woman in the *Monde*
III.  The Meaning of Illnesses
IV.   About What a Word Is
V.    The Reading of Russian Poets before the Public
VI.   On Helping the Poor
VII.  On the *Odyssey* Which Is Being Translated by Zhukovsky
VIII. A Few Words about Our Church and Clergy
IX.   About the Same
X.    On the Lyricism of Our Poets

There is no book of such originality and importance in Russian literature which is so seldom read or about which so little of significance has been
written. It is customary to suggest *Selected Passages* marks the last stage of
Gogol's decline, that it is noteworthy only as a psychological document showing how Gogol had become a half-mad reactionary, that it has no connection
with his earlier "realistic" (or, if the critic not a socialist, "pure art") works.
This tradition was initiated by Belinsky whose reviews and convulsive letter
to Gogol from Salzbrunn (July 15, 1847) have influenced Western scholars as
well as the Russian critics. Soviet scholars get into the queerest contortions
trying to explain away *Selected Passages*; their commentaries are all riddled
with interparoxysmal quotations from Belinsky—whose vicious attacks on
Gogol show that he had never read any of Gogol's works very carefully. (See
Gogol's unsent reply of July-August, 1847.)

Selected Passages, despite its faults (and the book does reveal serious
gaps in Gogol's education and vision), is a highly original book—in a genre
original in Russian literature. Apollon Grigoriev was the only critic to see the
connections between this volume and Gogol's previous works ("Gogol and
His Last Book," *Moskovskij gorodskoj listok*, No. 56 (1847)). Gogol himself
planned to publish a collection of essays from *Arabesques* (1835) with those of
*Selected Passages* to show how little he had changed in many respects. The
parallels between his "Petersburg Notes of 1836" and the essay on the theater
(No. XIV) are remarkably close and should be read by everyone who thinks
Gogol's views on the role of didacticism in literature were developed late in
his life.

It is natural that radicals of the nineteenth century, the Soviet-brand
Marxists of the twentieth century, and the literary critic searching for another

Volume One of *Dead Souls* should not be particularly interested in Christianity; but many of Gogol's essays are concerned with art—it is foolish to ignore these. He says much of value about *Dead Souls*, and his characterizations of Russian poets from Lomonosov to Yazykov show a gift of insight which cannot be squared with the view of Gogol as nothing more than a naive and sick fool who had exhausted his talents in 1841.

*October 20, 1846*

1. All members of the royal family.

*November 2, 1846*

1. Ivan Ivanovich Sosnitsky (1794-1871)—a well-known actor. He played the role of the mayor in the première of *The Inspector General*.

2. *Razvjazka Revizora*—a dramatic scene in which the characters (Shchepkin was to play the main role) discuss the nature of comedy and satire in general and offer interpretations of *The Inspector General* in particular. In it Gogol suggests the town be seen as our "mental town," the satirized characters as passions which pillage our souls, and that we be aware of the frightening Inspector General who stands at the doors of our tomb. The scene was written in 1846, ten years after the play itself. The allegorical interpretation does seem to have been an afterthought on Gogol's part (though that would be impossible to prove). I find the interpretation somewhat less preposterous than most critics.

3. Gogol wrote Shchepkin: "As for *The Denouement* (enclosed with this) which should follow immediately after *The Inspector General*—before giving it to the actors to learn, you yourself read into it carefully, enter into the meaning and force of each word. . . . These short lines should be said firmly, with complete conviction in their truth, because this is an argument, and a real argument—but not moralizing." Later, he told Shchepkin it was a clumsy piece and people would mistakenly think he wanted to make an allegory of the play: "I don't have that in mind. *The Inspector General* is *The Inspector General* and its application to one's own self is the indispensable thing which every spectator ought to do—with everything even, not just *The Inspector General*."

*November 24, 1846*

1. Gogol did not make his trip to the Holy Land until 1848.

*December 8, 1846*

1. The censors passed *The Denouement* for print, not for presentation.

2. Ivan Sergeevich Turgenev (1818-83). In fact, I. I. Panaev and N. A. Nekrasov took over *The Contemporary* from Pletnev. Belinsky and Turgenev became contributors, not editors.

3. *Northern Flowers* was an almanac published between 1825 and 1832 by Baron Anton Delvig (like Pletnev one of Pushkin's closest friends) and Orest Somov. All of the best poets of the time (among them Pushkin, Baratynsky, Vyazemsky, Batyushkov, and Kozlov), as well as Gogol, had contributed to it. With the passing of Pushkin's *Contemporary* from Pletnev's hands the role of the Pushkin circle in Russian literature was almost at an end; perhaps this is the reason Gogol suggests planting some more *Northern Flowers*. But his suggestion was not followed.

*January 15, 1847*

    1. In *Selected Passages*.

*January 25, 1847*

    1. Gogol's "Testament" was the first essay in *Selected Passages*. In it he wills (1) that he not be buried until his body had clearly started to decay [so he wouldn't be inhumed alive], (2) that no monument be raised to him, (3) that no one should grieve, (4) that any edifying passages from his letters after 1843 be published, (5) that all copies of a certain portrait of him be destroyed.

*February 6, 1847*

    1. Five essays were not passed ("One Must Love Russia," 'One Must Travel around Russia," "What a Governor's Wife Is," "The Terrors and Horrors of Russia," and "To One Who Occupies an Important Position") by the incredibly dull-witted censors. A number of passages were struck out of the surviving essays.

*February 11, 1847 (Rosset)*

    1. A weekly journal published in Petersburg from 1845 to 1849.

    2. Vladimir I. Dal (1801-72), later an important lexicographer, had published stories as well as ethnographical materials about folk beliefs and superstitions. Gogol praised his work on several occasions.

    3. Ya. P. Butkov, *Petersburgskie vershiny* (St. Petersburg, 1846). A collection of stories which betray Gogol's influence, something which he deplored.

*February 11, 1847 (Shevyrev)*

    1. Zinaida A. Volkanskaya had become a Catholic and settled in Rome in 1829. In 1838 there were rumors that Gogol, who was often in the company of Volkanskaya and her Polish friends, was going to become a Roman Catholic. As far as is known these rumors were totally unfounded.

*March 6, 1847 (Aksakov)*

    1. A friend of Aksakov.

*March 6, 1847 (Zhukovsky)*

    1. A main character in *The Inspector General*.

    2. *Selected Passages* did not sell as rapidly as Gogol believes here.

*April 27, 1847*

    1. Shevyrev made this accusation in his letter of March 22.

    2. The elder Dumas had a number of writers grinding out parts of novels according to his overall plans.

*June 20, 1847*

    1. *Selected Passages*.

    2. In "On the *Odyssey* Which Is Being Translated by Zhukovsky" Gogol said the "sick works of the century, ones mixed with all kinds of half-digested ideas" caused by political upheavals were beginning to appear less frequently. But he notes that some readers who "are accustomed to holding onto the tails of the leaders from the journals" have not noticed that "the goats who were leading them had stopped to ponder some time ago, not knowing themselves where to take their lost flocks."

3. Belinsky had indeed praised Gogol highly—because he could use his works for propagandizing, for advancing his own social philosophy.

4. Prokopovich replied to Gogol saying he was unable to find any relative or imposter, that he didn't know where Gogol could have heard such rumors.

*About June 20, 1847*

1. That is, the Slavophils.

*August 2, 1847*

1. A doctor in Paris.

*July-August, 1847*

1. This letter is the rough draft of a reply to Belinsky's virulent Salzbrunn letter. (It should be compared to Gogol's letter of June 20.) Gogol did not send this letter.

Nearly all of the fragments are translated here. In several places the Russian text is confused or incomplete.

2. The verses are from A. I. Polezhaev's "Four Nations."

3. Gogol interprets his own remarks correctly. This is what he actually said in "The Russian Landowner":

Your observations about schools are completely right. It is really foolishness to teach a peasant to read in order to give him a chance to read vapid rubbishy booklets which lovers of mankind publish for European peoples. The main thing is that the peasant has absolutely no time for that. After so much work no rubbishy booklet will penetrate his mind, and when he gets home he'll fall into a colossal sound sleep—as if a dead man. . . . The village priest can say much more that is truly necessary for the peasant than these rubbishy booklets. If someone truly gets a desire for literacy—and not at all in order to become a scoundrel-clerk, but in order to read those books in which God's law is outlined for man —that's another matter. Educate him like a son and use everything that you would use for a whole school on him alone. Our people aren't so stupid as to run away from any written paper as from a devil. . . . For the present they don't even have to know that books other than the sacred ones exist.

4. Russian is rich in diminutives which signify various shades of meaning from contempt to love.

5. "Living images" (*zhivye obrazy*) is the term Gogol regularly used for his fictional works and the characters in them.

*September 7, 1847*

1. Alexander Ivanovich Herzen (1812-70), writer, socialist, and revolutionary propagandist, left Russia in 1847.

2. Ivan Sergeevich Turgenev—his first stories had appeared in *The Contemporary, Notes of the Fatherland,* and *Petersburg Collection (Peterburgskij sbornik).*

*September 24, 1847*

1. Matvey Alexandrovich Konstantinovsky (1792-1857)—a priest under whose influence Gogol fell during the last five years of his life. It has become customary for biographers (except Mochulsky in his *Duxovnyj put' Gogolja*) to view him as a fanatical demon who drove Gogol to destruction and death.

There is some evidence that he was a fanatic, but there is virtually none that conclusively demonstrates his bad effects on Gogol; and furthermore there is considerable evidence that contradicts the few stories about his fanaticism. As is so often the case in Gogol's biography it is impossible to reach a certain conclusion on the basis of an evaluation of the evidence. I personally suspect that Konstantinovsky was a convenient scapegoat.

### January 10, 1848/December 29, 1847

1. The letter was not published, but Zhukovsky's lengthy epistolary reply ("On the Poet and His Present Meaning") was printed in *The Muscovite*.

Gogol's comments parallel what he says in his *Author's Confession*.

### January 12, 1848

1. *Selected Passages*.

### June 15, 1848

1. See note 2, December 29, 1847.

### October 29, 1848

1. V. A. Sollogub had started lecturing to his wife and sister-in-law (Anna Mikhailovna Vielgorskaya) on Russian history. It would appear that at this time Gogol was in love with Anna (see his last letter to her below—Spring 1850).

2. *The History of the Russian Church* (Moscow and Riga, 1847-48).

3. M. Yu. Vielgorsky—a wealthy relative of Anna.

### February 25, 1849

1. Zhukovsky's translation of the *Odyssey* began to appear in the fall of 1848.

### March 30, 1849

1. Anna Mikhailovna Vielgorskaya—sister of Iosif Vielgorsky. In the spring of 1850 Gogol's proposal of marriage was angrily rejected by her family.

2. *Domostroy* (*House-Orderer*)—a monument of official sixteenth-century Muscovite writing, attributed to the Archpriest Sylvester of the Annunciation (d. about 1566); it was first published in 1849. It provides multitudinous rules for a proper religious and practical life— under the strict control of a strong male head of the household. The duties of each member of the family are prescribed in minute detail.

This appealed to the medieval part of Gogol's mind. In fact his own letters to his mother and sisters rather resemble the *Domostroy*.

### December 3, 1849

1. Konstantin I. Markov—retired lieutenant, landowner, very minor critic.

2. In his letter to Gogol, Markov warned: "If you present *heroes of virtue,* your novels will stand beside the works of the old school. . . ."

### Spring 1850

1. According to Vielgorsky family tradition Gogol proposed to Anna Mikhailovna in 1850; the suggestion was met with incredulity by her haughty

mother. If this is so, Gogol had received the negative answer before penning this letter.—And it is his last to any member of the Vielgorsky family.

2. Probably Pletnev.

3. Of course what Gogol says about "living together" does not mean what it would today. There is no reason to suppose that his relation to Anna was anything but Platonic. (However, there is simply not enough evidence to justify some biographers' malevolently confident assertions that Gogol planned a marriage totally free of fleshly love.)

*July 10-18, 1850*

1. The letter may have been intended for Perovsky, P. A. Shirinsky-Shikhmatov, or A. F. Orlov. But it was never delivered.

2. In the last few years of his life Gogol gathered material preparatory to publication of a book on geography. Six notebooks full of this material have survived. This was a natural extension of his earlier interests in Russian history, folk songs and traditions, the compilation of glossaries of dialect words, and lists of plants, trees, and crops characteristic of various locales in Russia.

*August 20, 1850*

1. Gogol read the first four chapters of Part II before leaving Moscow on June 13.

*Summer 1851*

1. Professor of law at Moscow University and censor of *The Muscovite.*

*September 25, 1851*

1. Gogol searched morbidly for signs and omens. Father Makarius had said good-bye to Gogol once, then accompanied him to the gates of the Optina Monastery where he said, "For the last time, good-bye." Gogol took this as a sign of impending danger or death and wondered whether to continue his trip to the Ukraine or return to Moscow.

*February 2, 1852*

1. Zhukovsky's vision deteriorated in the last years of his life, but he was not totally blind. He died on April 19, less than two months after Gogol.

*February 6, 1852*

1. The day before Gogol had quarreled with Konstantinovsky before seeing him off from Moscow. After this time Gogol stopped his writing, slept little, and refused to eat. Exactly what happened is not known.

*February 10, 1852*

1. This is the last surviving letter of Gogol. He died February 21 (O.S.). Thousands of mourners came to see his body at the University of Moscow, and huge crowds accompanied the coffin to the cemetery. For reasons other than those he wished, Gogol was a national hero.

# Bibliography of Works on Gogol

*Abbreviations*
ASEER—*American Slavic and East European Review*
SEER—*Slavic and East European Review*
SEEJ—*Slavic and East European Journal*
ZSP—*Zeitschrift für slavische Philologie*

### ENGLISH

Baring, M. "Gogol," *Landmarks in Russian Literature. London*, 1916. Pp. 36-76.

Belinsky, V. "Letter to N. V. Gogol," *Belinsky, Chernyshevsky, and Dobrolyubov*, ed. Ralph Matlaw. New York, 1962.

Bezushko, V. *Mykola Hohol*. Winnipeg: Kultura i osvita, 1956. [An English summary, pp. 93-191.]

——. "Nicholas Gogol and Ukrainian Literature," *Ukrainian Quarterly*, XVI, 3 (1960), 263-68.

Birkhead, A. "Russian Pickwick," *Living Age*, CCLXXXVII (1915), 312-15.

Bogojavlensky, M. "On the Development and Concept of Gogol's Religious Thought." Diss. University of Pennsylvania, 1959.

Bowen, C. M. "*Dead Souls* and *Pickwick Papers*," *Living Age*, CCLXXX (1916), 369-73.

Bowman, Herbert. " 'The Nose'," *SEER*, XXXI, 76 (December 1952), 204-11.

Brasol, Boris. *The Mighty Three: Pushkin—Gogol—Dostoevsky*. New York, 1934.

Brodiansky, Nina. "Gogol and his Characters," *SEER*, XXXI, 76 (December 1952), 36-57.

Bryner, Cyril. "Gogol, Dickens and the Realistic Novel," *Études slaves et est-européennes*, VIII (1963), 17-42.

——. "Gogol's *The Overcoat* in World Literature," *SEER*, XXXII, 79 (1954), 499-509.

Charquee, R. D. "Nikolay Gogol," *Fortnightly Review*, 130 (New York, 1931), 230-42.

Čiževskij, D. "Gogol: Artist and Thinker," *Annals of the Ukrainian Academy of Arts and Sciences in the USA*, II, No. 2 (4), (Summer 1952), 261-79.

——. "The Unknown Gogol," *SEER*, XXX (June 1952), 476-93.

"The Cloak," *Lippincott's Monthly Magazine*, XCII (1913), 249-62.

Coleman, A. P. *The Humor in Russian Comedy from Catherine to Gogol.* Columbia University Slavic Studies, No. 2. New York, 1925.
Cook, Albert. "Reflexive Attitudes: Sterne, Gogol, Gide," *Criticism,* No. 2 (Winter 1960), 164-74.

Debreczeny, Paul. *Nikolay Gogol and his Contemporary Critics.* Transactions of the American Philosophical Society. Vol. 56 [n. s.], Part 3. Philadelphia, 1966.
Driessen, F. *Gogol as a Short Story Writer: A Study of his Technique of Composition.* The Hague: Mouton, 1965.

Eichenbaum, Boris. "The Structure of Gogol's *The Overcoat,*" *Russian Review,* XXII, 377-99.
Erlich, Victor. "Gogol' and Kafka," *For Roman Jakobson.* Comp. M. Halle. The Hague, 1956. Pp. 100-108.

Fanger, Donald. *Dostoevsky and Romantic Realism: A Study of Dostoevsky in Relation to Balzac, Dickens and Gogol.* Cambridge, 1965.
Finch, Chauncey. "Classical Influence on N. V. Gogol," *The Classical Journal,* 48, No. 8 (May 1953), 291-96.
Friedman, Peter. "The Nose," *The American Imago,* No. 8 (December 1951), 337-50.
Futrell, M. "Dickens and Three Russian Novelists: Gogol, Dostoevsky, Tolstoy." Diss. School of Slavonic and East European Studies. London, 1954.
———. "Gogol' and Dickens," *SEER,* XXXIV, 83 (1956), 443-59.

Gassner, J. W. "Chekhov and the Russian Realists," *Masters of the Drama.* New York, 1954.
Guerney, B. G. "Great Grotesque," *New Republic* (September 25, 1944), 376-78.
———. "Introduction," *Dead Souls.* New York: Modern Library, 1965.
Gustafson, R. F. "The Suffering Usurper: Gogol's *Diary of a Madman,*" *SEEJ,* IX, 3 (1965), 268-81.

Hasenclever, Nora. "Gogol and Dostoyevsky." Diss. Bennington College, 1951.

Juran, Sylvia. "Zapiski sumasšedšego: Some Insights into Gogol's World," *SEEJ,* V (1961), 331-33.

Kanser, M. "Gogol: A Study in Wit and Paranoia," *Journal of the American Psychoanalytic Assoc.,* III, 1 (January 1955).
Kaun, Alexander. "Poe and Gogol: A Comparison," *SEER,* XV, 44 (1937), 389-99.
Kent, Leonard J. "Introduction," *The Collected Tales and Plays of Nikolai Gogol.* New York: Pantheon, 1964.
———. "The Subconscious in Gogol and Dostoevsky, and Its Antecedents." Diss. Yale University, 1965.

Landry, Hilton. "Gogol's *The Overcoat,*" *Explicator,* XIX (1961).
Lavrin, Janko. *Gogol (1809-1852). A Centenary Survey.* London, 1951.
Lefevre, Carl. "Gogol's First Century in England and America (1841-1941)." Diss. University of Minnesota, 1944.

——. "Gogol and Anglo-Russian Literary Relations during the Crimean War," *ASEER* (April 1949), 106-25.

Littell, R. "Gogol," *The New Republic, XLVIII* (1926), 218-19.

Magarshack, D. *Gogol.* London, 1957.

Malkiel, Yakov. "Cervantes in Nineteenth-Century Russia," *Comparative Literature,* III, 4 (1951), 310-29.

Manning, Clarence. "Gogol and Ukraine," *Ukrainian Quarterly,* VI, 323-30.

——. "Nicolas Gogol," *SEER,* IV (1926), 573-87.

Markov, Vladimir. "The Poetry of Russian Prose Writers," *California Slavic Studies,* I (1960), 77-82.

Martin, Mildred. "The Last Shall Be First: A Study of Three Russian Short Stories," *Bucknell Review, VI,* 1 (1956), 13-23.

Masson, E. "Russia's Gogol: A Centenary," *Pacific Spectator,* VII, 3 (1953), 322-31.

Maurois, André. "Nicolas Gogol," *The Art of Writing.* New York: Dutton & Co., 1960. Pp. 265-95.

Mclean, Hugh. "Gogol's Retreat from Love: Towards an Interpretation of *Mirgorod," American Contributions to the Fourth International Congress of Slavists.* The Hague, 1958. Pp. 225-45.

Mirsky, D. S. *A History of Russian Literature.* New York: Vintage, 1958. Pp. 149-62.

Nabokov, Vladimir Vladimirovich. *Nikolai Gogol.* New York: New Directions, 1961.

Noyes, G. R. "Gogol, A Precursor of Modern Realists in Russia," *Nation,* 101 (Nov. 18, 1915), 592-94.

Passage, Charles. *The Russian Hoffmannists.* The Hague, 1963.

Perry, Idris. "Kafka, Gogol and Nathanael West," *Kafka,* ed. Ronald Gray. Englewood Cliffs, New Jersey, 1962.

Poggioli, Renato. "Gogol's 'Old-fashioned Landowners': An Inverted Eclogue," *Indiana Slavic Studies,* III (1963), 54-72.

——. "Realism in Russia," *Comparative Literature,* III, 3 (1951), 253-67.

Proffer, Carl R. *"Dead Souls* in Translation," *SEEJ,* VIII, 4 (1964) 420-33.

——. "Gogol's *Taras Bulba* and the *Iliad," Comparative Literature,* XVII, 2 (1965), 142-50.

——. *The Simile and Gogol's "Dead Souls".* The Hague: Mouton & Co., 1967.

——. "Gogol's Definition of Romanticism," *Studies in Romanticism,* VI, 2 (1967), 120-27.

Rabkin, Leslie. *Psychopathology and Literature.* Rochester, 1966.

Rahv, P. "Gogol as a Modern Instance," *Image and Idea.* New York: New Directions, 1958. P. 204ff.

Reeve, F. D. "Dead Souls," *The Russian Novel* (New York, 1966). Pp. 64-103.

Selig, Karl. "Concerning Gogol's *Dead Souls* and *Lazarillo de Tormes," Symposium,* VIII (1954), 34-40.

Setchkarev, Vsevolod. *Gogol—His Life and Works.* New York: New York University Press, 1965.

Simmons, E. J. "Gogol and English Literature," *Modern Language Review,* XXVI (1931), 445-50.

Spilka, Mark. "Kafka's Sources for *The Metamorphosis*," *Comparative Literature*, XI, 4 (1959), 289-308.
Spycher, Peter, "N. V. Gogol's 'The Nose': A Satirical Comic Fantasy Born of an Impotence Complex," *SEEJ*, VII, 4 (1963), 361-75.
Stilman, Leon. "Gogol's Overcoat, Thematic Pattern and Origins," *ASEER*, XI, 1 (February 1952), 138-48.
———. "Nikolai Gogol: Historical and Biographical Elements of his Creative Personality." Diss. Columbia University, 1953.
———. "Afterword," *The Diary of a Madman and Other Stories*. Trans. A. MacAndrew. New York, 1961. Pp. 223-38.
Strakhovsky, Leonid. "The Historianism of Gogol," *ASEER*, XII, 3 (October 1953), 360-71.
Strong, Robert L. "The Soviet Interpretation of Gogol," *ASEER*, XIV, 528-39.

Tilley, A. "Gogol, the Father of Russian Realism," *Living Age*, CCII (1894), 489-97.
Tsanoff, Radoslav. "The Russian Soil and Nikolai Gogol," *Rice Institute Pamphlet*, Vol. IV, No. 2 (Houston, 1917), 119-26.

Vlach, Robert. "Gogol and Hašek: Two Masters of 'Poshlost'," *Études slaves et est-européennes*, VII, 239-42.

Weathers, Winston. "Gogol's *Dead Souls*: The Degrees of Reality," *College English*, XVII (1956), 159-64.
Wellek, René. "Introduction," *Dead Souls*. Trans. B. Guerney. New York: Rinehart & Co., 1948. Pp. v-x.
Wilson, Edmund. "Gogol: the Demon in the Overgrown Garden," *Nation*, CLXXV (December 1952), 520-24.
———. "Nikolai Gogol," *The New Yorker*, XX (1944), 72-73.
Wittlin, Jozef. "Gogol's Inferno," *Polish Review*, VII (4), 5-20.

Yurieff, Zoya. "Gogol and the Russian Symbolists." Diss. Harvard University, 1954.

GERMAN

Adams, V. "Gogols Erstlingswerk 'Hans Küchelgarten' im Lichte seines Natur- und Welterlebens," *ZsP*, VII (1931), 323-68.
Anderson, W. "Gogols Porträt als Posener Volkssage," *ZsP*, XX (1950), 234-36.
Annenkow, P. "Meine Erlebnisse mit Gogol," *Corona* (June 1933), pp. 584-610.

Berdjajew, Nikolai. "Gogol in der russischen Revolution," *Wort und Wahrheit*, XV (1960), 611-16.
Blagoi, D., W. I. Strashew, K. Gudzi. *Drei russische Dichter: Leben und Werk von Puschkin, Gogol und L. Tolstoi*. Trans. J. Kieseritzky. Weimar, 1952.
Braun, M. "Gogol als Satiriker," *Die Welt der Slaven*, IV (1959), 129-47.

Čiževsky, D. "Nachwort," *Die Toten Seelen*. Munich, 1949. Pp. 475-94.
———. "Zur komposition von Gogols 'Mantel'," *ZsP*, 14 (1937), 63-94.

Dauenhauer, A. "Gogols 'Schreckliche Rache' und 'Pietro von Abano' von L. Tieck," *ZsP*, 13 (1936), 315-18.

Emmer, K. "Neuere Gogol-Literatur," *Wiener slawistisches Jahrbuch*, III (1953), 79-114.
Emmer, Karl. "Vergleichende Studien zu Gogols *Porträt*." Diss. Vienna, 1948.

Fischer, Ernst. "Nikolai Gogol—Roman des Bürgerkriegs," *Dictung und Deutung: Beiträge zur Literaturbetrachtung*. Wien, 1953.
———. "Nikolaj Gogol—Festrede zu seinem 100. Todestag gehalten am 11. März, 1952." Wien, 1952.

Gerhardt, Dietrich. *Gogol' und Dostoewskij in ihrem künstlerischen Verhältnis, Versuch einer zusammenfassenden Darstellung*. Leipzig, 1941.
Gesemann, Gerhardt. "Grundlagen einer Charakterologie Gogols," *Jahrbuch der Charakterologie*. I (Berlin, 1924), 49-88.
Gorlin, Michael. *N. V. Gogol und E. Th. A. Hoffmann*. Leipzig: O Harrassowitz, 1933. 89pp.

Harder, Johannes. *Der Mensch im russischen Roman. Deutungen: Gogol, Dostojewski, Leskov, Tolstoi*. Wuppertal-Barman, 1961.
Haertel, Emma. "N. V. Gogol als Maler," *Jahrbuch für Kultur und Geschichte der Slaven*. 5 (Breslau, 1929), 145-68.
Hippius, W. "Die Gogol Forschung 1914-24," *ZsP*, 2 (1925), 530-39.

Iwanow, Wjatscheslaw. "Gogol und Aristophanes," *Corona*, 3 (1933), 611-12.

Jilek, Heinrich. "Das Weltbild N. W. Gogols," *Zeitschrift für deutsche Geisteswissenschaft*, 1 (1938), 162-76.

Kasack, W. *Die Technique der Charakter-Darstellung bei Gogol*. Wiesbaden, 1957.
Kassner, Rudolf. *Essays*. Leipzig, 1923. Pp. 17-41.
———. "Stil und Gesicht: Swift, Gogol, Kafka," *Merkur*, VII, 8 (1955), 737-52.
Kessel, Martin. "Gogol und die Satire," *Romantische Liebhabereien*. Braunschweig, 1938.
———. "Satiriker der Weltliteratur: Gogol," *Neue Rundschau*, (August 1937), pp. 128-49.
Klempt, Heinrich. "Nikolay Gogol: *Das Porträt*—Ein Beitrag zu Behandlung des Problemkreises 'Kunst and Leben' auf der Oberstufe," *Wirkendes Wort*, XV (1965), 50-57.
Kraus, Otto. *Der Fall Gogol*. Munich, 1912.

Leiste, Hans W. *Gogol and Molière*. Nürnberg, 1958. 62pp. Bibliography, pp. 59-62.

Merezhkovskii, D. S. *Gogol und der Teufel* (mit einem einleitenden Essay von Juri Semjonow). Trans. Alexander Eliasberg. Hamburg, 1963.

Nilsson, Nils. "Zur Entstehungsgeschichte des Gogloschen *Mantels*," *Scando-Slavica, II* (1956), 116-33.

Pakosch, Hyacinth. "Der Humor N. V. Gogols." Diss. München, 1944.
Pietsch, Eva-Maria. "Gogol in der Publizistik Thomas Mann," in Günther Rienäcker (ed.), *Zum 90. Geburtstag Thomas Manns, Spektrum*, XI (1965), 187-91.

Pollok, Karl Heinz. "Zur dramatischen Form von Gogols 'Spielern,'" *Die Welt der Slaven*, IV (1959), 169-80.

Propper, Maximillian von. "Nikolai Gogols theatralische Sendung," *Dramaturgische Blätter*, Jahrg. 2, 2 (Berlin, 1948), 67-73.

Pypin, A. "Die Bedeutung Gogols für die heutige internationale Stellung der russischen Literatur," *Archiv für slavische Philologie*, XXV (1903), 290-306.

Richter, Sigrid. *Rom und Gogol': Gogol's Romerlebnis und sein Fragment "Rim."* Hamburg, 1964.

Roch, Herbert. *Richter ihrer Zeit: Grimmelshausen, Swift, Gogol.* Berlin, 1956.

Rost, P. "Gogol," in F. K. Mann, *Russland*. Königsberg, 1926.

Setschkareff, Wsewolod. *Gogol: Leben und Schaffen.* Berlin, 1953.

——. "Zur Interpretation von Gogols 'Nase,'" *ZsP*, 21 (1951), 118-21.

Stender-Petersen, A. "Der Ursprung des Gogolschen Teufels," Göteborgs Noskolas Arsskrift. Bd. 26 (1920).

——. "Johann Heinrich Voss und der junge Gogol," *Edda*, XV (Kristiana, 1921), 98-128.

——. "Gogol und die deutsche Romantik," *Euphorion*, XXIV, Drittes Heft (Leipzig, 1922), 628-53.

——. "Gogol und Kotzebue, zur thematischen Entstehung von Gogols 'Revizor'," *ZsP*, 12 (1935), 16-35.

——. "Der groteske Stil Gogols," *Welt und Wort*, XV (1960), 71-73.

Thiess, F. *Nikolaus W. Gogol und seine Bühnenwerke.* Berlin, 1922.

Triomphe, Robert. "Gogol und die russische Kritik über den *Revisor*," *Vorträge* (1957), 140-61.

Winkel, Hans-Jurgen. "Unbekannte Briefe von Gogol', Turgenev, Gor'kij und Sienkiewicz," *ZsP*, XXXI (1964), 261-64.

Wissemann, Heinz, "Struktur und Ideengehalt von Gogol 'Mantel'," *Stil- und Formprobleme in der Literatur.* Heidelberg, 1959. Pp. 389-96.

——. "Zum Ideengehalt von Gogol's 'Mantel'," *ZsP*, XXVI, 391-415.

Wytrzens, G. "Vjazemskij und Gogol," *Wiener Slavistisches Jahrbuch.* Graz-Köln, 1955. Pp. 83-97.

Zelm, E. "Ein Brief Gogols an V. O. Balabina," *ZsP*, 14 (1937), 54-59.

Zenkovskij, V. "Die ästhetische Utopie Gogols," *ZsP*, 13 (1936), 1-34.

——. "Gogol als Denker," *ZsP*, 9 (1932), 104-30.

### FRENCH

Cabanes, B. A. "Nicolas Gogol," *Grands névropathes*, III (Paris, 1935), 239-77.

Chaplenko, Vasyl'. "Les Ukrainismes dans le langue de M. Hohol," Augsburg: Ed. de les Soc. des amis de l'Académie ukrainienne libre des sciences, 1948. 27pp. (Essay in Ukrainian with a French summary.)

Clavel, Bernard. "La Politique dans l'oeuvre de Gogol," *Revue politique et parlementaire* (July-August 1965), pp. 65-76.

Eng, J. van der. "Le Personnage de Bashmatchkine," *Dutch Contributions to the Fourth International Congress of Slavists.* The Hague, 1958. Pp. 87-103.

Evdokimoff, Paul. *Gogol et Dostoievsky, ou La Descente aux enfers.* Bruges, 1961.

Gorlin, Michel, "Hoffmann en Russie," *Études littéraires et historiques.* Paris, 1957. Pp. 189-206.

Gourfinkel, Nina. *Nicholas Gogol dramaturge.* Paris, 1956.

———. "Gogol et le théâtre," *Révue d'histoire du théâtre,* Année 4, no. 3 (Paris, 1952), 189-219.

Hill, Elizabeth. "Une Lettre de Nicholas Gogol," *Revue des études slaves,* XXXVIII, 105-9.

Hofmann, Modeste. *Gogol, sa vie et son oeuvre.* Paris, 1946.

Juin, Hubert. "De Tarass Boulba à Tchitchikov," *Esprit,* No. 7-8 (1957), 144-55.

Leger, L. *Gogol.* Paris, 1914.

Marthe, Robert. "L'imitation souveraine," *Temps Modernes,* XVI (1961), 1124-49.

Merejkovsky, D. S. *Gogol et le diable.* Paris, 1939.

Merimée, Prosper. "La littérature en Russie," *Revue des deux mondes.* November 1851.

Mongault, Henri. "Gogol et Merimée," *Revue de littérature comparée,* Année 10 (Paris, 1930), 697-712.

Nilsson, N. A. *Gogol et Pétersbourg: Recherches sur les antécédents des contes pétersbourgeois.* Stockholm, 1954. 71pp. (Bibliography.)

Radoyce, Lubomir. "La Conception du 'Poète national' chez Gogol," *Langue et littérature* (1962), 343-44.

Rudnycki, Jaroslav. "Gogol et Chevtchenko: deux hommes—deux symboles," *Études slaves et est-européennes* (1956), pp. 158-63.

Sainte-Beuve, C. *Premiers lundis.* Paris, 1875. Vol. III.

Schloezer, B. F. *Gogol.* Paris, 1932 and 1946.

Shick, A. *Nicolas Gogol—une vie de torments.* Sceaux, 1949.

Smirnova, O. N. "Études et Souvenirs," in *La Nouvelle revue.* Paris, 1885.

Troyat, Henri. *Sainte Russie: Souvenirs et réflexions.* Paris, 1956.

Webber, Jean-Paul. "Les Transpositions du nez dans l'oeuvre de Gogol," *Nouvelle revue française* (1959), pp. 108-20.

OTHER LANGUAGES

Borghese, Daria. *Gogol a Roma.* Firenze: Sansoni editore, 1957.

Driessen, F. *Gogol' als novelist.* Amsterdam, 1955. (English summary. Also see above for English translation.)

Ferrer, Olga Prijevalinsky. "Las Almas muertas de Gogol y Don Quijote," *Cuadernos de literatura*, VII (July-December 1950), 201-14.

Giaconi, Claudio. "Gogol y Thomas Wolfe," *Cuadernos americanos*, XXI, cxxiii, 214-28.

———. *Un Hombre en la trampa* (Gogol). Santiago, 1960.

Lo Gatto, Ettore. *Storia della letteratura Russa*. Rome, 1935. V, 3-137.

Milano, Paolo. *Il Lettore di professione*. Milan, 1960.

Pacini Savoj, Leone. "La Povest' o Kapitana Kopejkine," Roma: Edizione di richerche slavistiche, 1958. 7pp.

———. "Il 'Revisore' e la 'Follia mistica' gogoliana," *Ricerche slavistiche*, 1 (Rome, 1952), 3-21.

Pappacena, Enrico. *Gogol*. Milan, 1930.

Vito, Mosca. "Il poema di Gogol," *Rassegna nazionale*, Ser. 3, 18 (Rome, 1933), 317-22.

# Index

Numbers in parentheses indicate the first page of letters addressed to a person; numbers in italic refer to pages giving explanatory material.